THE COMPLETE BOOK OF NUMEROLOGY

OTHER BOOKS IN THIS SERIES
BY LEONARD R. N. ASHLEY

The Complete Book of Superstition, Prophecy, and Luck
The Complete Book of Magic and Witchcraft
The Complete Book of Devils and Demons
The Complete Book of the Devil's Disciples
The Complete Book of Spells, Curses, and Magical Recipes
The Complete Book of Vampires
The Complete Book of Ghosts and Poltergeists
The Complete Book of Werewolves
The Complete Book of Dreams and What They Mean
The Complete Book of Sex Magic

Numerology A pseudoscience involving the study of the occult meaning of numbers, particularly the figures designating the year of one's birth, in the belief that these numbers have an influence on one's life or future. Like ASTROLOGY, this belief is unsupported by any creditable scientific evidence.

—Richard P. Brennan
Dictionary of Scientific Literacy (1992)

THE COMPLETE BOOK OF
NUMEROLOGY

Leonard R. N. Ashley

BARRICADE BOOKS / NEW JERSEY

Published by Barricade Books Inc.
185 Bridge Plaza North
Suite 308-A
Fort Lee, NJ 07024

Copyright © 2005 by Leonard R. N. Ashley

All rights reserved.

No part of this book may be reproduced, stored in a retrieval system, or transmitted in any form, by any means, including mechanical, electronic, photocopying, recording, or otherwise, without the prior written permission of the publisher, except by a reviewer who wishes to quote brief passages in connection with a review written for inclusion in a magazine, newspaper, or broadcast.

Printed in Canada.

Library of Congress Cataloging-in-Publication Data

Ashley, Leonard R. N.
    The complete book of numerology / Leonard R. N. Ashley.
    p. cm.
    Includes index.
    ISBN: 1-56980-270-X
    1. Numerology. I. Title.

BF1623.P9.A84 2005
133.3'35--dc21   2004041117

First Printing

In Memoriam
LOUIS A. de MONTLUZIN Jr.
27 September 1940–13 March 2003

Faust in his study, by Rembrandt.

Table of Contents

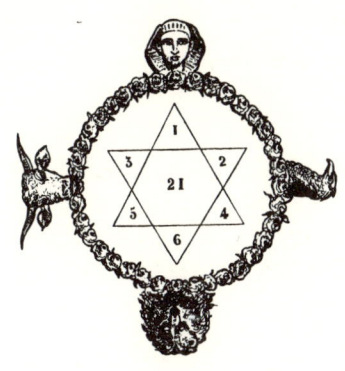

READ THIS FIRST 9

CHAPTER ONE
NUMEROLOGY IN THE CONTEXT OF SOCIETY 15

CHAPTER TWO
WHAT THE NUMBERS BASICALLY MEAN 23

CHAPTER THREE
YOUR FATE IS WRITTEN IN YOUR NAME 37

CHAPTER FOUR
THE PATH OF YOUR LIFE 49

CHAPTER FIVE
NUMBERS IN CHINESE ASTROLOGY 65

CHAPTER SIX
THE NUMBER OF THE HEART'S DESIRE 75

CHAPTER SEVEN
YOUR FAVORITE NUMBER 85

CHAPTER EIGHT
ODD AND EVEN NUMBERS 91

CHAPTER NINE
TRISKAIDEKAPHOBIA 103

CHAPTER TEN
PLAYING THE LOTTERY 109

CHAPTER ELEVEN
YOU'RE ON A ROLL 119

CHAPTER TWELVE
HOW MUCH DO YOU OWE? 149

CHAPTER THIRTEEN
YOUR COLOR SENSE 159

CHAPTER FOURTEEN
CAGLIOSTRO SPEAKS TO THE FREEMASONS IN PARIS 173

CHAPTER FIFTEEN
SEVENTH-INNING STRETCH 191

CHAPTER SIXTEEN
HEBREW LETTERS 205

CHAPTER SEVENTEEN
SUPERSTITIONS ABOUT NUMBERS 215

CHAPTER EIGHTEEN
"CHEIRO" 235

CHAPTER NINETEEN
PUBLICATIONS AND NUMEROLOGY 245

CHAPTER TWENTY
NUMEROLOGY IN LITERATURE 255

CHAPTER TWENTY-ONE
CONCLUSION 275

INDEX 281

Read This First

As the author of several dozen books, I am well aware that people seldom read prefaces. Publishers call it "front matter." Nevertheless, I keep trying to get people to look at an introduction before they take the next step in reading a book, which ought to be looking at the table of contents. Often people glance at the title and skip over the introductory pages. They look at the front cover and then turn to what Gillette Burgess termed the "blurb" on the back cover. Only then do they dip into the pages, often more or less at random or attracted by an illustration, or they go look for their own name or something else of personal interest in the index, if there is one.

The best rule is the one given to Alice of the Wonderland adventures. She was advised to begin at the beginning, go on until the end, and then stop. I hope you read the book through, but I have undertaken to organize it so that you can dip in at any point where you think you will find what you happen to be seeking. (Most readers will probably discover that for themselves, not by reading this.) Wherever anyone does read, he or she will get a byte that is not too great for the modern attention span. Because I cannot be sure all sections will be read through in order, I have to have a few repetitions. It will not annoy reasonable readers to see something repeated, especially if it is important.

That's an argument. A preface can be argumentative or merely positioning. It probably is best when it simply tells you what the author thinks the book is really about. That is a point that too many book titles these days fail to make clear. I think my title here is clear. Maybe right away as

10 *The Complete Book of Numerology*

the author I should explain the reason for the book as well as stressing that the first-person singular will appear often in this friendly text.

This book is about numbers. Pythagoras said numbers were the very basis of everything. There are many books on this subject, and nothing available, in my opinion, is adequate. As Cary Grant said in the film, *I Was a Male War Bride* (1949), "I'm writing a book about that," perhaps lacking his charm, but with some of his insouciance, if I can manage it.

The coin of numerology may be valuable. However, it has so been rubbed as it passed from hand to hand over the centuries that the information is sometimes unclear now, and some dishonest types have clipped

From Ur of the Chaldees.

the edges a little. The subject has been so repeatedly addressed that writers try to look original by selecting some small detail and inflating it into a padded treatise. I wrote the book you hold in your hand because a book seriously researched and yet presented in a reader-friendly way is needed. It cannot attempt to give even a partial history of mathematics or of mysticism. I wrote what I did as it is because I believe it will be welcomed by any general reader who happens to come across it and that it may well be read with enjoyment and maybe even profit. That would be perfect.

In mathematics, there is talk about perfect numbers. Apparently 6 (for example) is a perfect number ("the sum of its aliquot parts" if you want the jargon), and perfect numbers are even. Maybe there even are some perfect odd numbers. In any case, this book is about how many people—and some of my readers will think these people odd—who are not mathematicians or metaphysicians, but are involved with numbers, believe in numerology and believe that sometimes in superstition there is something that science cannot explain. Whatever the scientists say about this as a pseudoscience that is perfectly groundless, numerology asserts that numbers are perfect for telling us about our natures and our fates. Numerology says that there is vital information, even luck and magic, in numbers. It claims there is information of which mathematicians are wholly unaware. After reading this book, you decide for yourself.

As with my other books on what David Starr Jordan called sciosophy, the "shadow sciences" or the occult sciences (or pseudosciences, if you wish), I am no missionary with a gospel to peddle. I search the sources widely and write subjectively to be judged by believers and nonbelievers alike. What I myself am sure about is that millions of people do give some credence to the occult, always have believed in all its various aspects, however much reason or religion have forbidden that, and whether they are right or wrong to cling to their beliefs it is important to know what they are going on about and what that means to all of us. The cliché is a quotation from one of the ancients who wrote, "I am human, and nothing human is alien to me." There is something of interest in all human activities, even beliefs in things in which you yourself may not believe, even in practices in which you yourself do not engage.

I believe you will find it captivating to read about numerology, the science (or pseudoscience) of numbers and the occult. Enjoy yourself. I write deliberately not like what Melville would call a "metaphysical professor," but in a conversational tone. I hope it does not seem to the believers to be irreverent. I hope it does not sound silly to the nonbelievers. I have discovered that the public likes to be talked with, not at, not down to, and I would like it if you, the reader, would conduct a dialogue with me, pausing now and then to consider what you read and to collect your own thoughts on the matter.

Some people take numerology and superstition in general very casually. Others are extremely alarmed about their popular acceptance. Here are George Charpak and Henri Broch as translated by Bart K. Holland in *Debunked!* (2004):

> At every level society is infected with unscientific thinking, with potentially disastrous consequences. In the space of a few years, the occult has gone from an individual local craft to an international big business. . . . You can't lead people to accept the grossest errors, the biggest falsehoods, and the least justifiable reasoning without consequences . . . without making them doubt the validity of science and all the values that come from reason. . . . The geneticist Albert Jacquard said it very clearly in his forward to *Incroyable . . . mais faux!* [Unbelievable—but Wrong!] (by Alain Cuniot): "To transform citizens into passive sheep is the great dream of the powerful. There are many means to this end; poisoning their minds with pseudoscience can be very effective."

A useful tool to understand an aspect of your world or a sneaky plot to rule the world? You decide. Certainly *something* is going on in society with numerology, astrology, and all that so prevalent, something in popular psychology and the popular press, something that has followed upon ancient superstition's made-up explanations for coincidence and Jung's attempt to establish synchronicity in science. You may welcome it or despise it but you must agree that the occult, whether fooling with magical incantations or numbers, is a real fact of life, a social phenomenon, a daring attempt to explain the inexplicable and to manipulate the mysterious. "The magical forms of thinking," writes Lewis H. Lapham in his "Notebook" in *Harper's* (May 2004), "inhabits so many different quarters of the society that it is hard to read the morning paper, much less watch the evening news broadcasts, without coming across another instance of the broad retreat into the forests of superstition."

For a while at least keep an open mind. "People do everything," Louise Bogan's psychiatrist assured her. She agreed:

> All those odd things they do, like falling in love with shoes and sewing buttons on themselves and hearing voices, and thinking themselves Napoleon, are natural: have a place. Madness and aberration are not only part of the whole tremendous setup, but also

(I have come to believe) important parts. Life trying new ways out and around and through.

So numerology may be just another inventive tactic for just that.

So that will be the tone of this book, and as for the key to its theme I cite the fourth-century sage Appius Cæcus: "*Fabrum esse suæ quemque fortunæ,*" which can be translated as "Each man is the architect of his own fate."

Make of this book and of your life what is best for you. Enjoy both!

Brooklyn, New York
The Feast of The Assumption 2005

Prophecy by astrology in ancient Babylon.

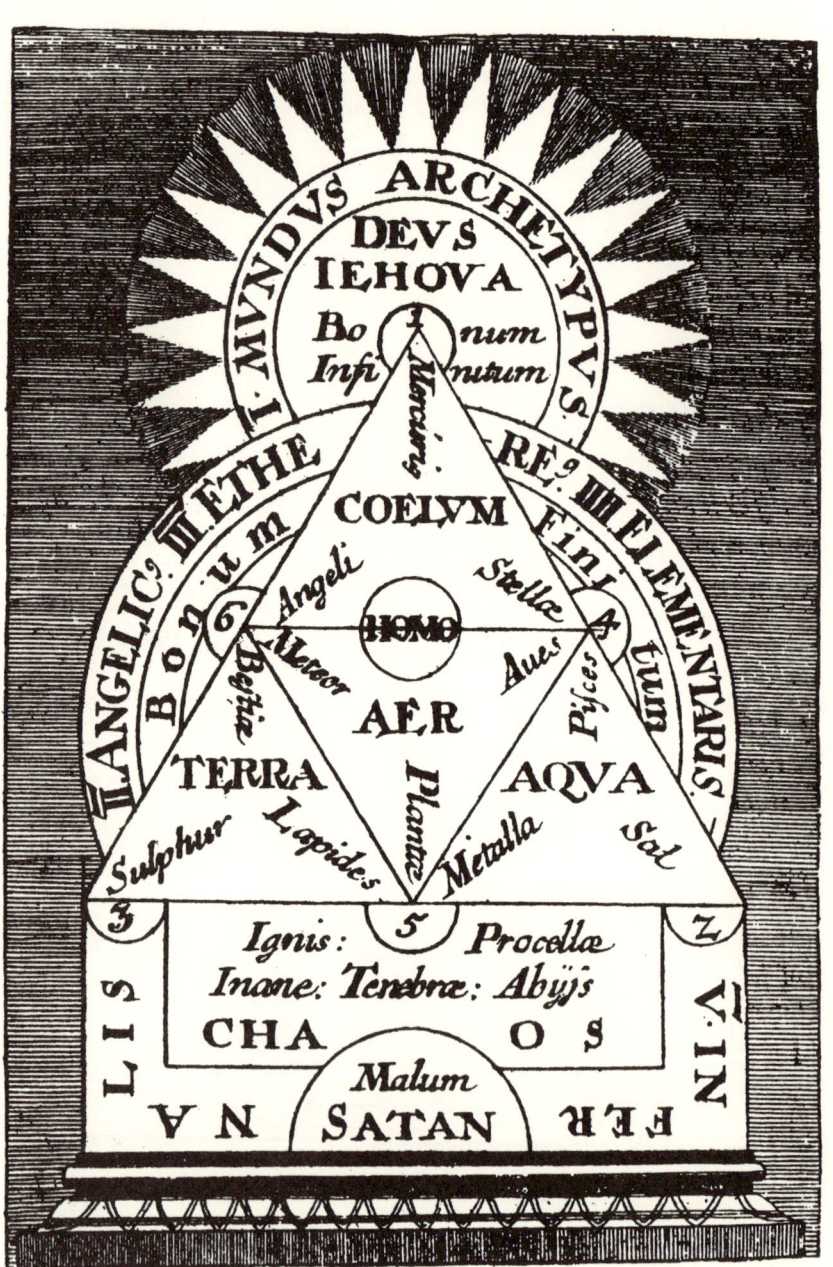

1
Numerology in the Context of Society

Your knowledge is not *to have* but *to learn to*. . . . So that you may be, both having and learned. Small are the Treasures of this world, in respect of the wisdom that judgeth NATURE. For unto him that judgeth truly, what secret is hidden?

—The Spirit Madimi to Dr. John Dee, 2 March 1584

This book, undertaking to do most things other numerology books do (if possible, better) and in addition addressing some things that other books on numerology sidestep, requires at least a brief mention of the sociopolitical and psychological dynamic of numerology. We start there. Other writers do not deal with this, but there is a need to tell you not only what numerology offers to tell you about yourself, but first how numerology can tell you about the nature and values of the culture in which you live.

So here is the context, as painlessly as possible, for Americans and for all of those who have fallen under the sway of the American global imperium, all of the world's people who more or less speak American and therefore (because language governs, expresses, and limits thought) think like Americans, more or less.

Obviously, right off the bat (as Americans say), what numerology principally tells us about society is that there has been since time immemorial a burning desire for hidden knowledge (as well as a love of the irrational).

From the Assyrians and the Chaldeans and their magic and the Chinese *chen* prophecies (that decoded the mystic content of names and other words), through all the ages, there has been a determined attempt to deal with the forces that control the universe and an unremitting urge to know, even to reshape, the future. Those who claimed to possess a secret knowledge of their own did not at all like the idea of others having *other* or even contradictory secret knowledge. They often encoded secrets, just as seventeenth-century mathematicians, doing real science, registered their discoveries in Latin anagrams so as to prove later, if necessary, primacy of conception.

Long ago the Roman Catholic Church completely banned all fortune-telling, and many Protestant denominations continue to instruct their adherents never to deal in fortune-telling in any way. Even devout churchgoers often ignore the prohibitions.

What the widespread popularity of numerology tells us now in the face of all objections is that many modern people are meat-eating vegetarians, or at least leather-shoe-wearing vegetarians, and that they by far outnumber the strict adherence vegetarians who will not even eat animal crackers.

What I mean is that moderns tend, when it comes to authority, to keep some parts of themselves in separate and sealed-off compartments, to hold contradictory opinions, to be of two minds. They believe in science and technology, and they believe in faith healing, superstition, and occult powers.

Most individuals, and moderns are more individualistic than people of earlier times, claim to respect authority. Most of them claim to belong to a religious denomination (and say that they attend services more than they actually do), but at the same time they reserve the right to do whatever they think best (about adultery, abortion, contraception, fornication, homosexuality, and down the alphabet of coital cravings, just about anything you can think of concerned with sex) despite what their infallible or revered and reverend authorities of sex-negative religions tell them. The majority of American men cheat somewhere (in business, on their wives, on their taxes, at the golf course), and yet they think of themselves as perfectly honest men (which to some extent they try to be). They and their wives grow obese and never think of the deadly sin of gluttony.

"I am concealed."
See *Job* 14:13.

They have selected from what I think now must be termed the Ten Suggestions such commandments

Numerology in the Context of Society 17

as they find convenient. They blithely ignore the ones that they find repressive. They usually reject whatever they think irrelevant to their lifestyles. They pick up from this or that faith a bright scrap of theology and sew it on their religious coats of many colors. They accessorize with flag pins or colored ribbons. Those are outward and visible signs of inner and spiritual ideas.

People used to be proud to be true believers but now are highly critical of uniforms and one-color outfits, especially sober black. They believe that such belief-suits are not chic and timeless like the little black dress, but simply indicative of a lack of style sense, of a dearth of creativity and a lack of individuality. They think such conformity marks the poor fashion victim as someone of a more uniform older time. They mock fundamentalist believers as uptight follow-the-leaders.

When told, even by a pope, that they absolutely must not dabble in the occult, their reaction frequently is, "What does he know?" When they consider luck and the claims of the occult, they say with the New York Lottery, "Hey, you never know!"

The one, holy, catholic, and apostolic church (whichever one that is) or the reasonable secular verities that all right-thinking, intelligent persons accept do not appear to be universal anymore. We have left "the fold," and while we do not like to think of ourselves as "black sheep," we do not like the idea of some bishop with a crook yanking us back into line. We like at least this much inherited from our Victorian forebears:

> I am the master of my fate.
> I am the captain of my soul.

Though our priests and ministers may demand that we give our children traditional Christian names, we go for *Brittany* and *Whitney, Jason* and *Tyrone*. Though the rabbis sensibly call for Jewish names for Jews, modern Jews may be content to have a Hebrew name and also another, American name (beginning with the same letter, so *Moishe* is also *Morton* or *Murray*—more recently even more assimilated as *Brian* or *Scott*). The dictates of an ecclesiastical authority when it comes to the likes of numerology we simply ignore. Indeed, his doctrines on gambling he (very seldom she) may have quietly shelved and bingo or a Las Vegas Nite or some other fundraiser may be going on happily in the church hall. The born-again go out and bet again, $5 billion on the Big Game, pittances on office pools. The church ladies who have had their changes of life sit down to tell fortunes with tea leaves or coffee grounds on a white plate, even cast the *I Ching* (Book of Changes). We have Buddhist Baptists and Ethical Culture Jews and Black Muslims.

So numerology is not all that transgressive compared to the rest of rule breaking in society. People think of numerology as not even as odd as Wicca or goddess worship. Numerology is regarded as a harmless hobby or a serious self-knowledge technique, no more dangerous than—the folk verse is old and Scots, as the rhyme makes clear—

> Rowan, ash, and red thread
> Keep the devils frae their speed.

Some people believe in numerology because they find it works for them and some in much the same way as they believe that silences occur in long conversations at 20 minutes past the hour and 20 minutes to the hour—because at those times an angel passes by. Some resemble the obsessed who must touch a doorknob three times, snap fingers three times, etc.

Numerology is regarded as just something that has been around as long as angels have so it may have value. It's fun to play with. Moreover, it is easy: All you need are letters and numbers, no magic wand, no consecrated dagger, no perfecting of the self to be pure enough to find and use the philosopher's stone, not even a pack of Tarot cards (kept wrapped in silk when not used, you know, or should know, to retain the "power"—if yours are not working perfectly, their psychic batteries may have run down). You can do it at the kitchen table, playing with numbers. You do not need blood sacrifices or the burning of pleasant- or obnoxious-smelling incense. Only numbers. Not even money.

We shall come to the basics soon. Here is some background.

The so-called Arabic numbers (which originated in India, as did the gypsies, who were once thought to have come from Egypt) are pretty much universal, but letters of the alphabet differ even when languages all use some form of the Roman alphabet, from the time when Rome was the ruler of the civilized world or at least when Latin was the language of the educated. We have 26 letters; the Romans had fewer.

English uses this version of the Latin alphabet (we now have, as the Romans did not, **I** and **J** and **U** and **V**, and we have thrown in a **W** for good measure):

ABCDEFGHIJKLMNOPQRSTUVWXYZ

Occasionally English has an accent on a word that we have fairly recently borrowed from a language that uses diacritical marks: *René, cliché*. I suggest for numerological purposes you simply regard that *é* as an *e*. I suggest that when you come to Swedish names with (say) an *Å* or *Ø* you just count them as *A* or *O*, although Swedish always lists those special letters at the end of the alphabet. You can do the same with French or Turkish letters such as Ç (which in French is sounded like the beginning of *swat* and in Turkish like the beginning of *chalk*) and all letters which in French, Turkish, German, or what have you that come with what the Germans call an *Umlaut*: ä, ë, ï, ö, ü. Just ignore the accents. If I were you, I would count Dutch *ij* as a single *i*. Don't worry about capitals and small letters. They are regarded as the same, although a female called *SuzAnne* is obviously not the same as even a *Suzanne*, let alone a *Susan* or a *Suze*

Some languages have more or fewer letters in their alphabets than English. They get by (except when referring to *Washington* or *Xerox*) without a **W** or an **X**, for example.

Of course, in numerology, you have to concern yourself with the letters that are there (to be translated into numbers) and not with what is missing. But an apostrophe in a name—and today you might encounter *Mich'elle* or something else unusual—raises a problem. I would ignore it, although the fact that there is a wild grab at attention in the name—not as bad as *Mike-L*, admittedly—is significant.

I'll leave it to your judgment to handle the hyphen in either *Mary-Lou* or the more offbeat *A'lone*. I think it was Tom Lehrer who said he went to school with a fellow who spelled his first name with a **3**: **H3NRY**. Do we regard him as having an *e* in his name or call that a **3**?

Just kidding, folks. In fact, this whole section is a riff with the sneaky purpose of putting into your thoughts the fact that all this numerology business, although it exists in cultures all over the world, is very culture specific. Though it has gone on for uncounted centuries, it exists today in various modern contexts. It inescapably reflects the age-old traditions and also the New Age concerns of the users. Naturally you cannot assume that you can "do" numerology only in English or that American ways and means are the only sound ones. Too many numerology books neglect to mention that, so I thought I should. But the numerology game can be played in any language with an alphabet, whether it has (say) no **W** (like Turkish) or a **W** (like Kurdish), a matter of bitter dispute these days.

There is always going to be something of the personal in numerological calculations, though not as much room for individual interpretation as in, say, the Tarot (which is why in my opinion the Tarot may be a better place to exercise your intuition and imagination).

Numerology likewise has no place for visualization, and visualization plays a leading role in the occult and can actually perform wonders. You, as Dr. Spock told mothers, have more information inside you than you think you have. Meditation can convince you of that. Numerology is not as calming and may not be quite as informative as meditation, but Americans don't like to sit still and meditate. They like to be up and doing. In American slang, even the verb "to say" is now "go."

Americans also like the quick and easy. The so-called rules of numerology are easy to get going with. They are much simpler in essence and much easier to handle in practice than the extremely strict demands of ceremonial or high magic or even fiddling with runes or concocting potions in love magic. You do not get into creepy situations such as the Babylonian "questioners of the dead," and you won't burn the house down as you might in pyromancy.

Perhaps the two principal reasons why you see so many people these days ready to sit down for a few minutes and work out a numerological "reading" is that it is simple and easy. So you see a lot of numerology buffs and very few creatures, huddled, hooded, and probably high on drugs, chanting *Zazas, Zazas, Nasatanada, Zazas* (the magical words to open the gates of Hell).

Numerology has an appeal for our user-friendly, in-a-hurry, if not actually dumbed-down society. We use a simple system and our familiar alphabet. We do not bother, as some did even in English in years gone by, to use the "Hebrew" system of numerology. I am going to describe that "Hebrew" system now. If you find this part boring, skip it.

The "Hebrew" alphabet covers only 18 letters of the alphabet of English. The letters we have in common are, with their traditional numerical "equivalents": **A** *aleph* 1, **B** *beth* 2, **G** *gimel* 3, **D** *daleth* 4, **H** *he* 5, **V** (or **W**) *vau* 6, **Z** *zayin* 7, **Y** *yod* 10, **K** *kaph* 20, **L** *lamed* 30, **M** *mem* 40, **N** *nun* 50, **P** *pe* 80, **Q** *qooph* 100, **R** *resh* 200, **S** *shin* 300, and **T** *taw* 400. You will find more detail on Hebrew letters later on in this book, but this is not the time to slow you down with those details.

You can see at a glance that this Hebrew-letter stuff is a lot more challenging than the system we use today with the letters in the "right" order for us and all of them accounted for. The "Hebrew" system required a little extra work to supply values for our **C, E, F, I, J, O, U,** and **X**. These do not occur in Hebrew. For reasons that I do not fully understand—get used to abiding mysteries in the occult—the following accommodation was made: **C** 3, **E** 5, **F** 8, **I** 10, **J** 10, **O** 7, **U** 6, and **X** 5 or 6. Numerologists seek simplicity, and "5 or 6" seems to throw what John Lennon would call

Numerology in the Context of Society

"a Spaniard in the works." It looks as if the "extra" letters mostly arrived for the benefit of the Greeks and had their names and numbers suggested by Greek (not Hebrew) words that began with the letters involved. The Greeks put vowels at the end of *aleph* and *beth*.

As if that were not enough, there is still one more complication. In Hebrew, letters can have different numerical values depending upon whether they are final letters in a word or not: *kaph* you have seen is 20, but as a final letter, it gets 500; *mem* gets 40, but as a final letter gets 600; *nun* gets 50, but as a final letter, it is 700; *pe* gets 80, but as a final letter, it is 800; and *sade* (coming between *pe* 80 and *qooph* 100) is 90, but has no equivalent in the English alphabet.

Every such detail tells us something about the different societies, their learned members, hermetic sciences, and popular enthusiasms, and the psychology of wanting to deal with the straightforward or valuing the complex. All you have to do is to look at the system I have suggested you use (because that is the one most people use today) and this older "Hebrew" system. The difference likewise reveals something interesting about the people involved. Today one camp likes the idea of everyone taking an interest in doing "readings" in numerology (and puts free offers and free programs on the Web), and another camp likes to shroud everything in mystery and be elevated adepts in a world of—this time a Yiddish rather than Hebrew word—*schnooks*. Those who like to wear the cloak of mystery as a magician's gown are the people who would prefer the occult to *stay* occult (hidden).

ד	ט	ב
ג	ה	ז
ח	א	ו

In numerology, it is my suggestion to you that you select the easy path or the difficult path and settle for yourself whether you are breaking rules of dictates you feel you should heed or not. If you see no harm in it, I do not think that numerology is going to do you any harm. If you do think of it as a truly forbidden practice, then you are introducing that sense of being on the dark side that black magic courts because necromancy thinks that generates power. In numerology, there is not so much of what Jean Bodin (*Demonomania*, 1580) found in witchcraft, which was a "very determined intention of attaining [one's] own ends" and antisocial ends at that.

Whatever you do, by turning to numerology you will be right on track in a society that is basically Ptolemaic, not with just the earth as the center of the universe but your country as the center of the world and YOU as the center of everything. Speaking of growing up, Piaget discusses what he calls (or what we translate as) "de-centering," which means learning to be less narcissistic, acquiring a broader perspective. Numerology is, we have to admit, self-centered. "Not that there's anything wrong in that!"

22 The Complete Book of Numerology

But enough about that. Let's now talk about you. Your birth name, your nickname, your Harry3866 on the Web, your credit card numbers, the number you want to play because you noticed it as the expiration date on the milk carton, your present and future.

I am going to try to stay off tangents such as what Julie Lockhart calls "cycles of divine order" and the cycles of biorhythms (which Marie L. Betz conflates with astrology and numerology). I am going to get to practical, you-centered numerology, the kind of thing Nicole Delongchamp called "*numérologie practique*" in her *Le Miroir des nombres* (*The Mirror of Numbers, c.* 1993) but in English, in fact insofar as possible with such an esoteric topic, I mean to write in what our shrewd, straightforward poet Marianne Moore called plain American "which cats and dogs can read." Up close and personal.

Move on to the basics.

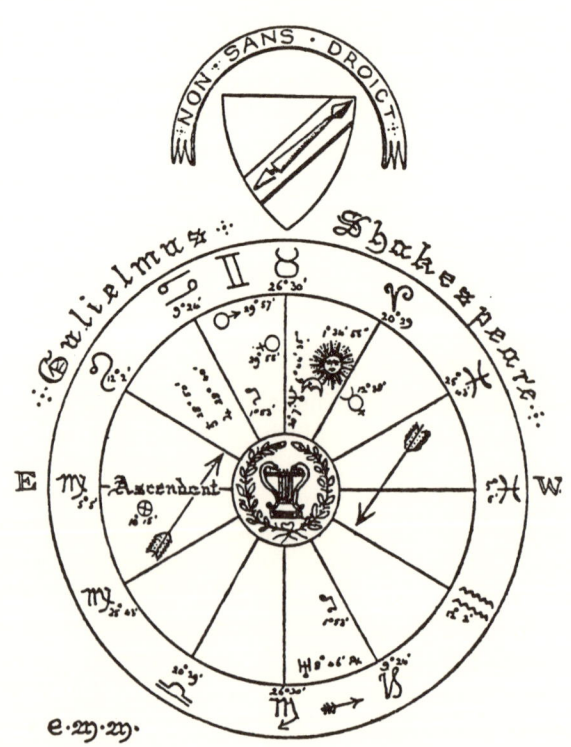

2
What the Numbers Basically Mean

Numerology sees significance only in the single digits 1–9 and in just two two-digit numbers, 11 and 22. (Anyone who tells you there are more and bigger numbers of power is unorthodox, and, in fact, the 11 and 22 are so rare as to be nothing to dwell on.) The single *digits*—a term that comes from counting on the fingers—are claimed to have lessons for us all. People have been thinking about this kind of thing for millennia, as you read in the previous section (and if you jumped in here, go back and read that before you continue here). Today, when interest in the individual is conveniently combined with never before seen opportunities for the individual to find out things about self and the world around, interest in numerology and all Me things is burgeoning.

The Me Generation (and the eras that have followed it) may balk a little at a system of psychology and prediction that deals in 9 basic regular types and 2 occasional exceptions. That may seem inimical to our desire for individuality. Think, however, that psychology has divided things into introvert or extrovert while sociology has divided people into those who are inner directed and those who are other directed. Remember that numerology is very old and tied to the planets the Chaldean astronomers and astrologers could see and was further influenced by the fact that Claudius Galenus (*c.* 130–201 A.D., called Galen in English) collected, as a Greek physician, philosopher, and anatomist, all the medical knowledge of his time and was *the* authority for a long time after.

Galen wrote more than a dozen treatises on Hippocrates, whom we call the father of medicine in the West. It was Galen who established the

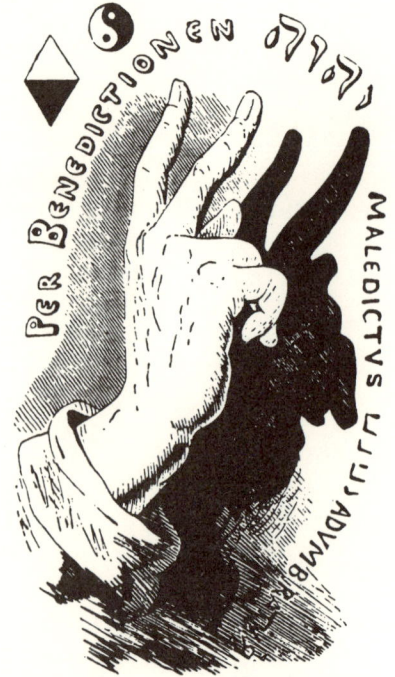

Éliphas Levy and indeed most writers on magic do not give enough attention to the fact that the gestures which go with the hocus-pocus actually refer to numbers and those numbers to mystical ideas.

idea of just four basic human types, based on supposed four elements (fire, water, air, and earth) and the four humours (liquids) in the human body. This was much more elaborate than the biblical explanation of Adam, fashioned by God (the Bible says) of earth. Adam's name translates Clay. But as early as Adam and Eve and their sons Cain and Abel, it was clear that people can have different personalities as well as different sexes. Numerology limits the basic identifications while at the same time stressing, as astrology does with its 12 basic personality types, that minor variations are almost infinite. It does not take sex into account. A male 3 is regarded as the same as a female 3.

If there are a handful of basic personality types, it seems natural that everyone would want to know if they are a 3 or a what.

Experts may introduce a series of "modifiers," such as the Expression number and so on, to as many as 20. I think they are catering to a desire of the individual not to have to face the limited number of basic personality types in which numerology traditionally deals. I think they are losing numerology's big appeal of simplicity. By the end of this section, I shall subject you to a bit of the complex shenanigans numerologists can get involved in as they make things more and more involved. If you really want that kind of particularity, you need an expert numerologist to play with "modifiers" for you. It is not something that you easily can do for yourself. If you will be content with the basics, I think you have enough in most cases. That is the thrust of this section.

Very few persons are capable of putting into effect the revelations of 11 and 22. Some numerologists not content with the rarities 11 and 22 posit a 33. I happen not to go along with them on this. There are so few perfect masters that I think we are off base harping on (say) Master numbers. Most people are just ordinary people like you and me.

In what one cultural critic has damned as the current culture of narcissists, some people are ready to believe that they are extra special, however, and may consider that they deserve the 11 label just as much as they think they deserve, say, the Gucci label. Or they want to regard themselves as a 22 or a 33 and would like a 44 if there were one.

I am going to give you the basic lowdown on the numbers 1 to 9 and 11 and 22 right now.

You will notice that the odd numbers tend to relate chiefly to the individual, the even ones to society or those who best serve society. You may also think that as the numbers get larger, the fates they promise get better, moving from the person all wrapped up in the self to the one serving the best interests of all mankind, from the person obsessed with his or her individual and temporary position on this planet to the person interested in the cosmos or at the very least whatever we can know of and do to improve and protect Spaceship Earth on which we are all passengers.

One could make a whole book out of the subject of this section, the way astrologers take (say) love signs and expand upon them, the way those who read palms go on and on not just about major lines, but hatchings and islands and stars and other singularities. We have need and space here only for concise, general sketches of each of the basic number personalities.

1 This is obviously the number of singularity, individuals, independence. It tells us that we come into the world alone and we leave the world alone and that we are responsible for our individual lives. Religion ties us together (as the word's etymology suggests), but in the Christian tradition it asks us, "What doth it profit a man if he gain the whole world and lose his immortal soul?" Your basic task on earth is one: to live your one earthly life so as to earn your personal life in heaven in the hereafter or just make your earthly life count for something good if there is nothing else. You are the only one who can save your eternal soul (if you believe you have one) and the only one who can make your life's journey good (if you believe the earthly existence is all that we have). One with God or all alone—that's you. If you do not believe in reincarnation, this is your one time around.

2 This speaks of the bipolar, the cooperative, the dependent, the contrastive, the extremes. We are social animals, and we must mate with another in order to create a family and that family exists within the larger family of man. No one lives a life completely on his or her own. Even those hermits who in early Christianity went off into the desert to live in solitude hoped in the long run to be taken into the company of the blessed.

They may have been solitary, but in their lives they attempted to keep God ever present. The Greeks had an interesting way of explaining why we feel incomplete without a mate, what the attraction of love was all about. They said that the gods originally created human beings as double individuals, but that, fearing the power of so complete an entity, the gods split us: We are engaged through sex in "the desire and pursuit of the whole," of completion as human beings. That's why, I suppose, men used to refer to their wives as their better halves. A twosome is cozy.

3 The individual must relate to God and to fellow human beings. He or she must acknowledge and participate in the connections and express gratitude and love. Matthew Oliver Goodwin (*Numerology: The Complete Guide* I, 1981) under this 3 writes: "The JOY OF LIVING can be expressed with optimism and enthusiasm. There can be a purity, even a naiveté here. (This is, perhaps, the most enjoyable lesson of all the numbers.)" Three has always been a mystic number. Christianity has the Trinity, three persons in one God. Superstition says that events come in threes. Numerology sees threes as powerful. Don't believe it? "What I tell you three times is true."

4 This is the number of a square, all four sides equal, secure, delimiting, fair. It reminds us of a building block of stone, of a cornerstone of an edifice. It speaks of rationality and proportion and strength and responsibility to be as it were on the square with oneself and on the square with others to whom we owe fair treatment and consideration. There is something complete about 4. Four-square. Four ways of getting out of jail, according to the criminal slang: "Pay out, run out, work out [do your time], or die out [by which is meant die *in*]." Numerology sees a 4 as stable, like a four-legged table or chair. It also sees a 4 as having something of a hard time in a world that is full of the unstable.

5 This is the number that makes us think of a star (unless we are Jewish and think of the two triangles that comprise the Star of David, which is six-pointed). The star can be our guide. In ancient days, the fearless explorer got into his craft and set sail saying, "I have chosen my star, and under that star there is land." The five-pointed star's odd number of points can remind us of the four points of the compass and also the point that says we should go not only to the four corners of the earth, but also upward, toward the heavens. The five-pointed star turned upside down is the symbol of the Adversary of God, Satan. It signals negativity. For some reason that nobody has ever explained, the 5 person seems to be more likely to know she or he is a 5 and to act more like a 5 than most of the other types that numerology describes do in playing the roles assigned to them by their numbers. Five turns up significantly in the lives of 5s more than other numbers do. The same is true for 5s and non-5s who are one of the three "fire signs" (the whole Zodiac having been tied, in groups of 3 "houses," to the 4 elements and 4 humours).

6 As you have read, if you looked at the preface, 6 is a perfect number. It stands for balance, for stability, for completion. It reminds us of the Trinity (Father, Son, Holy Spirit) in combination with the trinity that God has given each one of us: (body, mind, and soul). With these, religion says we must serve Him and our fellow humans for love of God and love of them. Sixes have perhaps a lot more work cut out for them than most other people, but 6s appear to be blessed with more gifts for doing their work than others have received except for the most exceptional.

7 This is the number most people associate with luck. You are going to hear a lot about that in this book. We often hear luck comes to those who are prepared to receive it. Luck seems to be irrational but, strangely, 7 is the symbol of the rational, analytical mind, the great gift that God gave particularly to mankind and not to the other animals of Creation. Tradition says that the seventh son of a seventh son (often called Doctor in the old days) has the gift of second sight. The seventh son may be a prophet and a healer. If you turn out to have 7 as your number, congratulations, but remember that being lucky is a "sometime thing." You can call your kid Felix or Fortunatus or Victor or Felicia or Felicity or Victoria, but luck . . .? We can name children from the time of their birth (those born at sunrise used often to be named Lucius or such, but now Dawn and Lucy and the rest are often given for other reasons) or make a try for a name that confers a power or writes a script (boys' names often emphasize strength, girls' names beauty), but time and chance happeneth to us all, as the Bible says.

8 This is the number of the material world and personal material success. It is double the practicality of 4. But it is not 9. It is about as much as hard work and talent can gain for anyone without the gift of grace or genius. This is about balance. Halved and halved again, 8 is balanced, and the final halving brings it down to basic 1. This sort of person is very reliable, but may be angry with those who slack off or who stand in the way of getting things done. Eights are usually a bit lacking in imagination and are better at tactics than at strategy. But if you want a great administrator rather than a charismatic leader, appoint an 8. Finally, 8s can be rounded individuals. They need all of what they can get because they are resident in a society that is often square, in the slang sense of the word, and a society given to elevating the eccentric to celebrity status if merely famous for being famous, if only for Andy Warhol's "fifteen minutes," which is not fair and always in our faces. On a more cheerful and uplifting note, think of the 8 Beatitudes of Christ's sermon on the mount, good advice seen earlier in Buddhism.

9 This is the number that goes beyond material success to an even greater power. It is the number of transcendence. It is the number of the spiritual, even the divine. As God loves us all, so the 9, with a touch of that, is a philanthropist and may, like 11 and 22 (through whom God tends to work more occasionally) open his or her heart to fellow creatures and serve their interests, sometimes doing well for himself or herself, but always striving to do good for others. The next two numbers are more powerful still and more altruistic. They are also even rarer than 9s.

11 This is the number of the rare individual who is not a 2 but doubly a 1, an extremely, extraordinarily outstanding individual who is gifted with some special insight and the ability to be the one to lead many others. To preserve his or her purity or individuality, the 11 has to some extent and from time to time to flee from the crowd and concentrate on the inner self, the personal illumination. Lacking true insight into the self, the 11 is in real danger of becoming something of a sacred monster and prone to think that those who are led are just sheep, perhaps not even worthy of the genius of an 11 to lead them. In great power there is great risk of power misused. The great villains of history are greatly gifted individuals gone wrong; most often, not people who by force and circumstances achieved more than their talents promised, but failures who did not live up to the promise of their best selves. There is both comedy and tragedy in that.

22 This is the number of someone doubly 11, you might say. Every once in a while, along comes someone who is more than a leader—a savior. This person is a doer, like an 11, but more than that; this person works miracles. This person is not so enamored of self as an 11, never without compassion and consideration for those less gifted. Here is responsible, loving genius, not genius too far above the masses to feel their pain and work for their needs rather than for personal glory. In a person such as this, the human and the divine are closely in touch. There is a spark of divinity in each of us, but a 22 radiates glory. The 22 may come to a bad end, but succeeds as a martyr, not fails as a villain. The world, sometimes, as George Bernard Shaw says in *St. Joan*, is not ready for its saints.

For a Power number, add the name number you get here to the Life Path number (which you will get later on in section 5), and that will tell you what your grip on reality and your force to act will be. Numerologists say that if the number derived from your name is not "harmonious" with the number that describes (limits? suggests?) the path of your life, there

What the Numbers Basically Mean 29

will be a discordant note struck. Maybe you don't want the Power number after all. The best thing is to stick with the number from your name, accept its advantages and disadvantages, and do the best you can with it—or change your name and fate and go ahead boldly. You are free, you know, to run your life, to some extent at least, and if you will learn to communicate with others and get their help you can be very happy here as a person, as a family member, in business or profession, in society at large, accepting, juggling, and balancing all your responsibilities and using all your talents, determination, and luck.

To some extent in this section, we have been considering the personalities of individuals. But essentially this has been not so much personal numbers, but you might say, group numbers, whether the groups are large (such as the 8s) or very small (such as the 11s or the 22s). For what interests the individual the most, which is to say his or her own private numbers, numerology derives (1–9, 11 and 22 again) from the name (whole, vowels only, consonants only, initial of the forename), the birth date, and other things very personal to the seeker. That seeker wants a lot more information to use in the understanding of personal life and fortune than the standard list, which goes something like this:

1 Self-assertiveness

2 Harmony

3 Self-expression

4 Stability

5 Adventurousness

6 Reliability

7 Mystery

8 Worldly success

9 Leadership

That is what I consider to be the most representative list of the type. Different writers say different things. Not able to cite them all, I make judgments. I confess that a certain subjectivity may have crept into my characterizing here, but my effort has been in this instance, and will continue to be as I move through this whole book, to report what is traditional. I am not attempting to revise numerology or to attack or defend it or expand it. I am trying to record a sort of history of numerology for the practical person who may wish to be introduced to it, maybe use it, maybe not. This book is not intended to attempt to reshape or correct numerology's historic ideas (or findings). I leave it to you whether to believe numerology is truly important or to side with Charles J. Cazeau: in *Science Trivia* (1986) he dismisses it as "an amusing parlor game" and states firmly "there is no scientific evidence on which its principles are based."

Over the centuries numerology, like any body of fact or opinion, has undergone change. Invariably the changes have been in the direction of attempting to make sense of the cosmos and mankind's place within it, the person and his or her place in society, and the cooperating and contradictory elements within the human psyche. Call them Eros (the desire for Life) and Thanatos (the urge for Death) or whatever you like, Reason and Emotion, Love and Hate, whatever. They are in flux and at work and perhaps at war within the mysterious self, with all its layers, all its secrets in the conscious and unconscious mind. Moreover, the individual, whatever the type, changes.

Mankind has certainly struck out in many directions over our time on this planet, and we have begun to reach out into infinite outer space. We should land some guys on Mars (why?) by 2020. But we still have not very much 20/20 vision when it comes to what I call inner space.

Numerology tries to address that problem. It tries to explain our lives, our world, and our universe. It is only right to admit that numerology is one of the most ancient of the occult sciences (or, as I suppose we must invariably add, pseudosciences). It predates even Pythagoras, a sixth-century-B.C. Greek philosopher who was interested in the transmigration of souls and also in what Bertrand Russell saw as the cold beauty of mathematics, both of which Pythagoras must have picked up from the Egyptians. They presumably got it from Mesopotamia. It is only in the last century or so that the psychological aspect of numerology has come to the fore. Before that, it went through stages of the magical and the mathematical, characteristic of other times.

Our times have in a number of respects had more than one Me Generation lately. A recent and notable one was the Beats, a generation which one of their number shrewdly said had chosen just one number and played it boldly. Today we are in love with technology (which may prove to be an unfaithful lover), but our favorite science is the science of the mind. We turn to psychology, psychiatry, mental therapy, and it is all very personal. The

Pythagoras.

physician gives orders; the psychiatrist gives advice. Unless he or she is nondirective. In that case, all you get for your money is someone to listen to you talk about yourself. You come to your own realizations and you are expected to adjust yourself. I have some quarrel with the idea of personal adjustment. Things are always in flux. It seems to me that mental health is not adjustment but the reasonable and continual adjustment to reality. I would not call someone maladjusted; I might call them badly adjusting.

In our solipsism, we don't even say we are being treated by a physician of the soul (or mind, if you prefer): We say not that he or she is working *on* us, but that we are working *with* our therapist. The patients may or may not be running the asylum, but they certainly want to direct their treatment, and they are tending to be drawn to alternative cures. Even the squarest old religion has turned the priest around to face the congregation, to work *with* rather than *for* them, you might say. Our respect for authority has weakened.

Psychiatrists are the priests of many people's new religion. I have always thought that, like Christianity and Islam and Mormonism and Spiritualism and Christian Science (these last three American creations), Freudianism was just another Reformed Jewish religion. The traditional religions have asked us to be God-directed and what David Reisman called other-directed (towards fellow mortals), but the newer, rather buffet-style religions for spiritual grazing have taught us to get very much wrapped up in personal problems and personal solutions. It is in a search for the self that most people who turn to numerology are engaged. People today are living their lives for themselves and not, like people in the Age of Faith, living their lives for God.

Numerology is a belief for the self-sufficient. Numerology is a hands-on thing the layman can learn to use without constant supervision and without expensive consultation, as I have said earlier. It is DYI (Do It Yourself). Its texts are FYI (For Your Information). It uses tools anyone can buy or rent and be shown how to handle. It promises cheap results in the comfort of your own home. It looks less superstitious than some other occult arts. It looks no more dangerous than crossing your fingers.

The people who turn to knowledge seeking and problem solving through numerology are on personal quests. They may believe that numbers govern other things, of course. They may believe, with the ancient Greeks, that numbers govern everything in the universe. They may be interested in the basic so-called Harmonious Numbers of the days of their own lives:

1 Time for decisive action

2 Plan your next move, but do not act yet

3 Time for small multitasking jobs
4 Time for routine work, nothing fancy
5 Time for surprises and calculated risks
6 Time to take inventory more than act
7 Time to reflect, maybe retrench, caution
8 Time to go for the gold
9 The big day! Aim high, and go for it

As always, you derive these numbers by adding digits time after time until you get a single digit. 20 March 2003 is 20 + 03 + 2003 = 2 + 3 + 5 = 10 = 1 + 0 = 1. Time for individual decisive action this day as I write = moving on to what you are truly most interested in, not the basic class of individuals to which you may belong, or the best advice on what to do or not to do today, but the ever paramount question: *Who the hell am **I** and what is going to happen to **ME**?*

One interesting, but often neglected aspect lies in the Challenge numbers, governing the self-imposed problems the person must face, whatever his or her basic number. These Challenge numbers work on the cycles of the Life Path (which is discussed in section 6). And once you find your Life Path number from 1 to 9, you start working with the cycles of challenges. They go like this, *followed* by the cycles for 1 to 9

Life Path **1** begins when you are born, second cycle at age 35, third at age 62—Growing up, gaining independence, impatiently, learning quickly

Life path **2** second cycle begins at 34, third at 61—Learning to socialize, becoming more other-directed, needing friendship and direction

Life path **3** second cycle begins at 33, third at 60—Socializing, enjoying life and creativity, seeking new adventures and knowledge

Life path **4** second cycle begins at 32, third at 59—Restrictions of earning a living, balancing work and play

Life Path **5** second cycle begins at 31, third at 58—Changing circumstances and goals, looking for instruction on self and society

Life Path **6** second cycle begins at 30, third at 57—Love and family or other personal relationships, perhaps outweighing career or complicating career

Life Path **7** second cycle begins at 29, third at 56—Search for a balance between the busy world and the need for solitary reflection, readjustment of values

Life Path **8** second cycle begins at 28, third at 55—Prosperity or acceptance of lot, maybe some dissonance or disappointment, maybe success

Life Path **9** second cycle begins at 27, third at 54—In a rut or inspired to creativity, possible major career or emotional shifts, movement in many aspects

You see that life presents changing circumstances over time and concomitant demands and challenges. There are Challenge numbers. You determine these not by addition, as is usual, the way you found your personality birth number, but by subtraction. You take your birth number (found by what is called fadic addition: as $1 + 9 + 8 + 2 = 20 = 2 + O = 2$) and now subtract to get a Challenge number. To get the number of your first challenge, subtract using birth date number (5 December 1985 is $5 + 12 = 1 + 2 = 3$, $1+ 9 + 8 + 5 = 23 = 2 + 3 = 5$, so what we have is 5, 3, 5, right? and that reduces to $5 + 3 + 5 = 13$, which comes to a 4, and fadic number of birth month ($12 = 1 + 2 = 3$). Take the smaller from the larger. In this case, if you are still with me, $4 - 3 = 1$. That is your first Challenge number, a 1.

For the number of your second challenge, subtract birth date from your fadic year of birth number. Here goes: year of birth number $1 + 9 + 8 + 5$ in our example and it is 23, $2 + 3$, a 5, and your birth day is $5 + (12=1+2=3)$ which is 3. Second Challenge number $5 - 3 = 2$, so the number you get is 2. For the third challenge—this is the big one—subtract your second Challenge number from your first Challenge number. The first was 1, the second was 2, and we cannot have a minus number so do it the other way, I guess, and we have $2 - 1 = 1$. Third Challenge number is a 1.

Have you got all that right? I promised basics, and this looks very complicated. I just want to make it clear that to the simple number you are about to get in "Your Fate is Written in Your Name" numerology has a lot up its sleeve to pull you in deeper and deeper with bells and whistles and computations and the Universal Year (that is what you got by $1 + 9 + 8 + 5 = 23 = 2 + 3 = 5$, that 5) and the Universal Month (that was your December $12 = 1 + 2 = 3$, a 3) and you add it to the Universal Year number (which was a 5, you recall) so that you have $3 + 5 = 8$, all of which is likely to make the beginner say it is a bit much, and can we just do the basics, please? Well, maybe I'll take a look at the challenges, because those are a bit worrisome, and I have fought my way to my Challenge numbers, first, second, and third.

Challenge **O** no specific challenge except inevitable change over time

Challenge **1** anxiety over the responsibility to be independent

Challenge 2 lack of sensitivity about the feelings and desires of others

Challenge 3 difficulty over balancing work and play, cooperation and creativity

Challenge 4 difficulty over becoming mired in habit or pushed by reality

Challenge 5 fear of letting go of the secure and familiar to attain the new

Challenge 6 the pressures of work and family responsibilities

Challenge 7 fear of one's true self and of what meditation might reveal of it

Challenge 8 sense of dislocation that power and possessions cannot help

I suggest that instead of the personal year, month, and day numbers driving you around the bend, if you really want a daily, weekly, yearly guide, buy a book of your astrological "house" for the year in which, you trust, someone has worked out what is likely to be the best advice for you as you make it through 2005, 2006, 2007, and so on. This is the kind of thing that a professional numerologist can do for you, but professional astrologers are easier to find, and books on (say) Aquarius for 2005 will not leave you personally carrying the can, as the British say, doing the hard work for yourself.

I say you should use numerology's simpler aspects to give you some insight on personality and life trajectory and leave the predictions to the stargazers and their mathematical computer programs. You don't know your trine from your ascendant, so get help if you trust in such advice at all. At the end of the year, look at the comments you have jotted down in your "house" book and tot up the writer's hits and misses. If you are sold on the thing, buy next year's edition. Otherwise, do not.

Later on I am going to say you can get something you may find useful by getting a number out of the initial of your forename (the one you usually use, if you have more than one; the first one on your birth certificate say some, even if you do not use that one), but numerologists, if you permit them, may want to fancy things up with asking you to "do" the first vowel and the first consonant, and really, is there no end to all this? Next they will be looking for last letter of name and God knows what else. Ayureveda? Love numbers? Cycles of Divine Order? Nine Star Ki? There are books on that and more. How deeply do you want to go into this?

I'll be glad if I can get you to play with the basic numbers derived from your name and the date of your birth. A big answer is said to be in your name, which may be altered and to some degree was arbitrary in the first

400 15. Booke.   The discouerie   *Art of coniuring.*

The characters of the angels of the seauen daies, with their names: of figures, seales and periapts.

The seuenth Chapter.

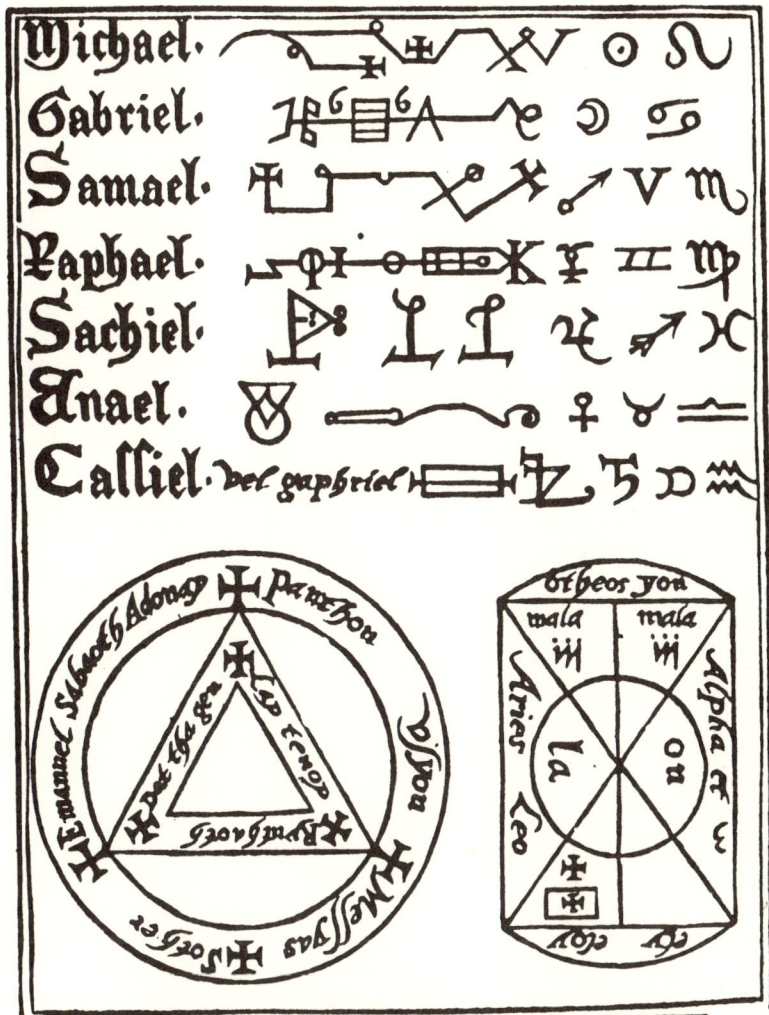

{ These figures are called the seales of the earth, without the which no spirit will appeere, except thou haue them with thee. }

From Reginald Scot's *The Discouerie of Witchcraft* (1595) the archangels related to the days of the week and astrology: Michael (Sun, Leo), Gabriel (Moon, Cancer), Samael (Mars, Aries, Scorpio), Raphael (Mercury, Gemini, Virgo), Sachiel (Jupiter, Sagittarius, Pisces), Anael (Venus, Taurus, Libra), and Casiel (Saturn, Capricorn, Aquarius). The seals at the bottom, left: names of God with Signs of the Cross, right: Alpha and Omega, crosses, Aries and Leo, &c.

place (unless you think there are clear reasons for everything even if we do not always know them all), and the direction of your life (determined by the unalterable fact of your date of birth), which basically is laid out for you and set.

Another element which is pretty easy to understand, if not to accept, that can easily be taken into account is the karmic debt discussed later in section 13 on page 150 the book. I'll give you just a taste of that elaboration right now. When you get a 1 from 19 (1 + 9 = 10 = 1 + 0 = 1) the karmic debt is 1; a 4 from 1+3, the karmic debt is 13; a 5 from 1 + 4; a 7 from 1 + 6. There is not much or even nothing that you can do about the karmic debt. So you may say you don't want to get into discussing it, but maybe you will want to be aware of it and make the best adjustment you can this time around in life—and keep adjusting as new circumstances arrive.

The whole thing can be as easy as finding out you are (say) a Scorpio or a 7. Like astrology, or a Tarot reading, or other such procedure, you are given certain "facts" and often but not always definite ways around any difficulties that might be said to be associated with them.

You work with what you are given and what can be made of it by yourself. Superstition, like religion, may spring from fear, but also, like religion, can be comforting and offer certain ways of undoing bad things. In religion, you can become a theologian or just follow the basic dictates of your particular faith. It is always nice to have some sense of support, some out.

If that black cat does cross your path or you do step on the cracks in the sidewalk, there are superstitious remedies. That gives people some confidence, and confidence is one of the great appeals of superstition as it is of a religious faith relied upon, even if you do not know all the details.

Next comes something gratifyingly simpler than the confusions I may have produced in the last few pages. You have a name. We can work with that. It can get you a number that will promise you that you are going to be comfortably independent (1, 5, 7, 8, 9) or financially well off (1, 4, 8), fine at fine art (3, 6, or 9) or literature (3, 5, 6, 8), psychic (2, 7, 9) or spiritual (same 2, 7, 9), lucky in love (2, 6) or marriage (same 2, 6) or sex (not the same thing, 3, 5), and so on. I am sure you will be interested. Much later on we let you in on 4 and 8 being rather hard to live with. Which number are you? Read on!

3
Your Fate is Written in Your Name

Your name is you. Magic says that it is as much a part of you as a lock of your hair or a fingernail clipping; magic undertakes to use it to get at you personally. More mundanely, your name writes the life's scenario. Everyone realizes a Bambi is going to be regarded (and regard herself) as very different from a Barbara. But your name can tell you more. Your name can give you an idea of your character type, very likely better than astrology can. You probably know if you are (say) a Virgo or a Gemini. Do you know your name number?

Here's how you can find it. For centuries, the universal numbers of Pythagoras (1 through 9, 0 not having come into use until the later, Arab, mathematicians) have been used to characterize and foretell fates through numerology. For English or any other 26-character alphabet, we construct this table. I do all the heavy lifting for you here!

1 2 3 4 5 6 7 8 9

A B C D E F G H I

J K L M N O P Q R

S T U V W X Y Z

There is an older system that violates the alphabetical order of English and leaves out 9 (as 3 times 3, 9 is a sacred number). The older system is more complicated and goes like this:

1 2 3 4 5 6 7 8

A B C D E U O F
I K G M H V Z P
Q R L T N W
J S X
Y

If you want to, you can use the older system, as I said in an earlier section. I prefer the simpler, modern one. But people turning to numerology and such often will try a second system if the first one does not give them the result they want, just as the $5 or $10 (or more expensive) "reader" may give you palmistry, the crystal ball, and the Tarot for good measure. Just deciding to accept that, you realize, reveals something about your basic character.

Here is how to proceed with numerology, which your "readers" seldom try. Using the simpler system, write out your full name in capital letters and check the number that corresponds to each letter.

K I M B E R L Y J O N E S
2 9 4 2 5 9 3 7 1 6 5 5 1

Add the numbers. The result for KIMBERLY and JONES is 41 and 18. Add those together. You have 59. Now, here's the secret: Keep adding until you get a single digit: 5+9 = 14 and 1+4 = 5. KIMBERLY JONES is a 5. If she thinks of herself more as a KIM JONES she may or may not have another number, just as if she spells her name (say) KIMBERLEE JONES or goes way out and has KIMBER LEIGH JONES. Sometimes you may be shocked to discover that your formal name and a nickname yield exactly the same number. The nickname in that case doesn't change things at all.

You should work out a separate number for all the ways your name appears, full, shortened with a nickname, before and after marriage, etc.

Each number has a character. After all, a Betty is different from a Lisa or a Liza or a Bette or an Elizabeth. Somebody who spells a name Barri or Daryl or Britney is deliberately trying to be very different from other people, even those with forenames much like those. A Smythe is different from a Smith. A Caan, Coen, Cohn, Kohan or Halévy, Levitt, LeVine rather than Levine is different from the Cohens and the Levis (inheritors of sacred duties in the old Jewish temple, by the way). As you see from these examples (such as *Smythe* and *Coen*), spelling may have different reasons for change. French *Halévy* suggests that Levites may face different circumstances in different countries. Names such as *Tyler* underline the difference we make between a job description and a name derived from an occupation that only an ancestor had, not shared by the bearer of the designation today, just as a *Short* today may be tall or a *Drinkwater* an alcoholic, a *Blackie* blond, even a *Charney* blond.

There are many aspects of forenames and surnames that have developed over the years that need to be taken into account, and many of these, numerology may or may not notice. It does not take cognizance that there is a difference between *Levine* and *LeVine*.

There is a lot of difference between the forenames of Yma Sumac and Amy Irving, but numerology sees *Yma* and *Amy* as exactly the same. In predicting social activities of name bearers, numerology ignores important facets of ethnic prejudices (a lot of American names were changed because of prejudice against immigrants), and it pays no attention to the "vibrations," as it were, that forenames create. These develop as society rolls along. *George* once was Greek for "farmer." Today *George* is a suitable name for an unsatisfactory husband. It used to be the general name for a Pullman porter.

That popular coloring of a forename is a big topic, but perhaps we have to have a brief look at the matter here despite the fact that numbers and not onomastics (the study of names) is our concern. Everyone knows at some level or another that every familiar name has acquired—who knows how in all cases?—a resonance, a reputation, a reaction. We somehow feel (rather than think) that a Mike must be more friendly than a Max, that anyone who calls himself James rather than Jim in everyday life must be stuffy, that Tracy or Tracey or (worst of all) Tracee or Tray-C must be loopy, and that Bertha must be fat. Whatever the numerological value of a name such as Tyrone or Cameron or Towanda, there is more sociodynamics at work in the forename than the number (which may equate it with a more "ordinary" name) takes into account.

It would take a large volume to insert here a full examination of the way forenames and surnames function in society, and indeed the findings would be fully valid for only a comparatively short period of time. The whole thing is constantly in flux and more so at some levels of society and in some regions of a country than in others. You may be a *George* named after a famous or wealthy relative whose forename registered differently in the past. Take a look at *Emily*. This was within living memory an old-fashioned name, but it has changed its status and its "meaning" in recent years and may do so again at any time. The idea of the meaning of any forename—in this the ubiquitous what-to-name-the-baby books are way off the mark—is static, is flat wrong. At any given time a name may be odd in one part of the country, common in another. Oral Roberts's forename was not a funny name where he grew up. Some names in one place or stratum of society sounded princely and in others funny or passé. Some people name only for dead relatives and others seek original names. The rich and aristocratic tend to retain old-fashioned names in something of the same spirit in which they furnish their houses with antiques; the middle classes may occasionally copy the upper classes, but tend to be conservative, while the lower classes are more inventive, sometimes wildly so, and get a lot of their forenames from television—*Ashley, Camryn, Yasmin*—and other pop culture rather than high culture sources.

At the same time, different ethnic groups in our multicultural society have different name preferences. You may have noticed the name choices of assimilating groups such as Jews (*Morton* and *Irving* as replacements for *Moishe* and *Isaac* have been replaced by the likes of *Stuart* and *Jason*—while non-Jews are favoring the likes of *Joshua* and *Joel*) and Asians (whose boys these days may be *Kevins* or *Keiths*), that many Italians and Greeks tend to hold onto ethnic forenames not common in the rest of the population, and that even within an ethnic group there can be regional and social differences. Some Hispanics will stick to *Roberto* while others attach *Robert* to a Spanish surname (in the U.S., only one, not the usual Spanish combination of father's plus mother's), and some Hispanics will choose *Teri* over *Dolores* now or keep on with *Rubén* or *Osvaldo*.

The sociolinguistics of it all, the psychology of it all, is fascinating. Names and naming (and humans are the only animals that name and claim) is immensely interesting. Here, however, all I really need to stress as I approach consideration of the "meaning" of names (from the numerological point of view) is the crucial fact that determining how one is regarded by others, and by oneself, does indeed depend significantly on names. Names are far more potent than mere descriptive labels, but all that lies in names as characterizing or predictive by no means is exclusively numerological. There is a great deal more in forenames than the old traditions and the new coinages that may come into fashion. There is a great deal more than the accident that a single celebrity can color a forename and affect its popularity. The importance and the impetus that personal names have lie in a number of factors, and only one of these, whatever numerologists say, is numerological.

With that caveat, we can turn to what numerologists claim a personal name can tell about the bearer of the name and, of course, about any new name a person may assume in order to take on a different personality and presumably a different result, an altered future.

For concise and authoritative character sketches of each name number 1 through 9, you can consult my book on names: Leonard R. N. Ashley's *What's in a Name?* (Baltimore: Genealogical Publishers, revised 1995). I can give you the essentials, however, right here. Of many aspects that could be included, I have decided to comment on one that most people will find of great interest, which is to say what kind of partner one will make in a marriage or other sexual relationship.

Your Fate is Written in Your Name **41**

The Moon. Fifteenth-century Tarot card.

1. If you are a 1, you unabashedly, aggressively want to be Number One, first in everything. You want to be somebody's only one. But an equally salient fact about you as a 1 is that you are shy about one-on-one relationships that might threaten independence. You like to stand alone. Or you like to think you do. A supportive partner who does not seek credit but is content with personal satisfaction is a godsend in a situation like this. That partner may be much put upon. If you are a 1, you may be a narcissist. You may hope to be unique. You ought to try to remember that individuals are far more like everyone else than they are different from everyone else.

2. If you are a 2, you have what some call feminine qualities. You seek equality, are cooperative and even submissive, cherish evenhandedness— and you like to get even with people. You can have two sides to you. The first consists of the elements of the reasonable maker of compromises and the gentle peacemaker and the inveterate second-guesser. This is the side most often in evidence. The other side is far less attractive and usually is concealed, but it can be resorted to with great speed and ironclad determination if the occasion is thought to have presented itself. Get out of the way! If anyone doesn't recognize your duality as a 2, they are sure to come in second.

3. Brilliant if erratic, this oddball makes a good leader and a poor follower. Anyone who can handle a 3's ups and downs and tantrums and triumphs is to be congratulated and held in a certain amount of awe. (Although the 3 may try to keep secret just how much is being accomplished behind the scenes to make the 3 performance look so good.) If 3s fail, 3s just start over. In this they may need assistance and encouragement, but they really hate to ask for assistance or to have the fact known that they need it. Threes like to look self-governing. A partner who is content to play along is a great asset to a 3 and will be held closely, some may think too tightly. Just watch out for the 3 deciding that, after all, he or she should dump you and strike out on their own.

4. Fours are four-square, foresighted, forthright, down to earth, for themselves, but also for good causes. If frustrated by being basic, however, they can get sneaky in their strong pursuit of the bottom line. The 4 makes a reliable partner but cannot stand indecision or nagging from a partner. If a person marries a 4, he or she can count on stability from their spouse. If you prefer excitement and variety to comfort and security, you might from time to time regret having thrown in your lot with a 4. A 4 can be a bore. If you want security above all, a little bit of boredom is acceptable.

5. Five adds something to 4 that makes it odd, maybe bizarre. Being unusual does get one attention—but then what? Being odd is awkward in a society as conformist as ours. It does, for some people, lend distinction and for others it seems to grant the freedom to color outside the lines that draws attention and sometimes applause. Fives like to be one up on squares. They may resort to silly differences to stand out. They may act eccentrically (off center). However, if they succeed, their fame gains them forgiveness. Five is an especially lucky number for 5s; it turns up in their careers in crucial details with astonishing frequency. If you are a 5, you probably have recognized that long before now. You are probably aware that 5 is your number.

6. Sixes have the coupling tendencies of 2s, the solidity of 4s. They add something that counteracts the occasional weirdness of 5s. Sixes are perfect. Now, being perfect is not all hearts and flowers. It can have unwanted effects that range from priggishness and coldness to putting off possible suitors who just don't feel they could deal with such superiority. Not a few people distrust calm and perfection, and 6s can lose out in life. Sixes love perfection and usually choose partners for their stunning looks rather than sweet natures. Choices like that are not perfect, of course, but a 6 wants others (who may not be affected by anything more than the superficial) to approve highly of his or her choice of partner. Privately he or she may berate or even degrade the trophy partner; lack of perfection is considered to be a cardinal sin by 6s.

7. Seven is widely regarded as *the* lucky number, and 7s are especially lucky in having more than their share of intuition, ESP, maybe even psychic powers. But 7s tend to be more scholarly than superstitious, though once in a while they will resort to gestures (reminding us of marching 7 times around the walls of Jericho blowing trumpets). Sevens' worst trait is that they absolutely cannot stand to be wrong. They resist admitting being wrong, and, when they simply cannot escape the fact, they get mean. That unfortunately comes right along with all their bright minds and sharp instincts. They probably should seek a marriage number that is even. If they marry a 3 or a 1, they will have to accept a tolerable amount of independence in the partner.

8. Eights are twice as four-square and grounded as 4s, and they can be twice as mundane, dull, and predictable. They excel in business or a profession where stability, solidity, and strength are preferred over showier qualities. Sometimes they can be twice as recalcitrant or stubborn as 4s. Call it admirable steadfastness or irritating bullheadedness. Eight good guys are well balanced and terrifically nice, but 8 bad guys (especially if they are aware that the enemy is superior in some way) can become extremely nasty. Eights make good winners and very poor losers. Fortunately for everyone, 8s more often win than lose. There would be a lot more trouble in this world if this was not so. Cross two 4s before taking on an 8.

44 *The Complete Book of Numerology*

9. As you read previously, an older system didn't have any nines because 9 is the sacred number (3 times 3) and, some said, not to be connected to mortals. Nine was often avoided in various situations. Nine people, nonetheless, do exist. They are proud, even pompous, and they settle for status rather than cold cash, but they have many talents to earn both. They like to get degrees, medals, awards, all kinds of titles and praise, even have people defer to them. To partner a 9, you must have this in common: You love the 9 passionately—and the 9 loves the 9 passionately, too. A person wrapped up in him or herself, they say, makes a small package. On the other hand, people say that good things often come in small packages. If you are attracted to a 9, just be aware of the risks as well as the rewards.

You have heard of 10s (perfection), but numerology doesn't play that game. A 10 is 1 + 0 is a 1. There can be, very seldom, an 11 or a 22 that should not be made into a 2 or a 4. The 11 or 22 are extremely rare. I keep repeating that. An 11 may be a prophet, a martyr, a savior, but even if not religious, the 11 is a prodigy of some sort (and thinks of herself or himself as a universal expert). In another book (that *What's in a Name?*), I say that the 11 is "insufferable but indispensable," and that about sums it up. I add (in that same book in a chapter on the names in magic and the magic in names) that the 22 is twice as world shaking (and much more than twice as rare) than the 11. "If you are a *TWENTY-TWO*," I write, you will go about your great work less flamboyantly, less famously perhaps, than the 11 but "the world needs you, in some fields desperately."

Now you have your name numbers for all the names you go by. You even have had a few hints about how certain numbers might go well with you. As in astrology, there are arguments that (for instance) certain signs can get along with (say) a Pisces or a Capricorn and certain signs cannot. The same thing holds for Chinese astrology, where the best partners for the Dragon or the Snake, etc., are suggested. I say a little something on Chinese astrology on 65.

You can find two more important numbers based on names. These are the Heart number and the Image number. (What you first found we redundantly call the Digital number.)

For the Heart number, just count the vowels in your name: **A, E, I, O, U**, and **Y** when it is used as in KIMBERLY. As before, keep adding until you get a single digit. This Heart number may reveal the more hidden side of you. This comes from a tradition of Hebrew (which was heavy with numerology, letters of the alphabet functioning as I keep repeating, numbers, so that the Name of The Beast in *Revelations* gave the number 666 for the Antichrist). The vowels, omitted in writing Hebrew (originally, except for beginners), are connected to the occult. They are hidden. The Heart number is the key to the most secret you, the hidden part of yourself.

Your Fate is Written in Your Name **45**

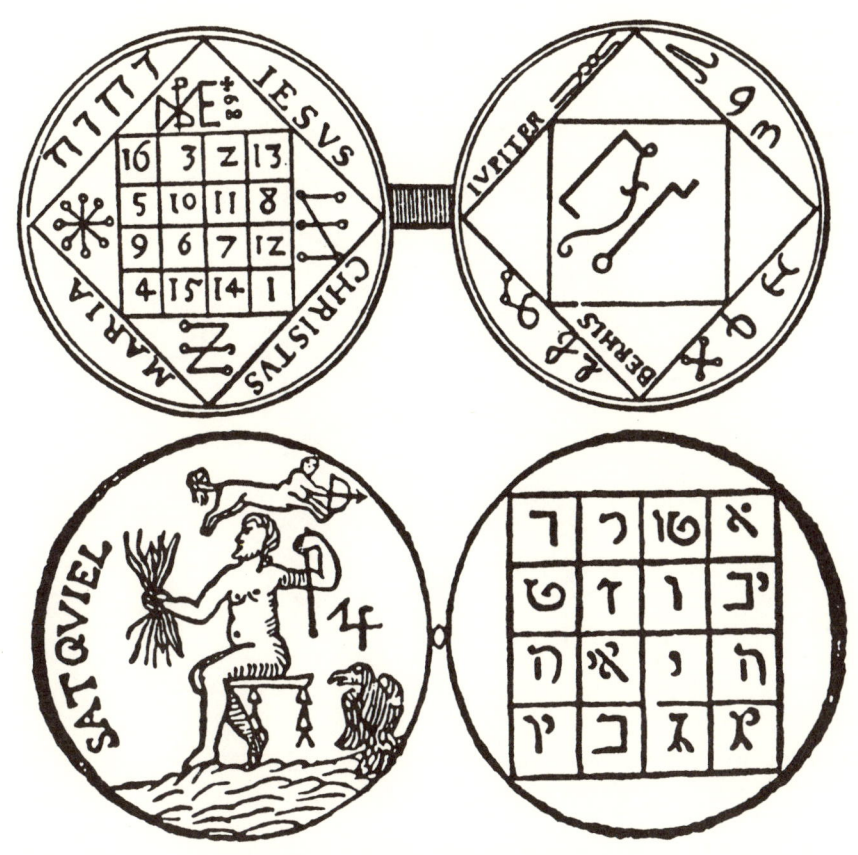

Amulet of Jupiter for peace and prosperity.

For the Image number, you add up the numbers of the consonants only. Keep adding until you get a single digit. This is the key to the you the world sees. This is the public you. It may not be the "real you" of the Digital number or of the Heart number, though things are usually easiest for people if the numbers jibe or are at least compatible. However, you have always been aware—haven't you?—that there is more than one you in there! As the poet says, we wear masks to face the people that we meet.

It is up to you to work with the information that your name numbers (Digital, Heart, Image) give you. Remember, numerology, just like astrology, charts a predilection, but does not dictate. Your fate is yours to shape. You can work with what you are given. You can play up your good points, play down your bad points. You can make your destiny and call it fate!

But first and foremost, you have to know what the basic materials are out of which you can fashion the you that you want to be, the life that you want to live.

Numerology claims, based on your name, to be able to tell you important facts. If you do not like the do-it-yourself kit you have been given with your name—change it. A change of name can change your life. Change is most successful, though, when the new character you play is not very bad casting. You may want to wear a certain kind of clothes, but do not have the figure for them. You could diet or build up your physique. You may want to sport a certain look but would be unconvincing in the part. Some hairdos may not suit your face.

Some things are beyond you, considering what you are given. Do not try to be an Amy if you do not have at least the ability to fake the qualities that people expect of persons named Amy. Or maybe you don't like being a Darryl, a Douglas, or a Donald, but can you impersonate a Brooke or Brad? As with the theatrical names people assumed for the movies, certain ethnic or other aspects may militate against the new name looking credible. What you want in an assumed name is credibility, just as you would not want to take on an alias that was obviously false. The idea is to take on a part you can play. So choose any new name with caution and be sure to take an honest look at yourself and what you truly can make of your-

Death, the fourth horseman of the Apocalypse.

self. Work with and on what you have. A personality cannot be redecorated successfully by throwing out all your old furniture and having an interior decorator come in and create something brand new.

Nonetheless, many a ninety-seven-pound weakling has become a Charles Atlas. Many a shy and retiring fellow has become a very believable, macho stud muffin. Many a homely girl in the old movies turned into a sex bomb when she removed her glasses and let her hair fall free. A name change might be equally magical. Many a Theodosia Goodman out of Brooklyn transformed into an exotic Theda Bara. But somehow Kirk Douglas never did look Scottish (though we appreciated his selecting a name we could pronounce and remember).

Changing your Digital number, your Heart number, your Image number can change your life, maybe a little, maybe a lot. If you are not happy with yourself and your reputation, how you see yourself and others see you, a change may be in order.

Maybe it is enough to change your first name—changing surnames is cutting your roots—if your parents started you off on the wrong foot in relation to karma. There is something you can do about that and about karma and the Cornerstone number of your first name coming later (page 156) in section 13, luckily.

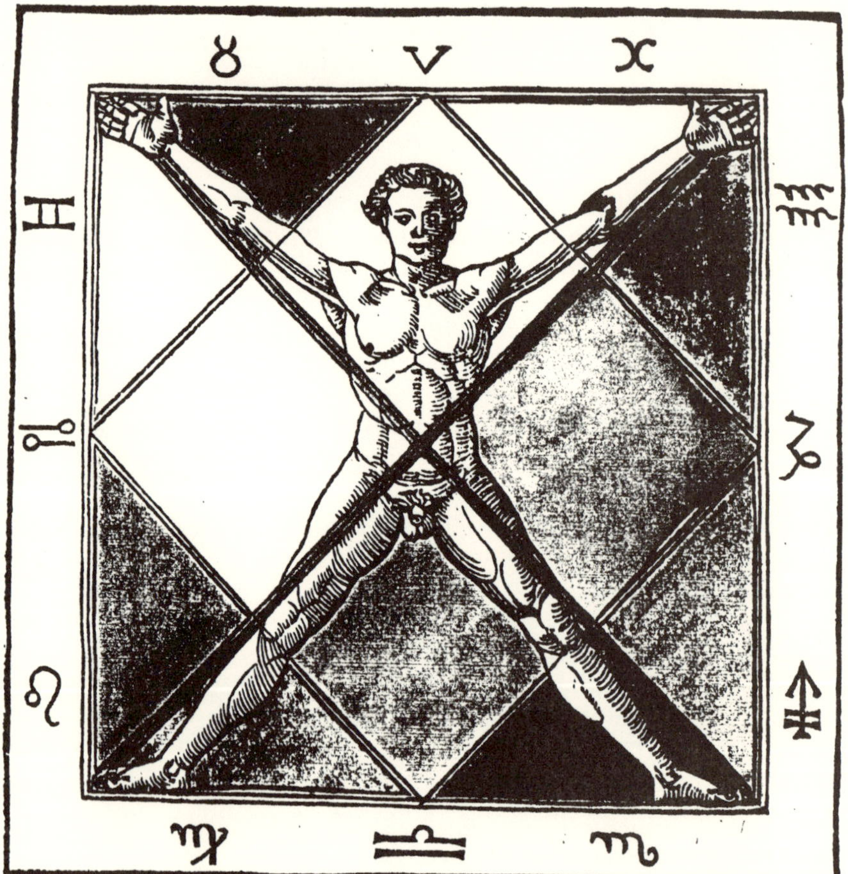

4
The Path of Your Life

ד

The journey of this life starts, of course, with your first appearance in this world. So the path of your life is determined, numerology says, by your birthday. That establishes, numerology and astrology say, the trajectory of your terrestrial existence. Michael R. Meyer in his *Handbook for the Humanistic Astrologer* (1974) called wisely if a bit awkwardly your natal horoscope "a seed-pattern, describing what an individual *may* grow to *become*, what he or she is potentially; though, of course, the person may not actually fulfill this potential to the fullest."

Whatever your Life Path (even if you were born at the midnight of India's independence and consider yourself exceptional), you can find its number. There is a simple way. It will presumably indicate a direction and not a doom. The average American now likes to think of himself (or herself) as a verb, not a noun, a process not a product. Margaret Mead testifies that this is not New Age but traditional, because her American (and she is old-fashioned only in saying *his* rather than *her*) is "always moving on, always in his hopes, moving up, leaving behind him all that was his past." The past influences us through karma—but that we deal with later.

The Life Path number is really about the trip, not the destination.

To find the Life Path number, start with the day of the month on which you were born. From 1 to 9, use that number. The 15th of the month is 1 + 5 = 6. For double digits, add the digits until you get a single digit. For example 31 is 3 + 1 = 4. If I were you, I would not bother with 11 and 22 as such; you are almost certainly a 2 or a 4, so face it.

50 *The Complete Book of Numerology*

The number for the month is to be treated in the same way. January is 1. December is 12 = 1 + 2 = 3.

The digits representing the year (example, 1980) are added up: 1 + 9 + 8 + 0 = 18 = 1 + 8 = 9. You're a 9!

Now add together the digits for day, month, and year. In our example,

$$6$$
$$3$$
$$9$$

That gives you 18 = 1 + 8 = 9. Nine again! There it is. There is the Life Path number. It's a 9 in our example. It is claimed by numerology that this is at least as significant as the astrological sign that your birth date gives you. Perhaps more significant. You decide.

There can be debate as to how much being born at a particular instant and place influences the path of your life, but no one can deny that the era and country into which you are born contribute in nurture to what your parents transmit in nature and upbringing. Indeed, though we like to think we can rise above our beginnings and achieve great things—some actually do—and that nationality and family are not so important when we consider how much some people differ from their compatriots and parents and even siblings. We are more determined by history and heredity than we like to admit. A daffodil bulb will always produce a daffodil, never a rose. You knew that.

My main problem with astrology is that it asserts that, basically, there are only a dozen varieties of flowers. It says that if the time and place of your birth determine that you will be a rose, you may be a red or white or even a blue rose, with or without thorns, climbing or not, and so on, but always a rose of some kind, and essentially different from the lily and the nasturtium, though part of the great garden of nature.

As you know, surely, astrology goes well beyond stating that there are 12 personality types and 12 fates dictated by the major houses, and four of what we may call personality clusters in the love signs, fire signs, water signs, and earth signs (three of each). Astrology traditionally does not take all of the planets into account that we know today. But it is said to be working on that problem. Most astrologers stick with old systems. Numerologists do also, though they may attempt to combine several traditions, as when they turn (why?) to the Kabbalah to say that this or that number also means Mercy, Justice, or whatever. I suggest you let them go their way elaborating. I suggest you want to strive to read out of, not read into, what you are dealing with as far as possible. Try to keep to numerology's fundamental attraction: simplicity. Don't take anything too far.

Astrology sometimes goes too far. It has from the first been interested not only in the character of individuals born under this sign or that, but

The Path of Your Life **51**

in the way that historical events, public as well as personal, might be predicted. You can cast the horoscope of a nation, such as the U.S., "born on the fourth of July" (in the words of George M. Cohan who said he was—but wasn't). I am especially dubious about political horoscopes. I tend to believe that history consists of a somewhat unpredictable, if not random, set of results deriving from causes that are never as clearly defined (and therefore never as predictive) as we should like. Logic cannot easily predict the illogical or the psychological.

The planets (wandering) and the stars (fixed) that were visible with the naked eye early tempted people to try to read earthly matters in the heavens. To my mind, the heavens, as the poet says, declare the grandeur of the formative force, the order imposed out of the chaos or whatever it was that exploded in the Big Bang. But the heavens can probably do no more to guide the paths of our lives than to stress the fact for us that we are a small part of a universe of staggering complexity and presumably of one simple essence and overall design (with a little chaos thrown in). The heavens can declare to us that we are subject to some sort of grand design that controls the evolving creation. Can we fathom that design? Can we penetrate all the mysteries of visible and invisible space? One writer has said that man (and woman) is the only creature with eyes that look up to the heavens rather than down at the earth. What do we see? Stay simple: What do we see rather than what do we imagine we see? We see constellations, and we have given them imaginative names, such as Orion and the Big Bear and we see Venus.

The signs of the Zodiac (a word that suggests animals, but not all the signs are animal totems) are certainly known to you. Let me remind you of them:

♈ **Aries** (Ram) 21 March through 19 April

♉ **Taurus** (Bull) 20 April through 19 May

♊ **Gemini** (Twins) 20 May through 20 June

♋ **Cancer** (Crab) 21 June through 22 July

♌ **Leo** (Lion) 23 July through 21 August

♍ **Virgo** (Virgin) 22 August through 22 September

♎ **Libra** (Scales) 23 September through 22 October

52 *The Complete Book of Numerology*

♏ **Scorpio** (Scorpion) 23 October through 21 November

♐ **Sagittarius** (Archer) 22 November through 21 December

♑ **Capricorn** (Goat) 22 December through 20 January

♒ **Aquarius** (Water Carrier) 21 January through 19 February

♓ **Pisces** (Fish) 20 February through 20 March

Each "house" or sign of the Zodiac has much more connected to it than just the dates (ignore the question of where the dates come from). First and foremost and why we must notice astrology here is the fact that occultists almost always connect astrology and numerology. One, in their view, supports and confirms the other. You can do either or both, and you can accept or reject other associations. There are, for instance, birthstones connected to each sign of the Zodiac. One common table goes like this:

Aries (Ram) Sardonyx

Taurus (Bull) Cornelian

Gemini (Twins) Topaz

Cancer (Crab) Chalcedony

Leo (Lion) Jasper

Virgo (Virgin) Emerald

Libra (Scales) Beryl

Scorpio (Scorpion) Amethyst

Sagittarius (Archer) Sapphire

Capricorn (Goat) Chrysoprase

Aquarius (Water Bearer) Crystal

Pisces (Fish) Lapis lazuli

I can discover no way in which numbers derived from the names of these gems, in any languages that are likely (which means in one case substituting onyx for chalcedony), can explain the choices made, not even if we substitute hyacinth for Sagittarius's sapphire, sapphire for Pisces' lapis lazuli, and so on, as is sometimes done. Fixing gems on signs is a sign of the fixing of characters on people born in the various "houses."

What you see above on gems is basically the work of Cornelius Agrippa of Nettesheim in his *Occult Philosophy*, following on a long and confused

The Path of Your Life 53

history of the supposed powers of gems in medieval thought and even earlier ideas. Note that diamond, ruby, opal, and some other stones mentioned these days in such lists do not appear in this early version. (Do we have different modern characters to match different modern gem choices?) Today you might get the following, and fewer people would be fobbed off with not so expensive materials such as crystal. Today crystals are said to have separate and interesting powers, though nobody explains how they might function.

You may be more familiar with

Aries	Amethyst
Taurus	Agate
Gemini	Beryl

And so on. *The Light of Egypt; or, The Science of the Soul and the Stars* (1889)—and more especially jewelers—may have done much to establish in modern times this scheme from that book.

♈ = Amethyst.	♋ = Emerald.	♎ = Diamond.	♑ = Onyx (Chalcedony).
♉ = Agate.	♌ = Ruby.	♏ = Topaz.	♒ = Sapphire (sky-blue).
♊ = Beryl.	♍ = Jasper.	♐ = Carbuncle.	♓ = Chrysolite.

For Sagittarius, I would stick with the older amethyst for December rather than the latest turquoise, if I wore jewelry. Are these gems arbitrarily assigned like, apparently, the gems representing the 12 tribes of Israel that are on the breastplate of the High Priest of the Jews (behind which are devices for casting lots and get "yes" or "no" answers!)?

I tried very hard when I was writing another book to get any rabbi to explain why each of the tribes got the stones they were assigned, and nobody knew. Rabbis explained to me that the synagogue was a *schul* (school), even if called a temple, and that unless/until the Temple was rebuilt in Jerusalem there was no need for priests in the Jewish religion, let alone a High Priest. Some of the rabbis even objected to the idea of a high rabbi. Congregations, they said, are autonomous, and the religion is Torah centered, not priestly, a faith with scholars rather than priests. It also, as you know, has many divisions, principally Orthodox, Conservative, and Reformed. One very reformed rabbi I consulted was female. Of all the rabbinical scholars not one was ready to discuss the fact that the stones in the breastplate were, according to magical traditions, in the wrong order, as I was aware because of non-Jewish sources. One said that was irrelevant—a good idea—because the breastplate was decorative rather than for magical use. The magic came from the devices behind the breastplate used for divination, not the jeweled front.

These birthstones, naturally, relate to our section 14 on colors as much as they relate to a Life Path determined by birth. They can, however, usefully be mentioned here as we discuss working out numbers for things as significant as the Life Path number. That is because the disagreements on which stones suit which sign (and it is generally agreed that wearing the birthstone of a "house" that is not your own is unlucky—opal for anybody but October born is supposed to be terrifically unlucky) bring to the fore a disturbingly unscientific aspect of this alleged science. This may make us all be more tentative about matters of numbers, too, even matters clearly based on definite things like birth dates.

Every birth date within (say) Pisces is different. There are gradations of (say) a Pisces. If you are born early in Pisces or late in the sign, you are said to be on a cusp, more connected to the nearest other sign, partaking of Pisces and also to some extent of its neighbor sign. That is just one of the reasons that unless you have a birthday smack in the middle of (say) Pisces you will not get much use out of the off-the-rack horoscopes that are so common in popular magazines and newspapers. The power of the "house" waxes and wanes (each period of a sign is divided into decans, so named because they last approximately 10 days). Thus exactly where within a sign one is born importantly matters. Similarly significant are the latitude and longitude of the place of birth, the precise hour and minute of birth (without these no one can cast any horoscope worth any serious attention), which planet is in the ascendant, where other planets are at that moment (I think especially of the moon), etc. You are much more than (say) "Pisces."

I know my own horoscope. Indulge me while I talk about it just a little despite the fact that I am a bit dubious about the whole thing and am also particularly intolerant of people who ramble on about *their* horoscopes. I tend to inform them that my reading for the day tells me to avoid people who discuss this subject, and I walk away.

Still, it seems to me that, as with religions, if something has been believed in by a great many people over a long period of time one ought to pay attention to the fact—whether one shares the faith or not. On horoscopes, I am of a suspicious mind. Many years ago, in connection with a book I was writing in which some opinion on astrology had to appear, I had my horoscope cast. It was done independently by three different experts, each one nationally or even internationally famous. What I intended was to present the three horoscopes side by side, without comment, and let readers judge for themselves what the differences, if any, communicated. Each expert was presented with the exact place of birth (pinpointing the hospital) and the time of birth (2:01 A.M. exactly marked my first cry). I did not indicate the fact that I was delivered by Caesarean section and had arrived months earlier than was expected (so that maybe I was supposed to be a Capricorn or something else instead of a Sagittarius).

The publisher's lawyers compelled me not to run the three horoscopes parallel as I had planned. The horoscopes were so different that I might be accused of libeling the experts, whom I had not warned might be held up to public mockery.

My own use of the three has been to select what I like from each and more or less go with that, if at all. I also read the newspaper advice and do not hesitate, if I see something nice in Virgo or Leo for the day, to take that under consideration rather than the Sagittarian communiqué. That is how I tread my personal Life Path.

Each "house" has its ruler. Mine (as a Sagittarius) is Jupiter. This is the best of all planets to have working for you, and it is said to be extra strong in the "house" of Sagittarius. When I was born, Scorpio was rising (some people will say that is not such a good thing). I was born in the second decan of Sagittarius and am thus supposed to be much shaped by the Moon (which introduces an element of change). So whatever you definitely deduced from that Jupiter influence now may be in doubt, or at the least there is a certain softening the influence of Jupiter; how much is a matter of dispute. I also have a touch of Mars, the planet of the god of war (which makes my rather effeminate amethyst or turquoise not nearly as suitable as bloodstone or something else macho red, red for the Red Planet).

My Mars introduces some belligerence, they say, strengthening Jupiter. Mars is said to dominate Aries and my own Scorpio and to bolster the powers of Jupiter. Also, my birth date falls within the 1909–1944 Cycle of Mars (but that is more about the path of the world in my early lifetime and less about my personal journey). But even after the basic "house" and the decan give fundamentals and some modifications, there are many other astrological aspects that go into shaping the individual born in a specific time and place on a certain date and day of the week. For one, the year of birth is about as important as the hour, day, and month. I was born in a leap year; that is another factor. There is still more. I get involved in this personal example so as to be able to hint authoritatively on just how difficult astrologers can be when it comes to authoritative statements. However, astrologers' clients want clear direction (and are impatient with the idea that astrology focuses but does not force) and clients want certainty. They are not at all happy with the idea that with all the detail, almost the only thing missing is some clear and credible explanation of precisely how the conjunctions of the planets and the constellations of stars *function* to affect human life. (I harp on that. I know.)

Father, Son, and Holy Spirit have given us body, mind, and soul, or evolution (if you prefer) has deliberately or blindly developed human reason, so that we want to *know*. When in theology or science we don't know, we make things up. In fact, both theology and science consist of a lot of propositions, hypotheses that may or may not be true. Astrology purports to be a body of knowledge, not a guess, and it has rules for casting horoscopes and predicting the future of men and women and the world. The rules are very complicated. You get planets in detriment and in decline, ruling and ascendant planets, masculine and feminine signs, planets in their own "houses" and out of them (including in cardinal signs), sidereal time and intervals and progressions, angular planets and exalted planets, trines, fixed signs and mutable signs . . . need I continue?

In recent times, computer programs have made casting horoscopes much easier for those who are not mathematical wizards. Still, without the precise moment and precise place of birth known—and one usually has only the likes of "early in the morning" or something like that—casting a real personal horoscope is theoretically impossible. If you do not know the exact time of birth, you can work with noon, and many astrologers do, but the result will be wonky, and naturally you are looking for correctness. Most people do not demand any kind of tailor-made horoscope; they are content to be lumped with (say) all the other Geminis in the daily "reading." Who writes these horoscope columns and what they know and how they know it remains pretty much obscure.

Numerologists step in. Numerologists tend to want something more direct.

They love numbers. They love the fact that 123456789×45 (5x9) = 5555555505. (Try it with 123456789×27 (3x9). Occultists are told in *Revelation* the size of heaven: a cube "twelve thousand furlongs" a side, and numerologists get working on $496,793,088,000,000,000$ cubic feet. How many Life Paths can lead people to that limited accommodation?

Numerologists just love numbers. The Buddhist numbers tend to get very big. We say astronomical. Numbers, say numerologists, are you! Maybe you ought to change your pickup line from "What's your sign?" to "What's your number?"

The first time I tried that I immediately got a phone number! (That's really "getting lucky.")

Instead of 12 signs you get 11 numbers in numerology. Elsewhere (page 152) you will find the brief personality sketches that go with the numbers 1 to 9 (and the highly infrequent 11 and extremely infrequent 22).

If you are going to go along with this, you ought to compare your Life Path number with your other significant numbers. You should note especially when it is the same as some other number, providing reinforcement. Major differences between the Life Path number and other significant personal numbers may alert you to conflicts or complications your personality may have in staying on the path that is basically most natural and easy

The Path of Your Life 57

for you to follow.

As with astrology, numerology basically promises that you are not stuck with a Life Path. Naturally it wouldn't be rather magical if there were not something you could *do* about it. If there is nothing to be done, you are involved with religion (with the elect and the damned) or superstition (but even that often offers a way out of difficulties). Both religion and superstition give you at least a sense of community. Magicians are loners, for the most part. They like to do their business alone and for themselves.

There are also other significant numbers, you will note, that can be deliberately altered by you. You change what you need to and work as well as you can with the rest, whether it is your DNA or your relatives or the troubled times in which you happen to live.

There is a saying that one often sees posted: "God, give me the power to change what I can, the power to accept what I cannot change, and the wisdom to know which is which." Otherwise sensible Americans like to say, "The difficult we do immediately. The impossible takes a little bit longer." This is charmingly confident. But it is foolish. The impossible, sad to say, is impossible. Maybe you can "dream the impossible dream," but really, honestly, unfortunately you cannot do anything about the impossible to change. A great deal of unhappiness comes from not tackling the tasks that are difficult but necessary, not doing what is doable. More misery comes from wasting time on the impossible.

So change what you can if you think you must. With numerology, you can make some changes in basics for which astrology does not seem as anxious to open the door. Learn to live with the rest. That may make numerology even more attractive to you. The date of your birth is fixed—and so is the path to which that birth date relates, so determinists allege.

Even if the determinists are right and there is nothing you can do about when you set out on the road, your trip can be somewhat managed, unless every single thing is determined and we are automatons. Along the road, there may or may not be (no thanks to you) some human creations such as a McDonald's or a HoJo or a quaint country inn. That can affect your trip as much as the children demanding that you stop or the charm of some place overwhelming you and a lover. Gas stations may or may not be near when you are running low. Over some things, from crowded freeways to paucity of rest stops, you have no control. Unless you take another road.

We like to believe that no matter what our DNA or anything else we inherit affects us, no matter how little control we have not only over our human nature but also our nurture, our whole fate is really not cut and dried. We like to think we have free will, and to some extent and with more or less success we can affect the conditions as we travel the road of life, whatever road we are set down upon at the start, however many malls or mountains or road repairs and detours we happen to encounter. You are often free to select a traveling companion who does not insist on stopping at every discount outlet or flea market or who will put up with your masculine urge to keep on driving for long periods and high speeds and your refusal to stop to ask for directions.

Your birthday seals your Zodiacal sign, astrology insists, I repeat. You are, for instance, a Libra or you are something else. But a Zodiacal sign is affected by many other things, and not all people born under Libra are exactly alike, as I said. Astrology may often be misunderstood, but astrology really says there is a basic personality associated with Libra (or any other sign of the Zodiac). Astrology says a "house" impels, but it does not compel. Astrology for all its dictates leaves the way open for you to make decisions that will alter your life. Astrologers assert, however, that, to start with, it is good to know all about the "house" into which you are born and also to find out as much as you can find out about the planets at the precise time of your birth. What was happening at midheaven then? What was going on all over?

Two people born in Baltimore at different times on the same morning of (say) September 12, 1978, will have different features and different lives. Two people born at exactly the same moment in Baltimore and Berlin or Baghdad will be very different. But all people, wherever and whenever they were born, that have a Life Path number of (say) 5 will have a great deal in common. Just as all human beings have a lot in common.

It is interesting to determine the birth dates of spouses and children and friends and business associates and so on and to see to what extent your Life Path number and theirs agree or disagree. It is not as simple a matter as saying that a 1 is as far as possible from a 9 or that two 2s are going to be an odd pair, but Life Path numbers shared ought to give you some basic connection, don't you think?

The Life Path numbers are said to have the following unpleasant connections:

1 arrogance, conceit, overconfidence

2 shyness, too much other-direction, oversensitivity

3 lack of focus, emotional vulnerability, moodiness

4 snap judgments, bossiness, vulnerability

5 impulsiveness, scattered interests, lack of discipline

6 dependency, sentimentality, bossiness

7 showing off, loneliness, selfishness

8 heedlessness, greed, impatience

9 masochism, lack of gratitude, sarcasm

Numerology so typically gives you so much of the good side of things, I thought for once you might like to see that every number has its obverse and reverse. Naturally each of these Life Paths is said to have an upbeat aspect and that is usually to the fore. The good side goes usually something like this, with every numerologist tweaking things to appear a trifle more knowledgeable than others:

1 originality, leadership ability, confidence

2 cooperation, friendliness, loyalty

3 creativity, innovation, wit

4 hardheaded realism, hard-working determination, pragmatism

5 versatility, assertiveness, talent

6 invention, reliability, helpfulness

7 spirituality, intuition, luck

8 independence, steadfastness, goal-oriented work

9 altruism, idealism, service to humanity

Now for the goal to which your Life Path directs you. It comes from the date of your birth and when you have worked that down to the single digit you are said to have:

1 command

2 friendship

3 creativity

4 success

5 freedom

6 responsibility

7 wisdom

8 wealth

9 love of humanity

For once we shall omit the compound numbers **11** and **22** whose goals are serving their fellow men and whose only major flaw may be that they hold the less gifted in a little bit of contempt even as they strive and sacrifice for their betterment.

חָדָה

The Life Path is most successfully traveled in the best years and on the best days, of course. There are said to be certain periodicities in dates that can affect both the individual's (nine-year) cycles and the history of a nation. "Cheiro" tells us of **14** in the history of France: 14 May 1029, the first Henri king of France; 14 May 1610, the last Henri of France assassinated; 14 letters in *Henri de Bourbon* (14th king of France and Navarre); 14 December 1553 (14 centuries, 14 decades, 14 years after the birth of Christ) birth of Henri IV, add 1 + 5 + 5 + 3 = 14. And on and on. I see a problem in that it has been well established that Christ was not born until a few years after the date from which we derive our modern calendar. But certainly 14 May is a red-letter day in French history: death of Henri II, birth of the first wife of Henri IV (Marguerite de Valois), start of the revolt of the duc de Guise in 1588, defeat at Paris (1590), Louis XIII died (1643), Louis XVI in the 14th year of his reign when he revoked the Estates-General (leading to the Revolution). You could try 14 July, but might not get as many hits. Also 14 December would be good. For you, the question is are there certain milestones along the Life Path that you have noticed that may be of some use in expecting events? Are there any lucky years for you, judging by your experience up to now? Reflect.

As for shorter distances along the way, what about months each year to look out for? "Cheiro" says in relation to health that the following personal numbers and days are connected:

> **1** (born day of any month 1 or producing 1 as 10, 19, 28 all producing a 1—and in subsequent entries the days of the month are added to get the entry number) eat a lot of honey, watch out for health trouble and October, December, January, health changes at ages that reduce to a 1: 10, 19, 28
>
> **2** (2, 11, 20, 29) watch out for stomach problems and January, February, July, eat lettuce, cucumber, cabbage, etc., health milestones ages 20, 25, 29, 43, 47, 52, 65
>
> **3** (3, 12, 21, 30) watch out for "overstrain of the nervous system" and skin troubles, watch out for December, February, June, and

The Path of Your Life 61

September and health changes at ages 12, 21, 39, 48, 57, eat beets, berries, borage, nuts, etc.

4 (4, 13, 22, 31) suffer "mysterious" and hard-to-diagnose ailments and melancholia, bladder and liver trouble, etc., should try hypnotism and electrical treatments, eat spinach, sage, Solomon's seal, avoid spices and red meat, watch out for January, February, July, and August and expect health changes at ages 13, 22, 31, 40, 49, 58

5 (5, 14, 23) should not overstrain mentally, watch out for insomnia and nervous prostration, get plenty of sleep and rest, eat carrots, parsnips, oats, walnuts and hazelnuts, watch out for overwork in June, September, December, and expect health changes at 14, 23, 41, 50

6 (6, 16, 24) are candidates for the ear-nose-and-throat doctor and may suffer upper-respiratory problems, need air and exercise and should eat spinach, apricots, walnuts, all kinds of beans, etc., and watch out for overwork in May, October, and November, and expect health changes at ages 15, 24, 42, 51, 60

7 (7, 15, 25) are worriers, so I hate to be the one to warn they are stronger mentally than physically and should be careful, especially in January, February, July, and August, eat chicory, endive, cucumbers, apples, grapes, drink plenty of fruit juice, watch out for rashes and digestive problems, and expect health changes at ages 7, 16, 25, 34, 43, 52, 61

8 (8, 17, 26) may have liver trouble, excretory system trouble (such as colon cancer), rheumatism, blood poisoning, etc., and should be as vegetarian as possible, eating especially celery, carrots, sage, etc., and watching out for difficulties in December, January, February, and July and health changes at ages 17, 26, 35, 44, 53, 62

9 (9, 18, 27) should eat onions, garlic, leeks, etc., ginger, rhubarb, mustard seed, watch out for measles and smallpox and all fever-producing illnesses, avoid rich food and alcohol, watch out for April, May, October, and for health changes—and *all* the changes I have been mentioning can be for the better or for the worse—at ages 9, 18, 27, 36, 45, 63

Sorry, for you in your late sixties or better, I have no information backed by the expertise of "Cheiro" and do not wish to guess at your coming health changes. I echo "Cheiro" in his statement that "herbs are nature's own remedies"—he names many more than I do here—but I would add, as he

SAGITTARIUS

does not, that some much-touted herbal remedies have as far as science is concerned no real effect on human health (echinacea is one, ginkgo balboa another, but there are many), and many tablets you can buy do not have powerful enough herbs to be worth putting much faith in them. There are actually a few herbs that can improve your memory—if you remember to take them. No herb needs to be gathered at a magical hour or in any magical way, they are all used soon after they are gathered. Like all food, they are most nutritious when fresh and uncooked. Spices not only spice up your food; they can spice up your life. Eat well, and travel at a reasonable rate.

Here is not a monthly or health-year calculation concerning the path of your life (or your terrestrial life), but information on the supposed really major stop along the road of years. It involves what numerology calls Vertical Tabulation, and it is simplicity itself. Here is something else numerology says you can find.

For Vertical Tabulation, write down the number of the year of your birth. Let us say 1965. Then, under the last number put down, one to a line, the year's number again. Like this:

1965
1
9
6
5

Add it up: **1986**

That, numerology says, was your Big Year. I hope you enjoyed it. Personally, I do not like to see anyone peak that early or have only one big year to enjoy. I like the idea that comes up in Chinese astrology (later on here) that every 60 years there is a whole great big new cycle. If you live to 60, wouldn't a new deal at that point be welcome?

But why wait until 60? Why not line up **1965** under the *present* year and look forward to something nice *down* the road of life? "It is better to travel hopefully than to arrive," they say.

Finally something else in connection with the road of life: those lucky days that may come along. It's easy. If you are a **1**, it's the first day of the month and also 10th, 19th, or 28th. From the work above, you can find the best days for **2, 3, 4, 5, 6, 7, 8**, and **9**. You cannot count on a lucky day each and every month, however, but keep an eye open over a period of time and see if the numerologists are correct. Just believing that there are some lucky days may be confidence building for you.

One nice thing about numerology: It fosters a positive, proactive outlook. One worrying thing is that it does not, for all its superstitious reputation, pay much attention to chance, and, as you may have heard, a great battle was once lost "all for the lack of a horseshoe nail," for little accidents or misfortunes can turn one's fortune upside down. Still, as we travel, we should not go along in fear or dread; a happy, hopeful attitude will make whatever the journey may be a lot more pleasant.

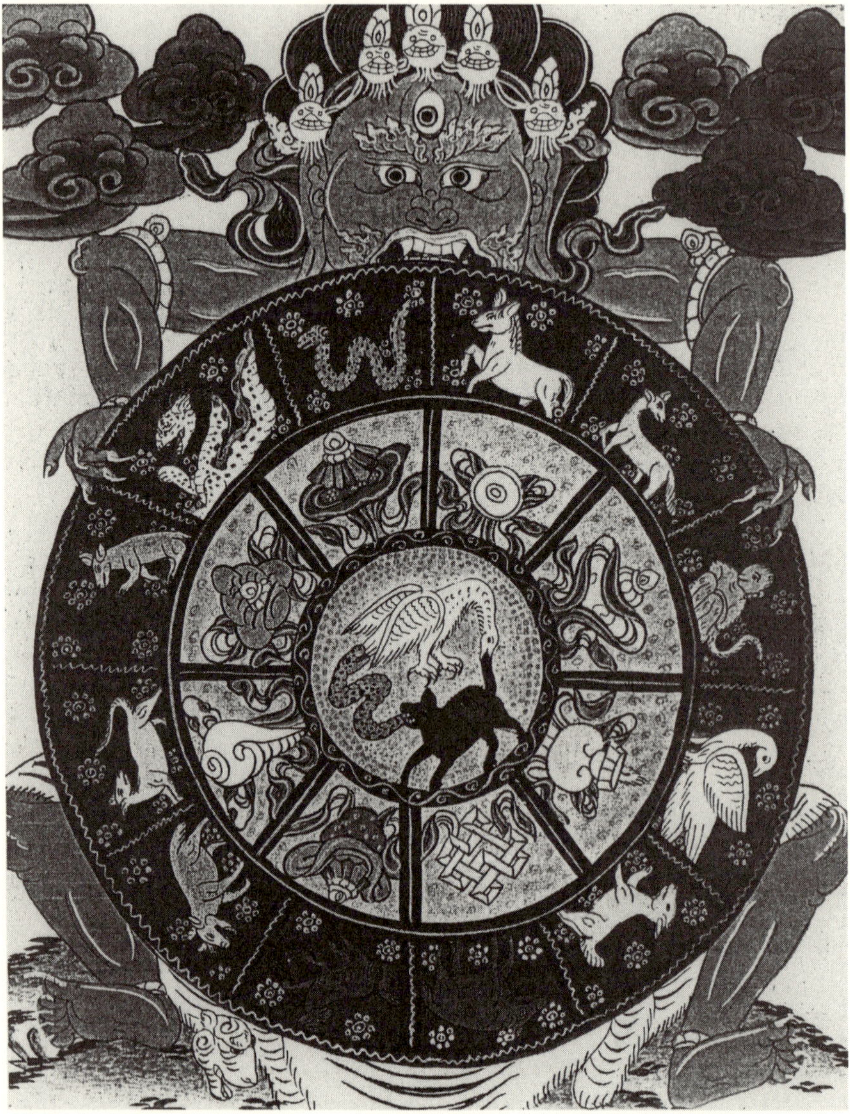

5
Numbers in Chinese Astrology

ה

Inevitably, in discussing the numerological method for determining the Life Path, we have had to take a glance as astrology. It was fairly easy to do that concisely because all readers will have at least heard of common astrology. But before we proceed here to more numerology *per se*, it seems wise to take a brief look at an astrology that also involves some connections to numbers. It is Chinese astrology.

Chinese astrology reminds us of the very ancient and also inevitably varied nature of predictive methods in different cultures. Chinese astrology, like the astrology with which you are more familiar, deals in 12 units. These are comparable to the "houses" of the astrology previously mentioned, but Chinese astrology is different in many respects. Anything in the Chinese occult holds much interest. The Chinese consider their occult teachings vastly superior to ours, just as they themselves are superior to us (having two souls, a *hun* connected to the *shen* or good spirits and a *p'o* connected to the *kuei* or evil spirits, in the better-known Eastern tradition of the balance of *yin* and *yang*) and China they stress is the Middle Kingdom, the central fact, the only country (the ideogram for *China* is just a square with a median line running through it, *the* country).

In English we have the expression "as hard as Chinese arithmetic," but, exotic as it may be, Chinese astrology, which involves a lot of numbers, is not really so difficult. There are, naturally, whole books on the subject. The best are in Chinese, but a few of them are in English. From them, I can let you have here a little introduction to the subject you may find worth reading and considering, and if

66 *The Complete Book of Numerology*

you are intrigued, you will be able to find more in other books. I trust this is not mitin (More Information Than I Need).

This will be a novel change from Western astrology. Western astrology in complex and professionally created natal horoscopes (based on the exact time and place of your birth and the conjunctions of the planets at that moment, as you know) and in the daily columns in newspapers. Americans tend to turn to them religiously, right after headlines and sports, sometimes because they have a bet on some game. So they are already familiar to you in some degree. Chinese astrology looks unusual.

As we noted, the name Zodiac suggests animals. Western astrology has, along with Virgo and Pisces, and such, Taurus the bull and other animals, and in the previous section you saw that Sagittarius (the Archer) is represented by a half-human figure, a centaur. The Chinese have a Zodiac that is all animal. Well, one bird. I shall later explain why that is so.

First, the signs or "houses" of Chinese astrology are:

The Rat

The Ox

The Tiger

The Cat

The Dragon

The Snake

The Horse

The Goat

The Monkey

The Rooster

The Dog

The Pig

There is some disagreement about this. The Japanese and some Chinese don't say the Cat, but the Rabbit, quite a different creature, the Cat being far more slinky and volatile—and very different in its sexual connections. The Egyptians had a cat god, but no rabbit god. In mystical writings in the West, the rabbit represents the wandering thoughts and unpredictable aspects of alchemy. In popular culture it is credited with breeding often. In any case, to find which sign you are in Chinese thinking, you only have to know the year of your birth, not the month, but the year. The Chinese emphasize the individual less; they concentrate on the cohort of a time as they see the person as part of a group. In Chinese thinking, everyone with the same surname (I cannot say last name because to stress importance of family, the family name comes first) is a member of the same family. They have *tong* associations for their approximately 100 family names.

Your sign, nevertheless, dominates your personal character, and as the years go by your particular sign-year comes around repeatedly in the endless cycle. The signs are in the order you see, and are of nonhuman creatures, legend says, because the Buddha, long ago, believing that China was in need of reorganization, called the creatures to a conference. They came in the order listed previously, first the aggressive Rat, finally the cautious Pig. The Buddha assigned a year of a 12-year lunar cycle to each in its turn.

You, if you were born (say) on or between February 17, 1969, and February 5, 1970, you are a Rooster. That does not mean you will be cocky, any more than someone born in the Year of the Dragon will have a fiery temper or someone born in the Year of the Ox will be big and clumsy. These creatures are just, as it were, your totems.

Each sign has its own character, just as our Leo (the Lion) is said to be bold and our Gemini (The Twins) likely to be a combination of two natures. The Rooster is frank and fearless, talented and resourceful, sincere and generous, stylish and popular, hard working and yet contemplative, self-assured and adventurous, tending to be conservative and yet enthusiastic. The Rooster has, as every sign of our Zodiac or the Chinese Zodiac, for that matter, defects or shortcomings as well as fine attributes. The Rooster can be pompous and pedantic, brazen and sharp tongued, didactic and liable to be nitpicking, wasteful, quixotic, shortsighted, and untrusting of people and events. The Rooster can be a strutting braggart. Whether the Chinese arrived at these opinions by magical means or by human observation, I cannot say. It is worth remarking that wherever the characterizations came from, so long as people believe them they powerfully control.

The Dragon, to cite another example, governs people born on or between February 17, 1988, and February 5, 1989. Dragons are said to be wise and intuitive, artistic and creative, lucky and successful, enthusiastic and sentimental, healthy and generous with both goods and information, independent, admired, ready to stick to tasks until completed. At the same time Dragons can be willful and stubborn, crabby and demanding, impetuous and melancholy, loudmouthed and complaining, sometimes without their feet on the ground, hard to get along with and often angry about that (among other things). The Dragon is a bellicose creature. You are aware of that. The Dragon in Chinese tradition is also a symbol of luck. The Chinese notably believe in life as being at one and the same time a matter of determined, and one hopes, lucky events.

As with Western astrology, the Chinese "houses" do not condemn a person to be of a fixed and limited character. They simply indicate inclinations; they do not dictate inescapable fates. But it is always best to know basically what you inherently are, what promise you may have been born with, what qualifications for life you happen to possess, and what weaknesses you have to overcome or be cautious in handling.

Our Aries is strongest in the head, our Ram. Our Scorpio (the Scorpion) is bold and fearless and with a dangerous sting. The Chinese Dog will be faithful, the Chinese Snake vengeful and a sore loser. But one can always have an Aries who is not very intelligent or wise and a Dog who is, as the Horse more often is, not only hard working but heedless, hotheaded, tactless, selfish, and inconsiderate. As with Western astrology, the particulars of the moment of birth and of the specific year matter. Tigers should sit tight and take on no risky ventures during any Year of the Ox, which is a bad time for them.

Chinese astrology pronounces that the individual is a complex creature and ruled by the heavens in ways distinct from others while there is also a mandate of heaven governing all. It deals in units of 12 and 5 cycles of them (60 years) ruled by 5 dragons.

So you might be well advised to check your birth date not just in the Western astrological cycle (12 units of time from a time in March of one year to a day later in March of the following year, for example), but in the 12 "houses" of the Chinese Zodiac.

The problem comes with the fact that the Chinese calendar moves these signs along as time passes. You need to know what sign covers which year of birth. Then you can pass on to consider what Chinese astrology says is the sign of the best partner for you.

Finally, you can determine that you are, for instance, born in the Year of the Goat (January 1979 to February 15, 1980), let's say, but have a cosign in Western astrology. This could be our Capricorn (the Goat). Capricorn runs from December 22 to January 20, you recall. Or you may even be our Cancer (June 22 to July 23). You would partake of both the Eastern and Western signs in this way.

Each of the two systems I have been discussing claims to be entirely adequate and unconnected to the other, but why not compare and contrast?

For that in detail, you must locate a good book on Chinese astrology. *Chinese Astrology* by Suzanne White was published by Tuttle in 1976. Also consult any one of the very many books on Western astrology (including some focusing on so-called fire signs, love signs, and so on). These crowd the shelves of any bookstore in America, proving the intense and continuing interest of the public in such things.

All the U.S. books look pretty much alike. The authors crib shamelessly from each other and repeat without apology or explanation. You can take your pick. There are even annual books that will tell each Aquarius (the Water Carrier) or the person influenced by any other sign what may be in store for him or her in any given year. Astrology dabbles not only in character analysis but also in fortune-telling, as you are well aware.

Many astrologers undertake to give you the numbers of the best and worst days for your sign each month, and a few tell you what your lucky numbers are. Some daily newspaper horoscopes give lucky numbers. Where they get these numbers, they never tell us. If you are willing to accept them, they may give you hope and confidence, if not actually good luck. A positive attitude going forward is always of some use. Many fortune-tellers never give any really bad news. Some say they keep it to themselves.

In a Rat year, the Rats are in clover. The Ox, Dragon, Monkey, and Pig all find Rat years good for them as well, for a variety of reasons. Other signs had better be careful in Rat years, lay low, be circumspect, and wait for better times. Favorable times come for every sign eventually. At this time of writing, the last Rat year was 1996. That was followed by Ox (1997), Tiger (1998), Cat (1999), Dragon (2000), Snake (2001), Horse (2002), and Goat (2003). Still to come as I write this are the next years of Monkey (2004), Rooster (2005), Dog (2006), and Pig (2007). In 2007 we shall start over with the Rat, with financial surprises as well as opportunities. That will be a good time to take stock (if not stocks) and stock up for hard times that may follow. If you are going to be born in a Year of the Rat, it is best to be born into the abundance of summer.

In these days when so many people set great store by astrology, it is a wonder that times of conception and times of birth are not fully planned. They now can be managed to a far-greater extent than ever before. Not only can you select, more or less, a good Chinese year and a sign of the Zodiac under which to have your child born, but the pregnant woman can get on a plane or a bus or drive and assure that the place of birth is the most favorable. Oddly, I do not find that even the most devoted believers in astrology, people who sincerely think that the exact time and place of

An Asian Aquarius not in the Chinese system of 12 creatures and the overarching Dragons which rule. 12-year periods and represent Wood, Fire, Earth, Metal, and Water. Every 60 years a major new cycle begins. Note that 60 the Babylonians used (whence our 60-minute hours and 360-degree circles) and the Egyptians connected 60 with Osiris.

70 The Complete Book of Numerology

their own births have done a lot to influence the direction of their lives and shape their successes and failures, take a great deal of care to give their offspring the best astrological chances.

Could it be that they only half belief in astrology, Western or any other? The followers of numerology appear to be more confident that they are onto something really good.

To return to the Chinese, they long have been rather more believing in the occult than we are, worshipping the ancestral gods and dealing with both *shen* and *kuei*, the good and evil spirits of which you heard, who can be fickle and surprisingly punish or reward. There are dozens of demons active in everyday life, they say. Alphonsus de Spina once calculated that Christians have to cope with millions of demons, but while our demons are immortal, some of the Chinese demons can be killed, and any of them can be frightened away (by the color red, by the noise of drums, gongs, firecrackers, and so on). Demons travel only in straight lines, the Chinese say, whence the zigzag bridges the Chinese build.

You may think the Chinese may be exceptionally superstitious (and inveterate believers in luck), but they are also a highly pragmatic people; the Chinese have many methods of dealing with devils and demons, with ghosts and poltergeists, with mysterious forces that bring good or bad weather and all sorts of supernatural creatures, including celestial dragons and other monsters. The Chinese predated both Joseph of Copertino (who demonstrated levitation before a pope) and D. D. Home (who amazed Victorian society) in levitation and flying. People swore these two (and some others, including Saint Ignatius Loyola, who had to be held onto while saying Mass) were seen levitating and flying through the air. The Chinese invented something like the Ouija board and other methods of divination, including the use of dried stalks of a magic plant for fortune-telling. They preceded the West in spiritualism séances (but the *wu* who acts as a medium is often avoided because only evil spirits would be at his call). There is one famous case at law in China that involved copyright when

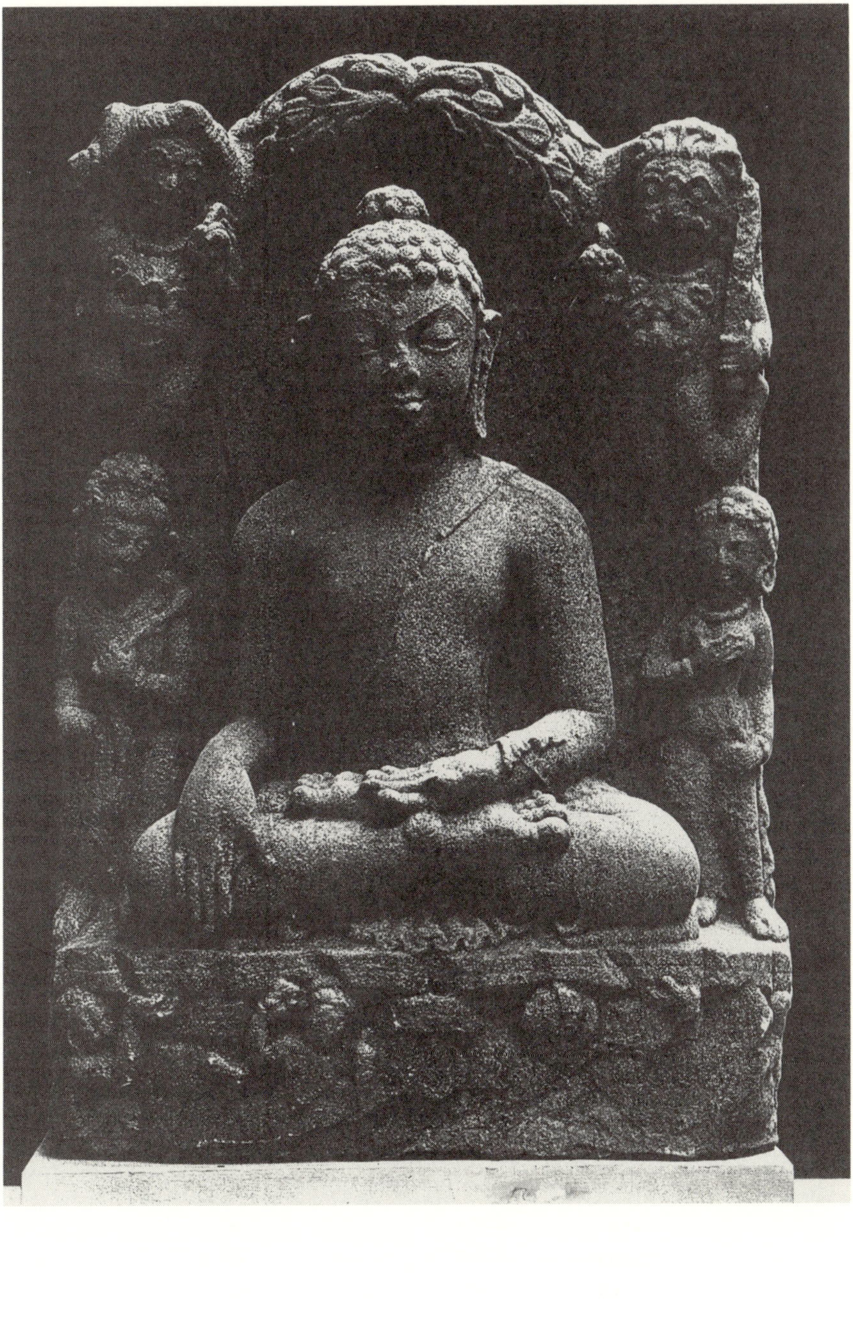

a medium published a book that was supposedly dictated by someone who had passed into the next world, and that dead author's living relatives sued the medium for the literary property.

The most prominent Chinese occult beliefs these days in the West may be the *I Ching* (which can give you some millions of different answers, though you must determine for yourself how to apply them to your needs) and *feng shui* (wind, water) manipulations of the movement of *chi* (energy). The West does not really "get" *feng shui* usually, and most people who practice it or hire so-called experts to redecorate their homes to suit *feng shui* principles cannot even pronounce the words. They are to be said in English as fung-SHWAH. It is all part of the connection between the world of spirit and the material world, the heavens above and life on earth, and at the heart of it all is some kind of energy not only in astrology but in the occult science of numbers, the basis of the physics of the universe.

"In China," says one encyclopedia of the occult, "the righteous man may be his own medium, and the professionals are not regarded with favor." You may need some advice on handling Chinese astrology or acupuncture, but numerology you can do all unaided, a great advantage in a world in which charlatans are numerous.

Stephen Karcher offers *Total I Ching* (2003), "myths for change" combing the Zhouyi version with the Confucian one. (The more common version is the so-called Confucian one and this is the first time the two have been well reconciled to produce a complete oracle. Karcher is also the author of another Warner Books (UK) guide, *The Kuan Yin Oracle* (reissued in 2003) and of *The Illustrated Encyclopedia of Divination*.

Chinese astrology and connected numerology are among the billions of items on the Web. See such sites as www.astroshasta.com, www.ebhasion.com/destiny/numerology, and www.namenumerology.com. There is a daily BBC Chinese horoscope on the Web and plenty of connections between numerology and the *I Ching*, *feng shui*, etc. You could learn on the Web of many books such as Bejan Daruwallah's *Star Signs, Numerology and Chinese Astrology*, Alfred Huang's *Numerology of the I Ching*, and M. Ward's *Gong Hee Fat Choy Book*. None of these is particularly good and many are worse. If you truly want to investigate Chinese systems seek out a Chinese expert and bring along an interpreter of the interpreter.

The Japanese are perhaps more rejecting of the number 13 than is true of most traditions but they do love numerology, even though their tradition does not include the 13 gates of mercy, the 13 heavenly fountains, the 13 rivers of balsam in paradise, the 13 paths of love, and so on. The Japanese oracle owes something to the Chinese (as do most things Japanese) but the Japanese have their own idea and it is called the Nine Yi astrological system and purports to deal with the energy of the date and time of your birth. The Nine Yi system undertakes to provide not only character analysis but prediction as well. It is well described in *Practical Astrology by Numbers* (Carroll & Brown, 2003) by Simon G. Brown.

Finally, when making dumplings for Chinese New Year do not count them. That brings bad luck.

坤 艮 坎 巽 震 離 兌 乾

prima ÿgo mathei

6
The Number of the Heart's Desire

ו

Whether you are seeking information for yourself from astrology or numerology, one of the driving forces behind your quest is your deepest heart's desire. You obviously have to know it if you are going to work to bring things in this life of yours nearer to your heart's desire. There is a number to be found for this just as there is a number based on your name or names and your birth date and a number for your Life Path. This section deals with the number of the Heart's Desire, as its heading promises. But you know that.

The number of your soul's deepest yearnings and most profound motivations is obviously crucial and yet often ignored by those who play with their name numbers and attempt by doing that to find out about their basic characters or even events that may happen to them.

The Heart's Desire number is easily found. I want to repeat how to get it and give it a whole section. Take the vowels of your basic name, the name in the form that you consider to be the most You. That could be William Ernest Henley Jr. (we always ignore the Jr. or III and such in using personal names) or William Henley or W. E. Henley or Bill, Will, Willie, or whatever Henley. If you use an alias or a pseudonym regularly, you may wish to see what the avoidance of your real name augurs. If you have a professional name (say in the movies or as a rap artist) you would want to check that. In fact, many people check such a name before adopting it to see if it will be a lucky one.

Extract the vowels from the name. For our purpose here, as is frequently the case in dealing with vowels in names, **Y** will be counted as a vowel when it is followed by a vowel and adds up to a single sound. It is also a vowel in *Yvette*. Count **Y** as a 7. For the usual vowels (for reasons you need not trouble with) the other values are as follows:

A = 1

E = 3

I = 9

O = 6

U = 3

You also need to know that **W** is counted as a vowel when it operates like a **Y**. Then **W** counts as a 7. For why it is 7, I have never seen any convincing explanation.

There you have it. Count up the vowels and keep adding until you get a single digit.

WILLIAM HENLEY
Write in the numbers yourself

OK, now add up until you get a single number. What is the number you have figured out?

The Heart's Desire number in this case is ___. Write it in here. Always write in books. It's called marginalia. Conduct a discussion with what you read, here or anywhere, with comments or ! or X or whatever in the margin. Just do not use a yellow marker to point up the good stuff; simply run a line along the margin, which makes the material you feature easier to read. I hope you want to mark a lot in this book. Make it yours.

Here is a sort of summary of conventional wisdom (though subjective, because I have not consulted every source available, of course, and naturally, I prefer some peoples' ideas to those of others and have made them mine) for the numbers involved in the Heart's Desire number. You will notice that where in another connection I put an emphasis on the kind of person one gets on best with in a sexual partnership, here I feature something else so as not to be overly repetitive. What you get this time is how each type works in social and business relationships.

1. Independent and self-starting, confident and even driving, but also possibly narcissistic (very complicated when the self-love for

reasons outside the self is a masochistic unrequited love), careless of the feelings of others, bossy and highly critical of others who lack 1's drive or talents, relies on a team but always wants to be in charge of it and may ride roughshod over opposition. A 1 does not ever want to be just one of the boys. A 1 wants to stand out. Great for a one-person business.

2. Considerate and self-effacing, indecisive and easygoing, 2 is the opposite of 1, cooperative and more comfortable as follower than as leader, companionable. Such a person may get you into a co-dependent relationship. The perfect "other half" in a sexual relationship or in a back-office, front-office kind of business, manager of manufacture/manager of sales arrangement. Remember that balance and second opinions are very useful in any important decisions.

3 Extrovert and hedonist, optimistic and ready to see the silver lining in any cloud that does happen to appear, a 3 is more likely to rely on intuition than preparation, to wing it and then to talk her or his way out of any trouble. One may add that while speech is located in the brain between thought and action (and it has been said that it often is substituted for either) nobody is sure where intuition is located. Note that the expression is *business sense*. The best happens to those who feel right moves and go with their gut reactions tempered by just a little caution (as much as is felt to be necessary) and also have the hard facts.

4 Sensible, no nonsense, a 4 has it all together and keeps his or her eye on the goal. But for all the organization and the determination the plan of a 4 may get bogged down in detail and 4 is not the type to call on or be able to get help from others who see the difficulties more clearly. A 4 often needs but won't ask for help. On the other hand, a 4 attracts by his or her reliability certain types that are more brainy, but more volatile and the combination of speedy hull and well-managed rudder may guarantee smooth and fast sailing. Hire 4s, and then find a way to make them not only cooperate with each other but to be competitive with each other for the good of the group.

5 Where a 4 was narrow-minded though focused, a 5 is versatile, open to suggestion, and more likely to alienate co-workers because they cannot share a 5's vitality and imagination. A 5 works by recruiting rather than by any martinet, dictatorial action, if 5 can possibly get what he or she wants that way. But a 5 does want his or her own way. They are sure they are right in most cases and, if wrong, are capable of coping. If obstructed, a 5 gets bossy, even petulant. You don't want to cross a 5. Well, well you might *want* to, and often, but be warned. You may have to trick 5s into the idea that it was their idea. Then you will have their talents working well for you. Give accolades.

6 Six shares 5's vital emotions, but is more solid, plodding, friendly, and open to direction, even correction, from others. Six may let kindness stand in the way of practicality and sacrifice effectiveness to creating a happy team. Some people see a feminine quality in a 6, but that is just sex stereotyping. There are some extremely macho types like Gouda cheese (blood red and hard outside and mushy on the inside) and there are some hard-as-nails drag queens. There are steel magnolia Southern belles and sentimental business girls and hell-on-wheels female company bosses and trial lawyers and lesbians in overalls that can burst into tears. Sex is on a spectrum. It's not all pink and blue in sex. Increasingly business wants to know what you can contribute to the company's bottom line, not whether you are in private life a bottom or a top.

7 Where a 6 was jazzed up by emotion and creativity and openness, a 7 is more analytical, critical, and secretive. Seven may be up to something that companions and colleagues are not aware of, not shared. There is a kind of delight even in unnecessary secrecy that a 7 seems to cherish. This can make 7s more interesting to people who like to imagine what is behind the façade, and even 7s with little back there can gain a reputation for deepness—but most 7s really do have hidden depths. This may make it difficult for their résumés to snag them the opportunities to shine as brightly as they can.

8 Like a 7, an 8 is cerebral but far less artistically minded or given to fantasizing. Eight has enough imagination for business success, but not much awareness that there is more to life than that. A true 8 truly is unaware or at the best rather uncaring that there are other paths, other goals, other rewards. Eights are the salt of the earth and often are a little amazed that some people want to be nuns or actors or ballet dancers or (as 8s see it) adopt other highly impractical professions. In this connection 8s' usual pedestrian or practical thinking does not permit them to understand vocation rather than occupation.

9 Nine is sensitive (perhaps too sensitive), spiritual (and maybe too unworldly), self-sacrificing, but sometimes ready to sacrifice others who have no desire to volunteer for that. Nine is loving, but true love allows the others to make their own decisions. The superior 9 likes to, often feels a 9 has the duty to, stay in charge.

The Number of the Heart's Desire

This can cause friction that puts a brake on progress. If you do not mind not leading the band or not riding on the fanciest float, a 9 in your life will bring a lot of color and happiness. There are some businesses in which imaginative 9s thrive and others in which they rouse suspicion and opposition. A 9 needs plenty of personal opportunity, but a 9 will reward employers.

As you will notice with personality numbers elsewhere, almost all people are somewhere between a 1 and a 9. Most 11s ought to be simply added up to 2s, but once in a blue moon the exceptional idealism and spiritual powers of a real 11 will surface. I apologize for repeating so much about 11s and 22s when I say they are so rare. I confess I regard them as far less usual than most numerology books, which tend to flatter, do.

It is not very comfortable being an 11, because the world misunderstands. This causes dedicated individuals some pain, even martyrdom in certain cases, but an 11 would not want things any other way: An 11 has a sense of mission and a dedication that can be astounding. An 11 is something almost as irresistible as a force of nature.

From time to time, but only once in a long while, a true 22 emerges, not a 4 in disguise but someone twice as powerful spiritually, twice as self-sacrificing, and twice as useful to humanity as an 11. This kind of person in business will do well for himself or herself and also benefit customers, clients, everyone with whom there is contact. The true 22 will deep down in the heart know of that status, that the two 2s should not be added to make a mere 4, that the 22 destiny is theirs, and that acceptance and personal dedication are demanded, never to be shirked. Almost no one has to face the demands that an 11 or a 22 has to face and most people would not want to pay in personal terms what it costs for exceptional people to realize their potential. Most people would like to take some time off to smell the roses. Some people rush along saying "there will be time enough to rest when I am dead."

Who knows what happens when you are dead? Those who are confident it is something nice have a good part of their heaven here—all of it if it happens that there is nothing after death for any of us. Those who are evil and know it may suffer most or all of their hell right here on earth. Or they may get most of the punishment later. The conviction that the evil will wind up like that helps the good, a little, to tolerate how the wicked prosper here on earth. But what comes next? We do not know in our heads though we may in our hearts.

Whatever the number of the inner You, as the ancient Greeks said, "Know thyself." Use your gifts, and be aware of your limitations. I do not want to appear preachy but I have to talk to you like this. Decide how much of your secret self you will keep to yourself and how much you are willing to reveal—and to whom. Make those confessions with great caution.

Always keep in mind that numerology claims that the inner You can be figured out by anyone who knows the vowels of your name!

As with Rumplestiltskin, once the secret name is known the power that can be exerted by the individual whose hidden self is open to inspection is finished.

You may want to pretend to a different number and have a different Heart's Desire by making the world think you are a Billy or a Willy or a Willie rather than a Will or a Bill or a William or (say) a Buddy or a Sparky or a Slim. Or by calling yourself (say) Werner Something or Tab Something. Down deep you will know who you really are, if you will stop kidding yourself. You will take off the mask only with great caution, if at all!

And one more thing about masks. Sir Max Beerbohm, I think it was, wrote a short story I keep thinking about that concerned an ugly man who wore the mask of a very handsome fellow. A young woman fell in love with this handsome fellow (as she thought him to be) and he fell in love with her. He loved her so much that he was ready to reveal his true nature to her. He whipped off the mask. His ugly face had grown to fit the mask. He really had the handsome face of the mask. The moral of all this, I suppose, is that one can become what one pretends to be if one sticks at it.

Presumably one could change not only one's basic name, alter the vowels and the essential nature of one's being, and live up to—become—the new person. Stranger things have happened. One of the permanently surprising things about human nature is how adaptable it is, how it can change. Another, as Kipling said, is that "the colonel's lady and Rosie O'Grady are sisters under the skin."

You cannot change the date of your birth, but you can take such care of yourself that the date of your death is put off, for a while, sometimes for a long while. Meanwhile, you can take actions not only to preserve your health but also to change the outer and even the inner You. Others may motivate or even be able to assist in the changes, but most of the work has to come from inside yourself. Numerology says you can do it. Make changes, with Mr. Right or Miss Clairol or whatever you need.

Finally in this respect, while we are dealing with a system that is based on extracting the vowels and giving them numbers, here is something else that relates to some people's "heart's desire," the desire for encoding (rather than decoding).

Now we somewhat digress on codes. Obviously a number code can easily be constructed by substituting for a letter of the alphabet the number of its position in the alphabet: as A = 1, B = 2, C = 3, and so on. But the purpose of encrypting is to hide, as the etymology says, and this is not hiding anything very effectively. So John Skelton (c. 1460–1529), the satirical inventor of skeltonics and a poet with a lively sense of language, is said

The Number of the Heart's Desire

to have invented a simple method of encryption in which you just take out the vowels and number them:

$$A = 1$$
$$E = 2$$
$$I = 3$$
$$O = 4$$
$$U = 5$$

The rest of the letters are given their regular numbers, as B = 2, C = 3, D = 4, and so on.

The result is not a very tough code to crack if one tackled it (and one would because the text is obviously in some kind of substitution code). The ideal code, of course, is one in which the text gives no hint that anything is encoded at all. With just the vowels disguised, as the simplest substitution (B= 2, C= 3, etc.) one would get a partly deciphered text that is pretty easy to read. Those who know Hebrew well can get along with just the consonants written, supplying the vowels that have been omitted. Indeed, to create a substitution code that is at all difficult to crack, you require some method to ensure that the most common letters don't give away any secret. In English, *e* is the most common letter—although I suppose someone has attempted to translate the weird French novel that was written with no *Es* at all. The challenge is not to permit letters in their accustomed frequencies to appear in the encrypted text. They must not appear in the same number in which they appear in the clear. The most secure codes substitute for the letters of the text to be encrypted numbers as random as possible, generated and read by complex machines.

Still the best codes depend upon preagreed signals. When I send you **237/14/5** you look at the fifth word in the fourteenth line on page 237 of a book I gave you to take with you (or one easily obtained, such as the revised standard version of the Bible in a common edition or the current New York telephone book for Manhattan). The big problem there is that someone clever might sense that the three numbers are of page/word/line (or possibly page/line/word), so right away you ought to find some method of making the three numbers an opaque one.

Even better would be for me to call you from a pay phone and say simply "Tomorrow" when you know that means for us Today or "Yes" when we have agreed that means No. Why lug around an Enigma machine?

I suppose part of the answer is that boys love toys. Males particularly enjoy coding and decoding, though females may have more patience at it. This playing with words and numbers is not wholly irrelevant to the

Soul and Spirit.

understanding of the attractions of numerology, the discovering of secrets hidden in numbers.

Suspicious minds may think they see secrets even in random numbers. They may, for example, think to play in the lottery some of the numbers they see on the dollar bill, chosen at random, they use to pay for their lottery ticket. I know people who play the numbers of horses and races and collect their so-called lucky numbers (rather subjectively) from the license plates of cars they pass on the way to the track. For one person I know this has worked surprisingly well, but so has (for several others) a habit of playing the market by throwing darts at newspaper pages of listed stocks. That is just about as good, maybe better, certainly cheaper than paying so-called experts at mutual funds who charge large fees for giving advice that is too often not nearly as good as this "random walk."

Random is the key word for encryption success. It may be that ingenuity too often sees significance in random numbers subjected to numerological scrutiny. People love to see a lucky result, to dig up a treasure. On the other hand, from centuries long past, we still cling to the idea that nothing is random, that chaos does not reign. The human body, we say, is a machine. The universe is a vast machine. God or whatever Force is in charge (or made it and lets it run unattended) is the Great Watchmaker. There is nothing random—or maybe chaos, the random, is a built-in and predictable part of the system.

Numerology says the key to it all is in numbers to decode. That is an attractive, even if wrongheaded, idea and appeals mightily to our hearts' desires.

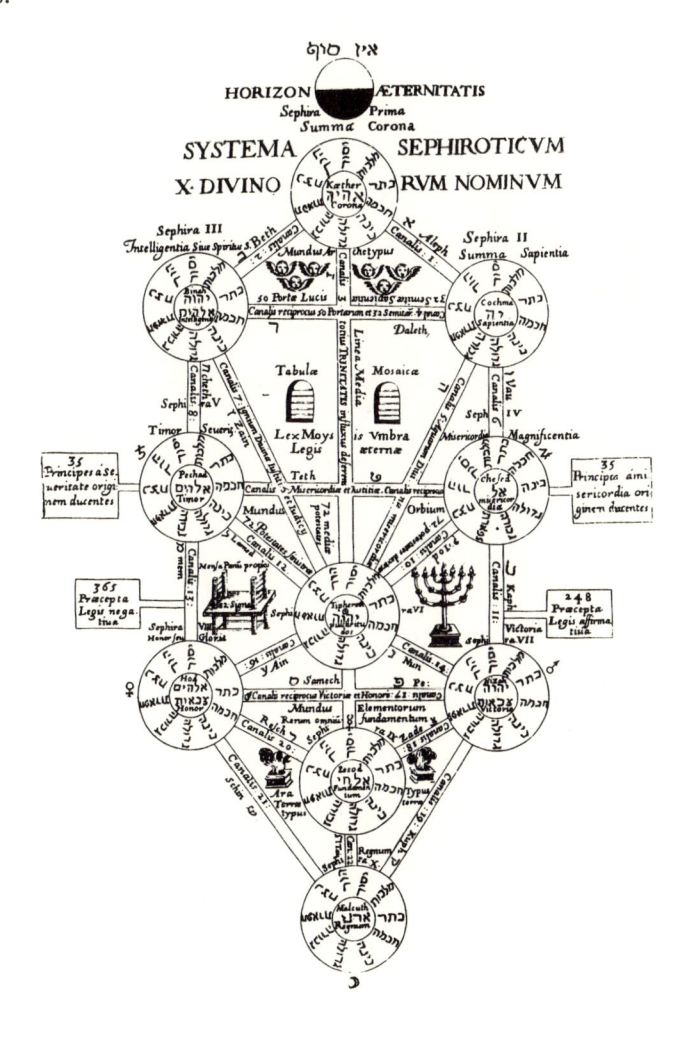

Chymische Hoch-zeit:

Christiani Rosencreütz.

Anno 1459.

Arcana publicata vilescunt; & gratiam prophanata amittunt.

Ergo: ne Margaritas obyce porcis, seu Asino substerne rosas.

Straßburg,
In Verlägung / Lazari Zetzners.
Anno M. DC. XVI.

An important milestone in Rosicrucianism: *The Chemical Wedding of Christian Rosencranz,* an hermetic allegory published at Strasbourg, 1459.

7
Your Favorite Numbers

ד

In discussing the Heart's Desire number we naturally considered the very personal. Now we turn to one of the commonest manifestations of some sort of belief in the power of numbers, the personal lucky numbers.

We all have personal favorites to some degree, no matter how much we say we do not believe in superstition and no matter how much we say we do not fear to walk under a ladder, mention pigs at sea, have a black cat cross our path, or break a mirror. Where we get these ideas is partly tradition and partly our own experience.

We may call them our favorite numbers. We may play them in the lotteries and wonder why they do not win. We may rejoice if they do and guard them carefully. As for winning at lotteries, there's another chapter on that later. I am sure that you will find it is interesting. I cannot say I am sure you will find it profitable. This chapter is about something else: not the numbers that may or may not turn up in the lotteries but the numbers that keep turning up in your everyday life.

In other chapters you may be given numbers for various purposes. Here *you* are the only one who can give the important numbers. Your life is unique. If you pay attention you will see that certain numbers can crop up again and again. I am sure of this much: If you think about it, you will find numbers that seem to have some very special meanings for you. On what basis do you designate them as lucky or unlucky or favorite?

You can and you should find those numbers. Become aware of what is going on.

It's easy to do. Read the chapter on names and numerology, and after you have worked out your numbers (Digital, Heart, and Image, as is explained to you there), work out the numbers of your parents' names, the names of your siblings, and other close relatives. Work out also the names of your best friends, maybe even those of your enemies. What you want are the numbers of the most significant people in all important areas and at every stage of your life. Try to remember any numbers especially close to you, whether the number of your first car registration or your first apartment on your own street address and number on the door or your ID numbers of all sorts.

Now, look closely. Do you detect any pattern? Are there any digits that turn up more often, in your opinion, than mere coincidence might explain?

Don't neglect to work out the numbers for the names, even the nicknames, of classmates, schools you attended, organizations that you have joined. All kinds of names. Get their personal numbers. Include, of course, numbers themselves. Is there a lot of one digit in your addresses, bank and credit account numbers, telephone numbers, and so on? Do you think there might be something in that? A numerologist would say so.

Many people neglect to look at the numbers (derived from that same table in the chapter on names and numerology) related to places. What about the ZIP codes of the place where you were born (even if it did not have such a ZIP then), the places where you have lived (town and city numbers, street names, maybe even the names of neighborhoods or apartment buildings, addresses where you have worked, and so on)?

Can you find any importantly recurring digit or digits in that information?

Search all the numbers derived from names that you can think of. Even the names given to your pets may hold some kind of information. Why disregard anything that might be useful?

Naturally you considered the date of your birth, and even the hour and minute of your birth. But people who pay a lot of attention to horoscopes based on birth numbers often fail to look for significant numbers in other respects. They neglect numbers that over and over mark important stages and events in their lives. Casting a detailed horoscope is a complicated procedure, as you know, and it used to take experts a long while to cast a horoscope. Most people got horoscopes that were off the rack, as it were, and just did not fit right. Today a huge amount of information can be fed into computers—with the caveat of GIGO (which you probably know means "Garbage In/Garbage Out"). Easier to cast than ever before though they may be, horoscopes when it comes to reading still is far more art than a science. They are complicated things.

But finding the digits that crop up often in your personal experience does not require any computer. Those are numbers that you can provide just by searching your memory. The art of memory was once considered a branch of occult studies.

Don't worry that you cannot remember all possible numbers that have touched you. Think of this: What you do remember is probably more significant to your way of thinking than what you forget. There must be some reason why certain things are in fact remembered and other things fall by the wayside.

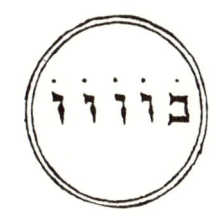

What you remember is you.

Are there any digits that you feel are basically you? Are there any numbers you consistently have found lucky? Is there any connection between them and the times and places and people that mean the most to you?

What you are looking for is a digit, or sometimes more than one digit, frequently important to you.

With that digit or that little collection identified, you may see patterns that can guide you, numerology promises, in making all sorts for future decisions and not just in connection with lotteries and such. Realize the simple truth of this: There is more than one way for you to "play the lucky numbers in your life"!

Having identified a digit or digits that are special to you, whether favorable or unfavorable, you may have in hand a useful guide to choosing a date on which to do something—or not to do something. You need not consult an astrologer for an opinion. You may on the basis of lucky numbers choose a partner in life or a firm to work for or an address to which to move—or avoid. That may be superstitious, but simply believing you are onto something can be supportive. It is never comforting to feel you are making some definite decision for no good reason. You may be falling for a mere superstition, but you will feel better about your decision.

Some people will tell you that the amazingly repeating digits in your life are just coincidence. They will tell you that it is silly and mindless to pay any attention to the recurrent numbers. However, you may be convinced that those doubters are flat wrong. You may say there is truth, even prophecy, in numbers.

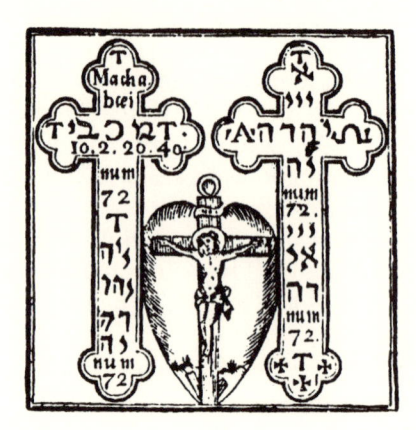

You may look at the numbers involved in, for example, the destruction of the World Trade Center in New York City on September 11, 2001, and see if the numbers of the two airline flights (or the number of passengers on the doomed airplanes) look unusually apt. There was, issued well before 9/11 (as we have come to call the date), a popular music album published which had a song about destruction called "September"—and it was the eleventh cut on the record. Just chance? Maybe. When you put all the 9s and 11s together, though, it really is astounding what appears to be going on. It may, nevertheless, be absolutely nothing but chance. Nonetheless, many people are going to say that there is "something in it" when coincidence stretches our credulity too far. What is, we ask, happening? Something strange? Superstition thrives on coincidence.

What has been going on with you? Are you like one person I know who considered her history and noted how astonishingly often the number 5 figured in her life, from her date and place of birth (in the fifth state to join the Union) as the fifth child in the family and given a forename of five letters and a forename plus surname that made her a 5? She attended five schools (one of them being a girls' school called Finch—five letters) before going to the university of Idaho (five letters), where she graduated fifth in her class. Five days after graduation, she married a man whose surname had—you're way ahead of me here—five letters in it. He was also a

5, maybe not the most compatible number for her, but that is the way it was. I won't go on and on with this, and I admit that she testifies, not without a certain amazement, there are many people and events in her life that have no connection whatever to the number 5, but it is certainly remarkable how often 5 has cropped up in her experience. That is the point. She says that she is not going to let 5 rule her life, and she is not going to go "too much out of her way" consciously to involve 5s with her activities, but it is when she acts quite unconscious of the 5s (she states) that, looking back, she sees how frequent and how much in the way of "milestones," as she puts it, those 5s are.

This is not to persuade you to run your life, choose your lovers and friends, guide all your actions by one or more digits significant to you that this chapter is written. All numerology asks you to do is to make a little effort to see whether or not there is some recurrent number pattern in what you experience.

The story is told of an old Jewish lady who saw from her window in Brooklyn that an automobile accident had taken place right in front of her apartment building. She had chicken soup on the stove in her kitchen at that very moment, and she quickly poured some into a bowl, grabbed a spoon, and rushed down to the street.

"Chicken soup!" she said to a policeman, who had appeared on the scene.

"Lady, I'm busy!" said the policeman.

"Not for you, for *him*! Chicken soup for the poor man who was hit by the car!"

"Lady," the policeman said, exasperated, "the man is dead!"

"Well," said the woman, "it couldn't hurt!"

That's it. In connection with finding out whether there is any significant digit recurring in your life or whether some particular number has been strangely lucky for you up to now—*it couldn't hurt*. Right?

So do it. Or come up with a reasonable excuse for not doing it. Think.

This is a short section because this time it is you who has the vital information, not me. You are the one and only expert on your favorite and recurrent numbers.

Finally on the subject of favorite numbers, there are those that are not surprisingly frequent in our experience, but that we have some special feeling for, somehow. Think about them. But do not be bound by them. Treat them fearlessly, the way that the actor Richard Gere says Tibetan Buddhism approaches everything, fearlessly. Gere, who has been involved with Buddhism since the age of nineteen or twenty, when he first started working as an actor—after an undergraduate degree in philosophy—and moving

8	58	59	5	4	62	63	1
49	15	14	52	53	11	10	56
41	23	22	44	45	19	18	48
32	34	35	29	28	38	39	25
40	26	27	37	36	30	31	33
17	47	46	20	21	43	42	24
9	55	54	12	13	51	50	16
64	2	3	61	60	6	7	57

The Kâmê'a of Mercury.

from Zen to the Tibetan vehicles, says that if anything, anything, does not work for you, disappoints your expectations, seems wrong even if you cannot explain why, you must "throw it away," fearlessly. So if your cherished favorite numbers do not work for you, toss them. Get new ones. You are in charge, in numerology far more so than in any other occult explanation of life and destiny.

8
Odd and Even Numbers

ח

In saying something about people's favorite numbers, it occurred to me that it is odd that the numbers people think lucky are not even—and may not even be lucky. This preference for the odd (in classical numerology, male) numbers has been around for a long time. Here are several historical comments selected from the very many available regarding odd numbers:

- "God delights in odd numbers."
  —Virgil, *Eclogues* 8
- "Why do we all believe that odd numbers are better?"
  —Pliny the Elder, *Natural History* 28
- "They say that there is divinity in odd numbers, either in nativity, chance, or death."
  —William Shakespeare, *The Merry Wives of Windsor* V:1, 2

Where does this superstition or observation about odd numbers come from? I don't know. Exactly how do odd numbers get to be luckier than even ones? Exactly how do odd numbers matter in terms of birth, death, and in between?

Typically, no one truly and convincingly gives reasons. That is the way so much in the realm of the occult works. People just make assertions, and people just believe. With some things, I believe. OK, since the recipe calls for *Atropa belladonna* or *Hyoscyamus niger*, I am willing to believe that the "magical" *Oleum angelorum* (Oil of the Angels), as the erudite magician writing under the pseudonym "David Conway" claims, "induces pleasant numbness of the body and a sweet langour [*sic*] of spirit." Why not, since the main ingredients (along with wolfsbane and wild celery, maybe a bit of poplar leaf) are, to give the common names of the two whose official Latin names I cited, deadly nightshade and henbane? Science has established that these are narcotics and hallucinogens. Necromancers and "wise women" had that figured out from the earliest times. In the Bible when we are told to kill all *witches*; what I think the word means is *poisoners*.

But concoctions that early apothecaries, alternative-medicine herbalists, and desperate weirdos put together were not just pharmaceuticals. They involved magic, as did regular medicines when astrology was involved: You see that "take it at the time of the full moon" is not the same thing as "take it on an empty stomach." The question is not whether you get languorous when you take a draught of the stuff that "Conway" describes. The question is whether there is any power in the promise that the user will perceive "astral forms" that are there, but are not ordinarily seen, as well as enjoy "gentle sleep during which his subconscious will learn many things about inner planes and their inhabitants" that are in some way truer than the usual experiences of our dreams. If such visions come, are they produced by autosuggestion? Maybe you have heard of the hippies of the sixties smoking dried banana peels to get high. It worked. It worked because they were told it would work, and they believed it, not because there was something hallucinogenic in bananas (as there actually was in the morning-glory seeds they were sometimes ingesting, not to mention the hashish brownies) but because of their faith. Faith healers really do produce results, but the power, in my way of thinking, is not in them nor (excuse me!) in God, but in the patient's own mind. True, that mind is a gift of God and the faith healer is a catalyst. I'll give him that.

From odd televangelists to odd numbers, then. Are odd numbers lucky in and of themselves, or do they seem to be because we have heard they are? *Are* there really any numbers luckier than others, and in fact, *are* there any astral forms and inner planes? Deponent saith not—or at least never troubles to prove scientifically that the assertions are valid.

There are many superstitions about odd and even numbers. When bringing gifts to the newborn (such as a clutch of eggs), bring an odd number for a boy, an even number for a girl. Hens should sit on an odd number of eggs if you want the hatchlings to thrive. Always, when presenting a bouquet, offer an odd number of flowers, so try to get the florist who is selling a dozen roses to throw in the extra as in a baker's dozen—or give one flower to someone else and present 11 in the bouquet. In Palma de Majorca, they used to count the letters or syllables in the combined names of the parents, maybe they still do, and they believed that if the number was odd the first child would be male. Around Scuratia, however, the usual odd = male/even = female rule does not apply when bringing gifts to the newborn.

The Roma or gypsies have plenty to say to us *gangé* folks about odd and even numbers, but their customs are very different from those of the rest of us. They need larger than usual coffins, for example, because they bury the corpse, often with some clothing on inside out, with her or his favorite things, sometimes with money. The story is told of a gypsy who died in England with 600 pounds. Relatives put various gifts and 600 pounds in bills into the coffin. The eldest son took out the money and put in personal checks, made out to his father, to the sum of 600 pounds.

Stephen Wilson's *The Magical Universe: Everyday Ritual and Magic in Pre-Modern Europe* (2000) is a vast mine of information, and on this he writes (page 194):

> In the Balkans, in and around Scutari, "all the women neighbours [*sic*] go at once to visit the [new] mother and take offerings of eggs. For a boy, two, four, six, or eight—an even number—are brought; for a girl, one, three, five or seven."

This may have some connection to the attempts to get the child started on the correct sexual orientation so that the child will not grow up to be effeminate if a boy or a tomboy if a girl. Wrap the child in the garment of the wrong sex, and they "will never marry"!

The symbolism and customs differ from place to place, but such guides as dream books do not deign to take that into account. They are written as if all cultures were the same or as if old customs (such as never marrying a person with the same surname as yourself—which seems to go back to very ancient fears of incest) never died. We still have holly and mistletoe at Christmas from the Druids and Christmas trees from the tree worshippers of the dark Teutonic forests, and we now have Kwanzaa, as well.

The writers of dream-symbol books pay little or no attention to anything but older dream-symbol books. The eagle to modern Americans does not mean what it did when some bishop wrote such a book in the first millennium after Christ. Times change and with them the vocabulary of dreams. Sometimes that vocabulary seems to pop up out of nowhere just to put at least a touch of freshness in the old recipes. Migene González-Wippler in a book on dream symbolism confidently writes: "**Dandelion**—Happy unions and prosperity. 79, 17." She claims that this is "the traditional meaning" of Dandelion in dreams and that "popular tradition" she gives those two numbers as "lucky in games of chance" and associated with this plant. But *where does this stuff come from?* What "popular tradition"? I checked **Dandelion** with a number of consultants who had set themselves up as professional or amateur interpreters of dreams when I was writing *The Complete Book of Dreams and What They Mean*, and nobody (as we say in New Yorkese, influenced by Yiddish, *but nobody*) said they had ever heard of the allegedly "traditional" meaning of the symbol. We all pretty much agreed on (say) **Snake** and **Naked**, and most pretty much were of one mind on **Water** and **Heights**, but when it came to **Dandelion** we thought Ms. González-Wippler had either pulled the "meaning" out of the air or, more likely, found it in a couple of off-center gypsy dream books that had copied from the same source and took for tradition what some writer who pulled it out of the air just a generation or less of gypsy dream books earlier had put down. "Traditional"? No. Right or wrong? How to tell? Suspicious, perhaps, on the face of it, but long established (which still wouldn't mean it was right), absolutely not!

My researches show that in this case and in almost all others the interpretation of symbols copied over and over in dream books that involve no real research and no serious thought are not consistent and do not go back to any clear and reliable or checkable origin. They just *say*. They pay little or no attention to what people actually report of their dreams and so personal "readings" are not compared (as they are in ink-blot tests, etc.). This is not science. This is not even pseudoscience, which has to claim some validity, even if falsely.

The occult is often very dismissive of science. Try telling a true believer in telepathy that science seems to have established that there is "rapidly diminishing intensity with distance" of everything radiated and that, therefore, brain waves couldn't reach from (say) Australia to England. The believer in mental telepathy will argue (as Felix E. Planer says in his book on *Superstition*) that "the law has been broken" by supercooled metals becoming superconductors. But we are talking mental, not metal. The defense is wrong. Seldom is any appeal to science attempted; usually assertion is all. When justification is offered—that "traditional" bit—it does not stand up to examination.

Most occult assertions do not bother with scientific details. They are unabashedly ignorant of science; they are cavalier about proof. The grand pronouncements about ghosts, demons, telekinesis, teleportation, PSI in general, etc., are nothing but arbitrary, just as when 7 is connected to "mystery, study, knowledge" and the menorah and the planet Saturn.

Let me be blunt and say that the design of the seven-branched candelabra probably came first and later the number 7 was introduced into an upbeat story about Jews being exceptionally lucky in their lighting-oil consumption.

Let me say on firmer basis of fact that the references to 40 days in the Bible, Old Testament or New Testament, does not mean one day more than 39. The language then was such that 40 days meant *any* rather long time, a remarkable time for a flood, or a retreat in the desert, or whatever. It is poetic, not exact.

Seven as special is also poetic, not exact. Who "discovered" that "as a birth number, 7 denotes a scholarly, poetic nature, often inclined toward the fanciful, though persons with this birth vibration are analytical as well"? It might be possible to back up such a statement if all the persons ever born "under Saturn" were to have their lives examined carefully. That work has not been done (naturally), and there has never been even a statistically valid sample examined with an eye to proving or disproving this.

This kind of assertion I find no more commanding of belief than the likes of: "Durand relates," reports Richard Burton in *The Anatomy of Melancholy*, "that he saw a wench possessed in Bononia with two devils, by eating an unhallowed pomegranate, as she did afterwards confess, when she was cured by exorcisms." I don't believe what Durand reported. I do not accept that dreaming of eating a pomegranate (or an orange) means that you will soon be ill. It may mean that your mouth is acid, the way that dreaming of deserts may mean you need to wake up, get up, and get a glass of water.

I do believe that certain male saints and a notable number of possibly hysterical nuns did truly believe that they saw visions of the Blessed Virgin (and some others deliberately lied and claimed to have done so), but whether these were delusions or facts is impossible to prove unless you have (say) miracle cures at Fatima or Lourdes *and* those miracles confound any conceivable explanation by medical science. Even then the cures may be explained later when medical science is more advanced. Faced with miracles, the pious will believe and the pragmatic will say either they disbelieve or bring in the Scottish verdict of "not proven," which usually means "we are fairly sure you are guilty, but we just can't nail you right now."

Lucky 3, lucky 7, unlucky 13. When it comes to the occult, do not be too ready to believe, nor too unwilling to believe, if and when there is evidence. Invariably demand evidence, and never believe until you see ironclad proof. On the subject of what cannot ever be proved or disproved, avoid conviction and keep an open mind. With those who are convinced and are not content to say they really do not know, question. Always, always ask: How do you *know* what you claim to know? A peasant kid told you that this portrait of the Virgin is from life? Some experts say this shroud bears the image of a dead Christ? Bring on the scientists. The textile of The Shroud of Turin is medieval.

The dead Christ lives in all of us. We are made in the image of the Blessed Virgin and of God. If you want to go by faith, that is mine. If you do not agree, that is fine with me.

Now, when Francisco de Quevedo y Villegas in his "visions" says that "[t]hings are admirably ordered in hell, and there is a place reserved for all," my faith is shakier. I ask *why* should we believe him? I shall not venture upon the touchy topic of magic performed by Jesus or the dreams vouchsafed to Mohammed. I have to confess that I am rather more impressed by the wisdom of mortals who claim no divine help and who put together the systems of the Buddha and Confucius. You can believe whatever you wish.

I do not mind asking if it is true when someone says that if we drop a piece of buttered bread or step on an ant or kill a spider there will be rain. Has anyone in any occult matter conducted replicable experiments? I want to know who first articulated any supposedly powerful incantation, where it came from, and precisely how it works, if in fact it does work. Faith is the belief in things unseen. I'm more from Missouri, so show me. That is what I believe.

What is the scientific explanation? *Why* and *how* does the conjunction of planets on 21 March guarantee that I will be bolder than usual and "coming out of the comfortable confinement in which [I] have been hiding" so far this year? You mean one-twelfth of all humanity, we Sagittarians, have all been doing that? No wonder the world is in such a bad state this particular month! But how and where did you get this information? Last month, my psychic friend told me I would face oppositions in March. Who won't?

Oracles like to be ambiguous; it is safer. But everywhere you go in the occult there are startlingly straightforward statements. "With a Dragon to love, the Monkey person will never be bored." A short index finger is a sign you won't be very forward. Look at your lines of affection/marriage/union on the side of your hand below your little finger: "If the lines have a downward slope then your mate will die before you do." "Dreaming of eating new-baked bread means imminent misfortune." "Chango will appear in your dream to tell you to move a flag from one side of your house to the other." "Pray to Saint-Expedite for fastest service." We are given explicit instructions:

> After sunrise, a black cock must be killed, the first feather of his left wing being plucked and preserved for use at the required time.

The eyes must be torn out, and so also the tongue and heart; these must be dried in the sun and afterwards reduced to powder.

The hideous *Grimoire of Honorius*, a manual of black magic fathered on one of the popes, goes on to sprinkle the powder on a parchment and perform a lot of superstitious and blasphemous acts, each stage of the scabrous game with its precise rules. Didn't work? You did it wrong.

With things such as these we may be dismissive or horrified. But they are no sillier, if perhaps far more dangerous to sanity, than believing one number is more lucky than another—unless we can say we have some explanation that reason can accept.

I cite advice and instruction in this book from so many obscure and ancient "authorities" that at this point I choose to go to a cult classic Western movie, something you probably know, the 1954 film *Johnny Guitar*. In it, the character played by Joan Crawford (whom the script describes as "thinks like a man, acts like a man") says:

> I'm not trusting in luck. A good gunfighter doesn't depend on four-leaf clovers.

I suggest that philosophy (or notion) is a very good guide.

When we are told that in telling fortunes by playing cards, the 5 of hearts means "indecision . . . desire to escape the issue"—*why*? How can that be proved?

Why is scarlet the color of " a nature more likeable or more spiteful than any other type"? *How* does that work? Don't just say it, prove it. More B.Sc., please, and less BS.

Don't tell me that you are a psychic and psychics just know. Don't offer to tell my fortune for money. That's illegal under N.Y.S. Penal Code 165.35, and the law is sensible.

How is it that psychics offering to help the police in criminal cases, even when clairvoyants "see" at a distance, it looks far more like guesswork than what anyone would see if they were at the spot? I don't want to tangle with the self-certified professional psychics who are advertising on TV, so let us go back in history and examine the evidence in the case of the Lindbergh baby in 1932.

Lindbergh was still at the time a great American hero, the man who flew the Atlantic solo; this was before Lindbergh was heading anti-Semitic, pro-Nazi rallies in Madison Square Garden and urging Americans not to go to war against Hitler. The infant was kidnapped and murdered. The police conducted a tremendous search. Out of the 4,300 messages from psychics who reported that they "saw" what had happened, only four contained the important facts that the baby was dead and buried under trees, and even these four psychics did not notice in their "visions" the most obvious and shocking fact that the pitiful little corpse was naked and mutilated.

But people still believe in magicians and visionaries and psychics. The world sometimes works as if even frauds were facts. Shakespeare and not a few others have noticed that what people believe to be true is the basis not only of their take on the world but of their actions in the world, and so generally accepted opinion, right or wrong, must be regarded as of great significance. Thus I find some religious fanatics and some zany witches and psychics and table-rappers and crystal-ball watchers and so on truly worth watching. They are essential for the fullest understanding of two of the most potent forces in human history: delusion and the madness of crowds.

Now, with all that out of my system, we arrive at what the title of this section promised. The several quotations I put at the top of this section prove that for a long time there has been the feeling that in odd numbers there is something special. Whatever the truth may be, that is the fact, we might say. Maybe that is why those famous numbers 3 and 7 are so popular and why 3 x 3 produces the number of divine power, 9. You should not be surprised to discover that numerologists go right along with this belief even if it may not have originated among them; it is something that cropped up for some other reasons in some other contexts.

Let us not pause long to ponder that. In this book I am not fundamentally interested in the speculations of metaphysics. The book is dedicated to being very practical for those who have or will have some interest in the efficacy of numbers study. This book assumes that. It is not designed or indeed able to cope with more abstruse and exotic topics. This book is not really about something unfamiliar. It is about your favorite subject: *You.* What do odd and even numbers mean in connection with you? Which crop up most often in your experience? What is your take on that?

I cannot give absolute proof of the validity of what I report others believing on the subject of Odds and Evens. I do offer the historical facts as I know them to you for what they may be worth. The only fact of which I dare declare that I am certain is that on the subject of Odds and Evens there has been in certain circles at least a good deal of agreement. Maybe you respect tradition, real tradition in this case.

Well, you have heard the word *oddball.* The odd numbers are said to express the independent and questing spirit, the loner, the leader who stands apart from the crowd, the other-directed but public-spirited person who believes that she or he is the one to figure out what is best and bring others that information. Those with odd Life Path numbers feel that they have something of a mission, in most cases, to stand apart and transform details into one big strategy. It is their privilege, their job to focus on ideas and to root out the causes that the many do not agree is important. This sense of a need to serve others is weakest in a 1 and strongest in a 9 and the rare 11. So they say.

Odd and Even Numbers 99

Naturally, the odd person can be not only a brave altruist but also the "odd man out." Individualists can encounter opposition and misunderstanding and rejection by the many. They can feel set apart or even set upon. Some of them actually enjoy being quite on their own, out of martyrdom fantasies or love of opportunities for self-reliance and quiet meditation.

The character of the 1 is simply stated: a 1 wants to be "the one." That is something said before, but worth repeating; it is something that is not to be said once. To the 1s of the world we owe much of what goes right and also, frankly, a lot of what goes wrong. For better or worse, they are the doers.

A 3 and a 5 and a 7 are said to have varying degrees of individuality, independence, and leadership qualities. The degree to which each group has doers among it is said to be unpredictable. It is not a simple matter of the fewest in 3 or the most in 7. We can expect various ways in which the persons who step forward to do or to lead others, to perform even if they must go against the grain, sidestep the conventional, stand out—and be put out. Particularly when rather than doing, they say—pointing out in a few well-chosen but impolitic words something others do not wish to face or take into consideration—the persons who act or call to action may be soundly rejected, either at first or later when things do not turn out as expected or desired. To twist an old phrase into a new realization, nobody loves a fact man. And nobody loves a failure.

The 9 and the 11 are regarded as less interested in personal acquisitions but share with all the others sporting odd numbers (whether derived from birth dates, names, or whatever) a quality of the exceptional, the unique, the singular. When faced with opposition, these people triumph, generally, not so much because they have more on the ball than other people have (which they do), but because they have the valuable talent of being able to rise above the mundane to a degree that other people, particularly those who pride themselves on being pragmatists, feet-on-the-ground people, cannot ever attain.

We come now to consider the group which, in our modern yearning for individuality in a situation in which we are all at some level aware is increasingly regimenting us, we somehow find a little bit less attractive than the Odds. I mean the Evens. The Evens tend to be more conservative, and in these days of entrepreneurship and risk taking on grander scales than ever before in history, conservatism looks to many like stick-in-the-mud. If I may revert to an abstruse quotation, here, from Baltasar Gracián, is an example of what he calls "the art of worldly wisdom." He writes: "A brand new mediocrity is thought more of than accustomed excellence." Think about it. Consider that the innovator of today is in the minority in the great democratic parliament of mankind, for there the dead are the majority. Consider that the person who marches along in step with the majority avoids a lot of difficulty or at least is spared a lot of criticism. One gets along by going along.

Those whose Life Path numbers are even are at least intended to work with rather than on others. They make good companions. They are almost by definition going to be more even tempered than others, or you might say they want to even out differences without regard to justice and even to get even in some perverted idea of justice. They like someone to lean on. You can also lean on them, too. They are helpers. They work well in teams. They do better in love than people ruled by odd numbers, except in those one-sided love relationships in which degradation or dependency is sought, masochistic marriages, self-abnegating sacrifices, trophy partners, that sort of thing.

However, as in everything else connected with numerology, no two people are precisely alike; all generalizations must admit of some notable exceptions, and in no case are broad generalizations completely reliable anyway. The 2 and the 6 are said to be particularly good at getting along with others, and the 8 is usually able to turn that into material success. The 8 is (some say) twice as reliable and twice as driving as the 4. That is why the 8 is expected to become richer. This could make others jealous. The 4 can also have troubles. The 4 is so four-square that she or he may annoy others with the square attitudes that appear to be the birthright. At the same time the 4 is someone to count on, someone as steady as a table with all four legs on the floor. The exception? The 9 is equally talented at getting along with others, and a 9 usually is more concerned than others with helping humanity and giving everyone an equal opportunity.

You have heard all this previously, but it needs repeating. I am also aware that some readers will not read straight through but dip into the book in search of certain answers to certain questions. I cannot put everything useful everywhere. I can attempt, at least, to put what may be wanted where it will likely be sought. If reiteration bores you, congratulations, for you are quicker on the uptake than most persons. Have some sympathy for your slower fellows. You ought to be happy, not irritated, at the results of your being one up on other people. That's lucky. Perhaps you go beyond that and are one of the very few extraordinary people. If that is so, your superiority will be comfortable and you will not be the sort to become antsy at the less fortunate, the mundane, the boring. You will rise, smiling and not sneering, calmly above it, right?

The acme of even numbers is the extremely rare 22, as you have often heard despite the fact that the phenomenon is extremely rare. A 22 is the perfection of serving others practically while at the same time exhibiting a wonderful spirituality. The 22 is credited with thinking in grand terms and very often in the abstract way so characteristic of the Evens. The Odds are better at brass tacks: they want the facts, not the reasons, the results and not the theories.

You might consider when choosing a profession or any kind of employment whether it favors and rewards the practical and individualistic Odds or the thoughtful and team-playing Evens. At the same time, every walk of life needs leaders and followers, doers and thinkers. Success comes to those who know how they are and conceive or cooperate as best suits their abilities and inclinations. That is pretty obvious, as obvious as the fact that an Odd and an Even will bring mystery as well as excitement to any pairing and that two Odds will battle more than two Evens in any relationship, raising a family or running a business.

Much of what numerology or any of the other so-called sciences of the occult have to say is, down deep, simply obvious. The obvious is often overlooked—like the envelope in plain view on the mantelpiece in Poe's *The Purloined Letter*. Whatever it is that makes you face the obvious is, for my money, good in and of itself. Whatever makes you quest and question is promising. Self-examination can be spiritual exercise.

Whatever makes you look inward for answers is excellent for you because there are little voices (you might say) within you that you tend to drown out in the hustle and bustle of daily life, and, when you quietly pause to attend to them, they can bring you not only serenity but wisdom.

That is where I find myself in full approval of (say) gazing into crystal balls (though a bowl of water will do quite as well and is a lot less expensive, even if your "crystal" is not crystal at all but just glass). So will laying out the Tarot cards. These things fire the imagination. They direct the interpretive intuitions to the deeper self. Personally, I do not consider this sort of thing blasphemous or superstitious. I think it is a perfectly reasonable thing to try to reach your inner reality. You are not, in my view, dealing with external and divine sources; you are delving into your own divinely given psyche. Nothing supernatural is going to happen. By concentrating, you will get to hear inner voices, whether you want to think of them as conscience or intuition or your personal unconscious mind or what Jung called the collective unconscious of the human race.

Oddly, Odds and even Evens can equally do this.

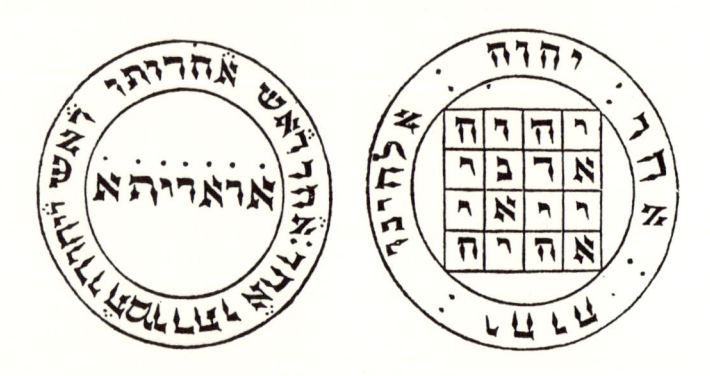

9
Triskaidekaphobia

מ

There's as jawbreaker for you. It's just the sesquipedalian (Latin "six-foot-long") Greek way of saying "fear of 13." Actually a lot of people enjoy learning the word and stunning their friends with it. You may want to do so as well. We needed a word of the sort, if not so hard a one to spell or pronounce.

The fear of the number 13 has been so widespread over so many centuries since Michel de Montaigne in the Renaissance first noticed people's aversion to it that in a book about numbers, lucky, unlucky, or neutral, there needs to be some attention paid to this particular number, in some cultures sacred and in some scary.

Montaigne remarked on the poor state of medicine in France in his time (he lived 1533–1592) because doctors were then taking astrology into account in diagnosing and treating patients and even permitted numerology to dictate how many pills a patient had to swallow while the stars dictated precisely when the medicine was to be taken. At the same time, things were not much better outside France and Italy, where early faculties of medicine were established. Things were about the same in British and German medicine. In Germany, Dr. Johann Weyer (or Weirius) was complaining about the persecution of witches, but he also was writing seriously on the hierarchy of demons. There were 7 kinds according to Peter Binsfield in 1589 (he wanted a number to go with the Seven Deadly Sins), down from 10 according to Alphonsus de Spina in 1460. Psellos later got the number down to 6, but then he added new stuff: 5 earthly demons and 5 infernal ones.

De Spina (somewhat moderate considering his time) was one of many Jews who became Franciscans or Dominicans and brought Jewish elements more into Christian beliefs while persecuting heretics with the special zeal of converts. Montaigne's contemporary Ambroise Paré (1517–1590) was establishing himself as the father of modern surgery, still the practice of medicine was riddled with ancient superstition. Doctors seriously discussed demonic possession, the incubus, the succubus, and witches.

Superstition still is rife. Even now ask anyone to think of powerful (masculine) odd numbers. Start with lucky rather than unlucky numbers. Ask anyone to pick a number between 1 and 10, and they usually come up with 3 or 7. To start with 13 might be unlucky. They think there are reasons for their choices even if they cannot give them. They like odd numbers best. Just do. A lot of people still cling to de Spina's prejudices about devils, demons, Jews, and infidels, and other dangerously foolish ideas.

This is not something peculiar to the Judeo-Christian and Islamic religions (all of which require believers to believe in devils and demons and many other such things). The Latin poet Virgil wrote that "God delights in odd numbers," as I quote elsewhere, and 3 and 7 might owe something to that belief. Ask anyone to name the basic lucky number, and they will in all likelihood say 7. At least in our Western culture. In China, people prefer 8. Where do different cultures get their different ideas of what is lucky and what is not?

Ask anyone for the classic unlucky number here and you are almost certain to get 13. That's true not only in Western culture, but also, for instance, among the Japanese. They not only avoid naming a 13th floor in buildings (as you know we in the West often do), but to a much greater extent than Americans the Japanese refuse to have a gate numbered 13 at the airport or a 13 in any other place where it can be avoided. Asians often believe that certain words and numbers are to be avoided because they sound like other words meaning bad things or are written with an unlucky number of strokes.

The Japanese are avid believers in the power of numbers. Mr. Toyoda, whose car you know as the Toyota, is said to have selected the name *Toyota* because in Japanese it is written with a numerically more auspicious number of strokes than the name *Toyoda*.

Why are people so down on 13? What's wrong with 13?

Let's look at some of the origins of this particular and very ancient superstition.

Looking at the question from our Christian perspective in the West, 13 is the number of the group at the Last Supper, the Lord Jesus Christ, and the traitorous Judas Iscariot. Those whose religions claim to be older than Christianity would ask why there were indeed 12 apostles. Was Christ following the ancient pagan tradition of the covens? Did Christ perhaps

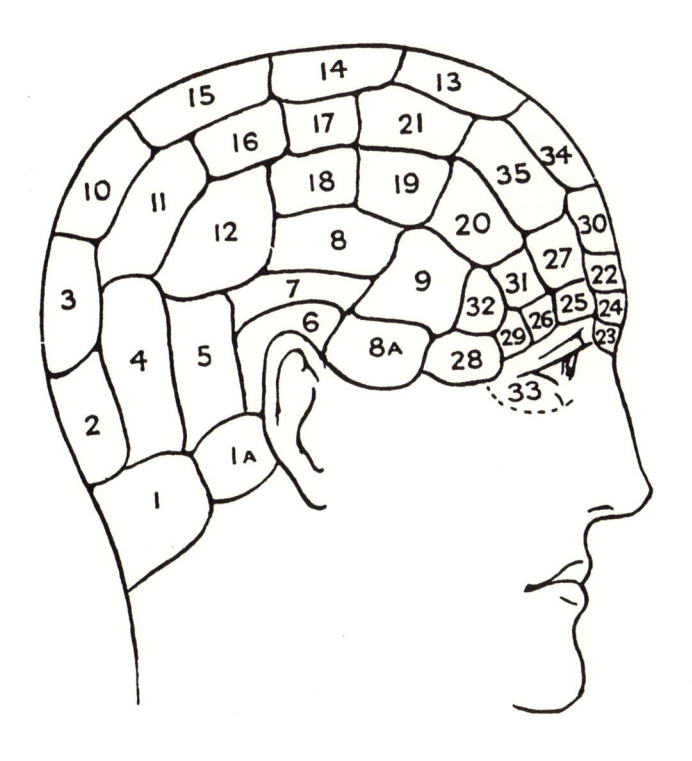

Propensities

1. Amativeness
1a. Self-preservation
2. Philoprogenitiveness
3. Inhabitiveness
4. Friendship
5. Combativeness

6. Destructiveness
7. Secretiveness
8. Acquisitiveness
8a. Alimentiveness
9. Constructiveness

Sentiments

10. Self-esteem
11. Approbativeness
12. Cautiousness
13. Benevolence
14. Veneration
15. Firmness

16. Conscientiousness
17. Hope
18. Wonder
19. Ideality
20. Mirthfulness
21. Imitation

INTELLECTUAL ORGANS
Perceptive

22. Individuality
23. Form
24. Size
25. Weight
26. Colour
27. Locality

28. Number
29. Order
30. Eventuality
31. Time
32. Tune
33. Language

Reflective

34. Comparison

35. Causality

Area 13 is supposed to be the site of Benevolence.

have fewer or more than 12 disciples and later reports choose what they considered to be a significant number? They certainly got some other things wrong.

When you put together the 13 at the Last Supper and the day of the Crucifixion you get Friday the 13th, considered by many to be a day when misfortune is pretty much to be expected. Very ancient traditions, dating from well before the time of Christ, considered their equivalent of Friday to be a day chock full of bad luck. Well into modern times people even in the most advanced nations of western Europe would never set sail on a Friday, never begin any important project on a Friday at all. Friday was bad news and combined with the 13th day of the month—the day, as a matter of fact, that is a Friday the 13th more often than any other day is—it constituted something to fear long before there was a long string of horror movies called *Friday the 13th*.

Of course, a lot of superstition arises out of simple coincidences. When a tradition that 13 is unlucky exists, every time a Friday the 13th rolls around or anything bad occurs with the number 13 somehow connected to it people will say, "There, I told you so! Thirteen is unlucky. Always was. Always will be."

Still there are some people who like to swim against the stream. There are people who think that whatever most other people believe has got to be wrong. Or perhaps the naysayers are basically oppositional by their very nature. If other people try to avoid the number 13, those contrarians will hug it to their hearts. Thirteen, they'll say, is their lucky number. They will bet on it, and they will know that not many other people will have chosen to bet on it.

The story is told of the man who dreamed that a great big number 13 hovered in the air above his bed. This dream recurred night after night. When it happened for the 13th time, the dreamer could not help but rush to the racetrack and place a huge bet on the 13th horse in the 13th race. (Naturally the odds were very much in his favor; he stood to win a fortune.) The 13th horse in the 13th race came in—13th.

When it comes to whether 13 is lucky for the rest of us or not, the Founding Fathers of the U.S. did not have much of a choice. They had, with the Thirteen Colonies declaring American independence, to embrace the number 13. From the coat of arms of George Washington, I guess, they got the stars and bars idea. The flag was to be 13 stars in the canton and 13 stripes, red and white alternatively, one for each of the 13 original states. The Great Seal of the United States is an orgy of 13s. There are not only the 13 stars and 13 stripes, but also the noble eagle—the suggestion that the nation's bird be a turkey was turned down—with 13 feathers in each wing and 13 feathers in its tail. The eagle reigns over peace and war, and on one side its talons grasp the olive branch of peace (with

Triskaidekaphobia 107

13 leaves and 13 berries), and on the other side, there are the 13 arrows representing war. This is THE COAT OF ARMS OF THE UNITED STATES OF AMERICA. More accidentally than the rest of all this, I think, that adds up to 39 letters or 3 times 13.

So far our great nation seems to have been especially lucky in world history, whether because of or in spite of defying the old idea that 13s are especially unfortunate. Our fortunes as a nation can be, astrologers say, easily "read" if you take the moment of the founding of the country and regard that as a birth date basis for a horoscope.

Have you personally found 13 to be an unlucky number for you? Or do you perhaps deliberately sidestep it so that it does not get much of a chance to work any baleful influence on your life? Are you one of those who claim that, for you, 13 is lucky? What has your experience been?

Would you hesitate to have 13 in your ZIP code or telephone number or home address? If you were issued a credit card with a 13 in its number, would you use it?

As with all kinds of numbers, we can refer to Hamlet's idea in Shakespeare's play that there is nothing wrong or right, lucky or unlucky, "but

Just show this third pentacle of Venus to someone and they will fall in love with you. If you are holding a large sum in bills, that helps. Good luck!

thinking makes it so." Thinking, belief, also helped those doctors work "miracles" with their patients. Doctors still put up their confidence-inspiring diplomas on the wall and may even wear white coats and sport stethoscopes and use impressive words like *oncology* and *protocol*. Confidence gives strength; fear births weakness.

If you are afraid of 13, it can probably have a bad effect on you. If it makes you uneasy or leads you to expect the worst it is indeed doing you no good. If you are stuck with it, you may panic or you may come to mock the superstition. Louis XIII's (1601–1643) mother (Catherine de' Medici) was regent of her son, who ascended the French throne when his father was assassinated and the boy was only about nine. She set up an unpopular alliance with the pope and with Spain and arranged the marriage of young Louis XIII to the daughter of Philip II of Spain. That young lady was Anne of Austria, and when she married Louis XIII she was thirteen. Coincidence?

I have resisted citing too many other books in this book that you will never consult, but for once, I cannot resist a bibliographical reference, even if it is in German and you are not at all likely to dig it up even if you read German. It is Ernst Böklin's *Die "Unglückzahl" Dreizen und ihre mythische Bedeutung* and it is an exhaustive (and exhausting) Teutonic tome of what he calls (using quotation marks) "unlucky" 13. It was published in 1913.

So far we have not had Israel broken up into 13 kingdoms with one for the Messiah to rule, which the Talmud promises and which will bring the end of the world uncomfortably close, nor have we heard of anyone winning the lottery 13 times.

10
Playing the Lottery

ל

In a recent volume, *The Complete Book of Dreams and What They Mean*, I mention playing lottery numbers:

> Some people try to dream of lucky numbers. You are truly lucky if you are not one of those who play lotteries where the odds are ridiculous. The influence of the cabala . . . introduced numerology into the interpretation of dreams. Some dream-books give numbers for the symbols. Forget that. Just play the same number an infinite number of times and it will come up. Or take your dollar and give it to someone needy.

Millions of Americans are not going to take my warning that the odds are millions to one. They will play the lotteries, which in many places are now legal. Before that, people supported organized crime by playing the numbers games. They just want to have fun, preferably profit. No, there is never something for nothing (they think), but every once in a blue moon there is a lot for very little. So we have casinos, racinos, and more.

People will even enter the Reader's Digest or Publishers Clearing House or other sweep-

Would the numbers on this bill be useful not only in paying for tickets or make you a winner in a lottery?

stakes. They realize that there are stupendous odds against them but they say to themselves that it costs only a postage stamp—companies no longer are allowed by law to restrict sweepstake entrants to paying customers—and they are willing to give it a whirl. Why not? Moralists will say that this is trying to get something undeserved and that it sets a very bad example for your children. Otto plays Lotto anyway.

Moralists or not, people play for money and will one way or another choose their lucky numbers and even try prediction. These are the people who will see something terrific in adding to **1794** (climax of the French Revolution) the numbers **1 + 7 + 9 + 4** and deriving **1815** (Napoleon defeated at Waterloo). This draws, by the way, on the history of France, a country where the revolutionaries of the Age of Reason suppressed all lotteries by decree of the national convention (15 November 1793). Louis XIV had tried to suppress superstition even earlier. He failed.

Here is an important point: Even if the dollar for a lottery ticket doesn't make you fabulously wealthy, you do get something for it. You get hope. At least for a short time the poor person has the dream of becoming fabulously wealthy, of hitting the jackpot. A little hope, a little raising of the spirits if only temporarily, may give the poor person some considerable bang for his or her buck

In Harlem, policy slips (12 numbers chosen at random from 78—figure out your odds of getting 12 numbers right!) were one of the major industries in the twentieth century. The Hispanics play *bolita* (one ball selected at random out of 99, but the payouts are only about 70 to 1). Such "gaming" is good business for a few; they make lots of money at it. In Mexico and France and Spain, for instance, the governments pull in bundles of cash this way. They prey on citizens utterly convinced that all their troubles would vanish if only they had big money, and those citizens avidly scrape up the cash to play the lotteries, regularly. They scrimp and save to make the price of a ticket.

When I was a child, I asked why, in certain countries I visited, the persons who sold lottery tickets were blind. Was it just to give the indigent jobs, like the war widows collecting tickets in the Métro? No, I was told. The blind were favored because that way they could not identify the lucky numbers on the ticket and keep the winning ones for themselves.

Also, when I was a kid—and probably people still do this—I was astonished that one could buy a piece of a ticket: Those who could not afford the rather expensive tickets in the Irish Sweepstakes bought a portion of a single ticket, hoping to win and share their luck with others who owned shares of the winning ticket. This gave them some promise of happiness. They kept on doing that, and very, very occasionally, one of those tickets hit the jackpot. My family knew two different winners of some stake in the Irish Sweeps. The Irish State Lottery began in 1780 and something like it is still going strong.

Lotteries long ago were about luck. The Romans distributed prizes such as slaves or ships taken in war by lottery—but the chances were free, and now governments have lotteries that sell tickets, so you are betting.

You may be contributing to good causes. The London lottery that distributed prizes every date from 11 January to 6 May 1569 raised cash for repairing the coastal fortifications. The British Museum (or British Library) owes its existence to a lottery of 1753. Irish Sweepstakes supported hospitals. The U.S. state lotteries fund various causes, which taxpayers rather than gamblers should finance. It is a tax on the ignorant. Some lotteries apparently are fixed. I believe one of my favorite artists, William Hogarth, was involved in one of those. In 1750, Hogarth, who was a major supporter of London's Foundling Hospital and had donated some wonderful pictures to it, painted *The March to Finchley*, and 2,000 lottery tickets were sold. Somehow the Foundling Hospital won the picture, and I believe Hogarth had always intended the hospital to have it. It seems to have been just one more lottery (a fixed one) for a good cause.

Some races tend to produce more gamblers than others. Americans like to take a chance. I don't think the Irish are as accused of being gamblers as they are of being drunks. The Chinese are said to be inveterate gamblers. However, I do not believe that gambling, which can be fun if one does not bet the farm, if one does not risk more than one can afford to lose, is confined to any one race or indeed any one class of people. Everyone takes some risks. The English have been legally gambling for money since 1630 and at various times have passed laws permitting or forbidding lotteries but have never been able to control gambling in card and dice games, betting on bear baiting or dog fights or rat killing by dogs, horse races, and other sports conducted basically for bettors.

"Mozan" has a book called *Racing Numerology: A Standard System of the Science of Numbers Applied to Horse Racing* (1998). If you want to be a track star, try it. This section is headed "Lottery," but really we are all over the map here on the subject of wagering, gaming, betting, putting your money where your hunch is.

Everyone gambles in some way. Some people call it investing as they play the stock market, but it is still gambling, if of a sort not quite as blatant as sitting at the one-armed bandit with a bucket of coins to feed into it. Hordes of people go to Las Vegas, or Atlantic City, or one of the swanky

112 *The Complete Book of Numerology*

new gambling establishments that have brought extraordinary wealth to the Amerindians. At this time twenty-eight state governments who know full well what social damage gambling can do, how terrible an addiction it can become for some citizens, have put aside moral objections in the desire or the pressing need to raise money for social good such as education. Harvard and Columbia in the Ivy League and Dartmouth, set up in the wilderness to teach the Indians, were early assisted by lotteries. Governments benefit from gamblers as they do from alcoholics and smokers and others whom they condemn but would severely miss if those tax flows dried up. As the Irish Sweepstakes supported hospitals, the notorious Louisiana Lottery Company, which got a license after the Civil War and which, Benjamin Harrison said, by 1890 had "defrauded and debauched the people of all the states," was established ostensibly to raise money for the Charity Hospital. More tolerated everywhere, well before New Hampshire was the first to establish a big state lottery, were the little raffles and lotteries and "chances" at dinners, dances, fairs and fêtes; these were all for "good causes."

It's nice to think you are doing something most religious people say is moral (supporting good causes) when you are doing something the same people if you press them will have to say is immoral (gambling).

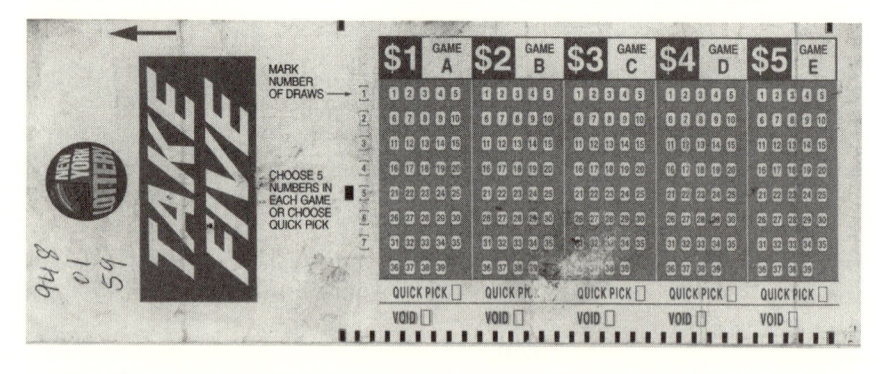

In all such gambling, but especially the lottery, numbers are very seriously if oddly chosen. What player ever took a flyer without a system or a hunch?

There are plenty of books on playing the lottery. Surely all of them give advice on choosing numbers. If you follow instructions and do not win, perhaps you will wish to sue the authors and the publishers.

I have no desire to set myself up as a purported expert on selecting lottery numbers. My own gambling career was too short to qualify me for any expertise, though I was lucky.

Maybe you would like to hear about it briefly. Gamblers love to talk about their experiences, and for balance, here is something from a non-gambler, you might say, but it is about a Big Haul. Many years ago, more than I want to remember, I was teaching at the University of Utah and on weekends myself and friends would pile into a car in Salt Lake City and team-drive either to San Francisco or Los Angeles, both about equal distances away. On the way to or from San Francisco, we would break our trip at Reno and stop for a free drink or a show or just to "stretch our legs." On the way to and from Los Angeles, the stop was Las Vegas. Those places were then as they are now glittering oases of entertainment, and then they were dirt cheap if you didn't gamble.

To encourage you to start betting—they call it *gaming* there—in those days on entering a certain establishment you were given a free silver dollar. My friends put theirs into the nearest machine and that was the end of it. I put mine in my pocket. As we were about to go out the front door—such places always have slot machines near the doors and it turns out these often pay off more than usual, just to create good publicity—my friends insisted I play, not keep, my free silver dollar. So I put it in the dollar machine. I hit the jackpot. I got a river of silver dollars. I wish I had kept them because each would be worth much more than a dollar today. I excitedly took my heavy winnings to be turned into bills, and I have never gambled again. Here is one guy who is way ahead on Vegas! But that does not make me any kind of gambling expert.

Talking rights, the fun of trading stories, whether of wins or near misses or strange occurrences, may be an attraction of gambling that those who study the psychology of the addiction have too much overlooked. The lingo abounds in what used to be called gambling dens or hells and now (to use a name a hotelier put on luxury) ritzier. The gambling subculture has its own language. It has its own and long-established traditions. Under **Lottery**, Thomas L. Clark in his lively *Dictionary of Gambling and Gaming* (1987) writes (he uses capitals to direct readers to cross-references):

> There are many variations in purchasing chances to win prizes or a share in a money POOL. POOL GAMBLING usually requires the selling of numbered TICKETS such as a KENO TICKET or LOTTERY TICKET. The NUMBERS GAME (also called POLICY) is an illegal betting scheme similar to lottery (sometimes called CHINESE LOTTERY) or SWEEPSTAKES.
>
> KENO WRITERS use a KENO GOOSE (formerly a WOODEN GOOSE) or RABBIT EARS. They rely upon a KENO CALLER to coordinate the KENO RUNNERS' activity in the rooms adjacent to the KENO LOUNGE where KENOISTS may be dining or gambling. INSIDE TICKETS and

114 *The Complete Book of Numerology*

> **Hertz**®
> CDP# 0109682
> Must appear on rental record
>
> **ONE CAR CLASS UPGRADE**
>
> Take advantage of coupon savings in the U.S. or Canada
>
> Call your travel agent or call:
> 1-800-654-2210 in the U.S.
> 1-800-263-0600 in Canada
>
> Mention this offer when you reserve a mid-size through full-size car (Class C, D, or F) for a day, weekend or week to enjoy a one car class upgrade while taking advantage of your membership discount. At the time of rental, present your Hertz Member Discount Card for identification and surrender this coupon. If a car from the next higher class is available, you'll be driving it at the lower rate!
>
> COUPON EXPIRES 06-30-03
> U.S. & Canada PC# 168081
> Puerto Rico PC# 168070

Do you think this number might be lucky or unlucky for your trip?

OUTSIDE TICKETS record the wager. Some KENO TICKETS are dispensed from WRITER MACHINES. HOUSE TICKETS and WAY TICKETS (also called COMBINATION TICKETS) are based upon groups of numbers in contrast to a STRAIGHT TICKET. In either case, one hopes for a WALL TICKET.

Many governments operate LOTTO from a LOTTERY OFFICE which supervises the selling of LOTTERY TICKETS through LOTTERY DEALERS and the drawing of winning tickets from a LOTTERY WHEEL. At a NUMBERS DROP or POLICY SHOP a bettor may PLAY THE NUMBERS with a STRAIGHT-NUMBER BET (or a STRAIGHT-POLICY PLAY) or may choose a WASHERWOMAN'S GIG [a selection of the grouped numbers 4, 11, 44], a MAGIC GIG [same], or a SINGLE-ACTION BET. The bettor gets a POLICY SLIP or, perhaps, a SHORT SLIP. Only some players resort to a DREAM BOOK.

Clark, linguist and folklorist, will tell you everything about gambling except how to find winning numbers and get your ticket number recorded up on the Keno wall as a bonanza. Dream books and other sources of that useful information will never explain to you *why* such and such a number is related to the dream image (though you might try numerology to see if there is any connection between letters and numbers), nor will anyone explain to you how to dream the numbers that count. But dream books like to offer numbers that may *win* you (the verb suggests a contest when actually you are quite passive, suggests you deserve what you get when it is sheer luck and nothing to do with merit) everything you ever dreamed about having.

Gamblers have to have for some games a great deal of skill. Think of poker or bridge, card games at which at least two of our fairly recent and surely trickiest U.S. presidents excelled. Others may have nothing but Lady Luck on their side, or a system, whether it be for *chemin de fer* (French "railroad") at Monte Carlo or having a go at a low betting shop in London. In Britain, bookies are called "turf accountants"!

I do not have a system, and gamblers, as I said, all seem to have systems. I do not follow any gambling field with the wondrous expertise of horseplayers. I do not suggest you bet on the racing of horses, cars, or contestants in the Olympics, but I do have one practical suggestion for you players of the lottery rather than what the British call the fruit machines. With the slot machines what you want to do is to wait until someone who has been pushing coins in and winning nothing gives up and walks away. The more the machine has been played, the more likely it has been primed to gush out some winnings. I mention this little observation because I want to add that with the lottery the opposite is true. You want numbers that not too many people are playing. There is just one big payout, and you don't want to share it (though Uncle Sam steps in to take a big tax bite out of your winnings).

There is not much you can do about the taxman but, as for your share, you want to stay away from those that tend to turn up in the selections of those who play dates (of birth and such). I do not think that there is any chance that there are lucky numbers in the lottery other than the ones that turn up at random. Some numerologists may disagree. If they have become exceedingly wealthy, I am prepared to listen to them.

This is not to say that I do not find the psychology of gambling interesting and the long history of lotteries and such full of colorful stories. As with fishing, the stories are mostly about the big ones that got away. Every once in a while it warms the heart to see that some young fellow in a Korean grocery store has won forty million bucks in the New York State Lottery. When someone already very wealthy wins, it's a bummer. But a dream come true? Always a delight for all but the incurably envious.

I disagree especially with the Italians when it comes to playing lotteries. Mario Pei writes in *The Story of Language* (1949) of "Italians, who go by lottery numbers from one to ninety, each of which has a special symbolism that serves well when it comes to playing your dreams on the state lottery. . . ."

Italians not only think 13 is unlucky, but also that 7 = "misfortune" and 17 = "mishap." Every culture has its own ideas about lucky and unlucky numbers. Every national lottery has its adherents and superstitions. I have listened for hours to Mexicans talk about their national lottery, but I have never bought a ticket in it. Most Mexicans need to strike it rich more than I. An American walking away with the big prize would go even further to convince the Mexicans that the tragedy of their country, as one of their wittier presidents said, is that Mexico is "so far from God and so close to the United States."

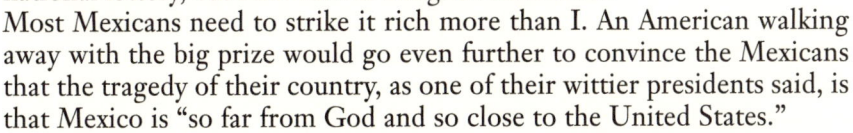

As for the Italians, I mentioned some obscure Italian dream-book pamphlets in my book on dreams and their interpretation: Two of the "classic" guides were Luigi Chiurazzi's *Smorfia napoletana* (1876) and the anonymous *Libro di Sogni* (which had reached a seventh edition in Italy by 1882 and was often found in other printings in the tenements of first-generation Italian-American immigrants pursuing their dream of prosperity in America).

There are many other books that purport to tell you the numbers connected with the symbols that pop up in your dreams. Dream books also say that dreaming of winning the lottery means "you harbor foolish hopes of reward without effort. Wake up."

Thus I can see no reason to recount for you or recommend to you their lucky-number systems. The main thing about numbers in Italian is that they make so clear (as one Italian writer noticed as early as the sixteenth century) that the language is, with many other European languages, anciently derived from Sanskrit. If you want lottery numbers from dreams and if you have a very old Italian grandmother, she may be able to help you with that as she has helped you, perhaps not without resistance from you when it comes to Old Country things, on other matters.

Or you can play the day, month, and year of any special event or your credit card bill, the amount owed, and the (excessive) APR (rate of interest). Remember that words, any words, not just names, can be turned into the single digits of numerology. But single digits, as far as I can tell from the television spots announcing the lottery winners in the state where I live, do not seem to appear as often as two-digit numbers. Those are more frequent in certain Chinese fortune cookie slips.

The lotteries of New York and New Jersey differ. In New York's Take 5, there are 5 numbers to choose out of 39. Your odds of winning are 1 in 575,757. The average jackpot is $45,000. In New Jersey's Cash 5, there are 38 numbers, the average jackpot is $40,000, and the odds are roughly the same. New York usually sees a winner every day. New Jersey often does not. When no one guesses the correct 5 numbers in the right order, the person(s) guessing 4 out of the 5 winning numbers wins. That happens only 12% of the time in New York but 75% of the time in New Jersey. So play NJ for the best chance at a second prize. Get 3 numbers right out of 5 and you win third prize and that happens about half the time in New York with odds of 1 in 103 and a payoff of a mere $25.00. In New Jersey, third-place winners get 26% of the prize, a mere $12 each on average, reflecting a better deal than New York: 1 in 95 odds. Pick 2 of the 5 numbers right in New York and you get a free play. That is not available in New Jersey. The odds are not very good for anyone but many subscribe to the New York motto, "Hey, you never know!" If you worry about odds, you never put down even a dollar, of course.

If you insist on playing the lottery, when you choose single-digit numbers avoid the lowest ones and especially the popular 7 and when you choose double-digit numbers make sure that at least 4 of your numbers are over 31. Many people believe in picking double-digit numbers ending in 0, 1, 2, 8 or 9, and once again avoid 7. In fact, 10, 20, and 30 are seldom selected. Information like this may be of some use in determining whether you are going to have to share prizes with others but naturally have no connection at all with what chance may turn up. Perhaps you may decide to dabble in what Mason Claire calls "personal and spiritual numerology" (in *Spiritual Years*) when taking a flyer on a lottery, if you can spare the time from googling the several hundred thousand entities on the Web, taking "tests" for love, getting free courses or history in numerology, contacting "metaphysical practitioners" who advertise, etc., or checking your *chakras* and so on.

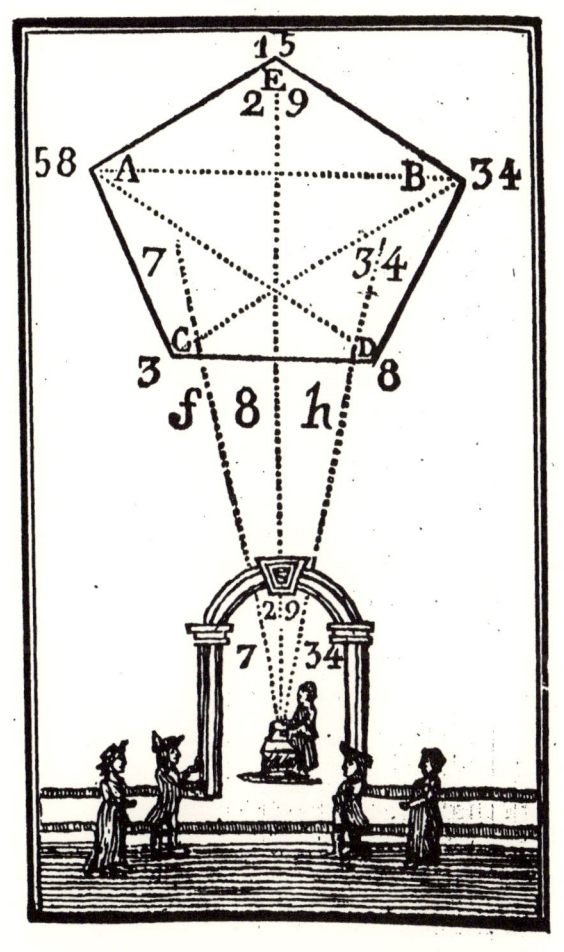

A figure for winning lotteries. From Albumazzar de Carpentari, La Clef d'or *The Golden Key*, (1815).

When playing the lottery and wishing to choose numbers others will not choose, always avoid 19, which occurs in most birthdates and other personally important dates.

The lottery, like Bingo (unless you play a lot of cards at one time), demands no skill, so go ahead and be superstitious about it if you wish. In games of skill, such as poker (says Andy Bellin in *Poker Nation*), "It's unlucky to be superstitious."

In everything, what you have earned by your skill is better than what you got by accident. The story is told of Margaret Thatcher (then little Margaret Roberts, the grocer's daughter) who at the age of seven won a prize for her piano playing. "You were lucky," her teacher said, "to win that prize." "I *deserved* it," retorted little Maggie.

In lotteries and life, may you get what you deserve. In that I am not certain numerology can play a part, but insofar as it gives you encouragement, it is not a bad thing if you do not stake all on luck but try to help luck along by your own effort.

90 8 52 9 71 7 77 8 5 74 29 8 14 57 37 2 34 60 62 13 63 45 35 56 69

11
You're on a Roll

כ

We are well into the book now, and it is time for a change of pace, a diverting game. So let's play a game. Get out the dice, and I'll tell you how numerology is connected to what Americans used colorfully to call African dominoes, though that is not politically correct now and never was sensible because throwing bones or dice or anything to tell fortunes went much farther back than black slaves in America. It went farther back than Roman soldiers playing dice to see who would get the seamless robe of the crucified Christ. It went back before the High Priest of the Jews tossed the gadgets kept behind his jeweled breastplate (one stone for each of the 12 tribes of Israel) to get a yes or no from God. I told you about those.

People have been rattling the bones as a game and even for fortune-telling since time out of mind, and there is no reason why you shouldn't put down your Tarot or *I Ching* or pack of playing cards and seek advice on present and future by throwing dice. You can use dice not only to win at the craps tables at one of America's casinos but also to answer your personal questions without risking a dollar.

All you need is a pair of dice and you can have answers to your questions. No one can guarantee reliability. What divination device can? Try it and see.

This will take up quite a few pages although I have limited the questions posed to thirty (as some others have done before me) for each different combination of dice. So the answers—and I try to give the answers most agreed upon, though there will always be debate in any such area

120 *The Complete Book of Numerology*

where the subjective is unavoidable—will have to be thirty. I think this is worth the space it takes and may, in fact, be a very entertaining feature of this book.

See what you think. It may be better than having an 8 Ball or some other device that randomly gives you a Yes or No to questions posed. It may be a change from the many items you have to deal with in the *I Ching* and more attractive because the answers in this dice game are usually more direct, less ambiguous, than the *I Ching* offers.

You don't need sharp intuition. You don't need some swami or some guru or some psychic at dollars per minute to give you any kind of advice. Numerology says that all you need is the following list of useful questions and the following list of no-nonsense answers to those questions.

So, if you want to know if someone you love loves you, you can just ask them (for heaven's sake) and interpret the response for yourself. OR you can roll the dice, and if they come up snake eyes (1 + 1), you get "That depends more on you than them." If you don't like that answer, I suppose you can roll again. Some people who got the same answer twice in a row would be impressed. Or two out of three.

Just roll those dice, and get answers to any one of the following questions:

?

1. What business or profession is best for me?
2. Shall I be successful in love?
3. Am I in any danger?
4. Where can I find what I lost?
5. Will my plan work out?
6. Will my wish come true?
7. What should I concentrate on now?
8. Whom shall I trust?
9. Should I change my job?
10. Does or will the one I love, love me?
11. Should I take a case to court?
12. Am I right about a certain person?
13. Will I get money owed to me?
14. What does the coming year hold for me?

15 Shall I receive what I hope for?
16 Shall I hear from a certain person?
17 Can I expect an excellent adventure?
18 Will my dirty secret become public?
19 Should I travel?
20 Shall I succeed?
21 If I marry, or am married, what happens?
22 How can I recognize Mr./Miss Right?
23 How many love affairs shall I have?
24 What's coming next?
25 What is the best thing for me to do at this point?
26 When will the wanderer come back?
27 Where shall I find fulfillment?
28 What will be the best time for me?
29 Will I ever be rich?
30 Should I stay put or strike out on a new path?

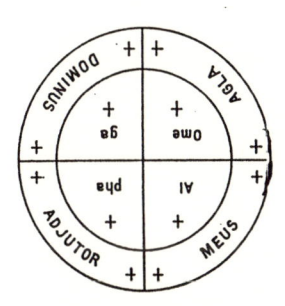

You choose your question, roll two dice, and look up the number of your question for the answer in each case. Nothing to it—and there may be in another sense of the phrase nothing to it, but just maybe.... Remember that all answers resemble oracles, and oracles often have been said to present answers that need to be interpreted.

In days of old, you used to be able to go to an oracle (say, at Delphi), and there a priestess, high on hallucinogens, would offer an answer to your question. But even the answers obtained like that needed decoding, as it were. The story is told of an ancient ruler who approached the Oracle at Delphi and asked if he should engage the enemy in battle. He was told, "If you fight, a great empire will fall." So he went into battle, and sure enough, his empire fell.

So here are the responses you can work with for yourself.

If each die has a single dot, the answers are as follows. For 1 + 1:

1 Stick to your present job.
2 Yes, if you are unselfish.
3 Not if you are circumspect.
4 In a small place.
5 Yes, if it simply depends on my efforts alone.
6 That depends on you alone.
7 Self-improvement.
8 The one who is frankest with you.
9 Only if you can make progress.
10 That depends more on you than them.
11 Going to court is always perilous—think twice.
12 Probably not.
13 Only if you find a way to compel.
14 It will be a time of flux.
15 Possibly not.
16 Not until you make the first move.
17 No, but the few should be exciting enough for you.
18 Not if you are careful.
19 Think again.
20 If you work hard enough.
21 Possible security and happiness.
22 If you are doubtful, seek another; if not, commit.
23 If you are unlucky, too many.
24 The unexpected.

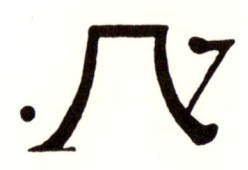

25 Better safe than sorry.
26 Not soon enough.
27 Not where you are now.
28 Your birth month.
29 Not if money is not of primary importance to you.
30 Change always improves opportunity.

For 1 + 2:

1 Consulting or teaching.
2 Why not? Aren't you lovable?
3 Not now.
4 In a drawer or closet.
5 Yes, if you can rely on others.
6 No.
7 Your future; it is never too early to be concerned about it.
8 The most realistic.
9 Not now, but perhaps next year.
10 Just ask her or him; why have you not done so?
11 If you do, the matter is not crucial.
12 Probably not.
13 Maybe never; don't count on it, but move on.
14 Nothing special.
15 Your expectations will not be met.
16 If you do, very suddenly.
17 Maybe none for a while.
18 It's already out for those who have looked closely.
19 Not soon, maybe never.
20 You aim too high.
21 A chance at peace.
22 Look for a *yang* for your *yin*, or *vice versa*, compatible difference.

        23 Enough. Don't fret.
        24 Some good and some bad times, not boredom.
        25 Just do it.
        26 When ready and not sooner.
27 In acceptance.
28 Summer.
29 Only if you marry money.
30 Do not stray too far from home base.

For 1 + 3:

1 In any plodding work. Try accounting.
2 Yes, if you do not expect too much.
3 No.
4 Do you really need what you have misplaced?
5 Not a lot.
6 After it doesn't matter anymore, maybe.
7 Personal relationships.
8 The friend who most trusts in you.
9 No. Work to improve what you are now doing.
10 Not really, but you knew that.
11 Stay away from lawyers.
12 You're mostly wrong about them.
13 Soon—but don't waste it.
14 A worse year than this year, but not in every department.
15 Yes.
16 No.
17 You don't really like surprises.
18 Who cares besides you?
19 Yes.
20 Probably, if you refine your goals and work harder at them.

21 Constant work at it.
22 You know you'll know, so why do you ask?
23 Enough—you are not all that romantic.
24 Surprise.
25 Step by step, the road is traveled.
26 Unexpectedly.
27 Not this year.
28 Next year holds no big surprises at any time.
29 You will never have as much as you want.
30 Stay home and make the best of it.

Here's 1 + 4:

1 Flexibility.
2 From time to time.
3 Not really.
4 You may not find it.
5 Eventually, so stick to your guns.
6 Are you sure you'd be happy?
7 Security.
8 The most experienced.
9 Decisions will be made for you.
10 Some.
11 Yes. Sorry.
12 Not anymore.
13 No.
14 Changes, mostly for the better.
15 No.
16 Maybe, but move on.
17 Yes.
18 Yes, but it doesn't matter much.

19 Reconsider, then act decisively.
20 Not the ambition you have now.
21 Domestic strife on and off.
22 The eldest or only child (as you possibly are).
23 Lots, but few will mean much.
24 Insecurity.
25 East, West, home is best.
26 When good and ready. Don't hold your breath.
27 Helping others.
28 Summer.
29 You can't hold onto money.
30 Strike out for the frontier, if you have the courage.

1 + 5:

1 Science or technology.
2 Not completely.
3 Not importantly or permanently.
4 Someone else will find it, if it is to be found.
5 Not as much as you wish.
6 Not if it is not within your own power.
7 Secrets.
8 A cautious one.
9 Only if you, not others, think change is best.
10 Why question?
11 No.
12 Positively no.
13 Maybe some.
14 Totally unexpected circumstances.
15 No.
16 Indirectly but importantly, maybe finally.

17 Yes.
18 Not if you don't tip your hand. (But you may really want to.)
19 Not just yet.
20 No. Rethink.
21 Family squabbles that are mostly your fault.
22 In your case, it is going to be a huge surprise.
23 Few.
24 Big change in a small matter.
25 Things are seldom what they seem.
26 Be honest: Do you really care?
27 In contemplation of what is truly important to you.
28 Spring.
29 No. You will have higher, more difficult goals in time.
30 Stay put. Redecorate emotionally or physically.

1 + 6:

1 Something energetic.
2 Yes. Why not? Do you know something I don't?
3 The worst is over.
4 Wait.
5 Plan more before you invest time, effort, money.
6 Probably not.
7 Uncertainty about your estimate of others close to you.
8 Nobody you now know. Expand your circle.
9 Not if you don't have to.
10 Somewhat, but don't bet everything on them.
11 No.
12 No.
13 No.
14 Finally a positive response: unusually good luck.

♏.
15 Yes.
16 No.
17 Yes. But how many really make a difference?
18 Yes, you bet.
19 No.
20 Change your goals for some more firmly grounded in reality.
21 Another marriage.
22 Someone you have yet to meet. Be patient. Keep looking.
23 Many. You are still in a flighty stage because you lack self-love.
24 Nothing great for a while yet.
25 People don't think you are as great as you think you are. Who's right?
26 Soon.
27 Not in this life.
28 Late fall.
29 Possibly, but you want fame more than money. Much more.
30 If you travel, you may get homesick.

2 + 2:
1 Entrepreneurship.
2 Yes.
3 Yes, but don't panic.
4 Among unrelated objects.
5 Yes.
6 Not for a while yet.
7 Health.
8 Go your own way, and blame only yourself.
9 Always be ready for opportunity if and when it knocks.
10 No. Stay cheerful.
11 No.
12 Not for love or money.

13 Now or never.
14 Distraction. Try to stay on track.
15 No.
16 First build a bridge.
17 Yes.
18 Not if you are careful—but why do you care?
19 No.
20 Increase your expectations and then work and hope.
21 Divorce.
22 Someone who admires your business skills rather than looks.
23 As many as work allows time for.
24 Business risk.
25 Strike while the iron is hot.
26 Who cares?
27 In winning over others, especially when failure was forecast.
28 Spring.
29 Yes. After you are rich, then what?
30 You would be better off to work at home.

2 + 3:
1 Advertising, brokerage, insurance.
2 More than now.
3 Yes. Get help.
4 In an obvious place
5 Too risky. Pull in your horns.
6 Only if you take the wishes of others into account.
7 Entrepreneurial opportunities.
8 Someone who has experience and experience with you.
9 Only for a much, much better deal.
10 If you ask, you may find out. But you may not believe the answer.

11 Not now.
12 Yes. You understand others better than yourself.
13 Fortunately you don't really need it.
14 Another step (or two) up the ladder of success. Don't look down.
15 What is it you want and why?
16 Forget it.
17 You don't want any upsets.
18 No.
19 No.
20 Not for a while, if ever,
21 Security.
22 Someone never expected.
23 One too many—however, you'll get over it.
24 A time to prepare a springboard to success.
25 Don't make a move unless it guarantees progress.
26 You don't care.
27 In another state—of mind, too.
28 On a rebound.
29 Yes. You already know that.
30 If you go, don't come back.

2 + 4:

1 Traditional retailing, unusual manufacturing.
2 You want contentment, not passion.
3 No. Why are you anxious?
4 Why worry about trivialities?
5 No. Take another look at your strengths and weaknesses.
6 Yes.
7 Family.
8 No one. You are all alone in this.

9 No. Just make minor adjustments.
10 No. You already regret a decision.
11 No.
12 You do not see people all that clearly.
13 No.
14 One terrific surprise.
15 No.
16 No.
17 No.
18 Yes, probably, but just go on as if nothing had happened.
19 Yes.
20 Yes.
21 A demand for compromise, which is never easy for you.
22 Someone who helps you cheer up when you are depressed.
23 Concentrate on one right one.
24 Stay focused.
25 If you are not for you, how can others be?
26 Soon enough. There is no hurry.
27 In being much admired, whether you deserve it or not.
28 Late fall.
29 If you get rich, you will eventually give most of it away.
30 Are you comfortable? If so, why move?

2 + 5:

1 Creative, constantly challenging if risky, occupations.
2 On and off—but you like roller coasters.
3 Always.
4 Not in any usual place.
5 No.
6 The one after this will be successful.

7 Stability.
8 You are on your own; it is your peculiar angle of vision that is core.
9 Why not? You love risk (way down deep), but hate to admit it.
10 No, not as much as you love yourself. You're something of a loner.
11 Never.
12 Trust your own instincts.
13 Not likely.
14 Still another scheme your friends will be amazed at.
15 Forget it.
16 You are still at odds.
17 Always.
18 You don't even know the deepest secret yourself.
19 No.
20 Not until you are ready to take bigger risks, if ever.
21 Breakup.
22 You want a partner, not a lover.
23 Up to you, if you don't get involved just to impress others.
24 False friends (maybe business representatives, agents, or the like).
25 Talent is the ability to use ordinary gifts extraordinarily.
26 What traveler?
27 In being in the spotlight.
28 Spring.
29 You would settle for fifteen minutes of fame—or independence.
30 Travel is a vacation from talent.

2 + 6:

1 People-oriented occupation.
2 The mystery will soon evaporate.
3 Coming!
4 It's gone.

5 Not likely, but your life is full of surprises.

6 No. Get a new goal, and do it soon.

7 Self-improvement.

8 Take any advice offered, and make your own choices.

9 Why would you want to? Want to start over on something completely new?

10 You can make gratitude substitute for love.

11 Sometimes. Consider costs, emotional as well as financial.

12 You think you are never wrong when it comes to people. Wrong, wrong, wrong.

13 No.

14 Minor setbacks actually increasing your determination.

15 No.

16 No.

17 Yes. You wouldn't want it any other way.

18 What secret?

19 If you can afford the time and money, why not go?

20 Yes, but you will find your aims changing as you go along.

21 Fasten your seat belt; it will be a bumpy ride. You get on best with strangers.

22 There is not just one pebble on your beach.

23 See 22.

24 The biggest challenges of the last three years. You will be OK.

25 When in doubt, make a decision, and stick to it through thick and thin.

26 It doesn't matter much.

27 In becoming more and more your true self.

28 Spring and summer.

29 Health is more important, especially in late years, than wealth.

30 Don't go far because you may have to come back.

3 + 3:

1. Executive and administrative positions.
2. Most of the time.
3. Yes. Rise to challenges, and never give up.
4. What is really missing is acceptance of what has happened.
5. Yes.
6. Yes. Congratulations!
7. Old age—plan for it, finance it, for it will come, barring accident.
8. Trust no one, not even your partner.
9. At least two or three times over a lifetime.
10. Yes. This will cost you.
11. Now and then you may be tempted.
12. No.
13. No.
14. A change of pace.
15. You realize you must earn what you get.
16. Probably not when you want to do so.
17. All the time. Stay optimistic, and remain open to new things.
18. You have no secret of any real importance to others.
19. No.
20. No.
21. Excitement.
22. You need not. They will choose you.
23. Too few to please you, more than you need.
24. Opportunity to change direction.
25. When one door closes, another door usually opens.
26. No matter. She or he will never be the same as when the traveler departed.
27. Pretty soon. Get ready now.

28 Fall, but next fall is not the big one.
29 If you subordinate a lot of other things to getting rich, yes.
30 Travel only for vacations. You are happiest at work.

3 + 4:

1 Anything where you can be in charge. You hate bosses.
2 As long as your partner is not bossy.
3 Next season.
4 You won't find it.
5 No.
6 When you come up with something more sensible, yes.
7 Daily contentment.
8 You have no friends you think truly wiser than yourself. They are few.
9 You may have to.
10 Not much. Want to start all over?
11 No.
12 No.
13 No.
14 Harder work, less than satisfactory rewards for the time being.
15 No.
16 No.
17 Not while you stick to the old grind.
18 No. Even you are not much concerned with it.
19 Not now.
20 Not for quite a while.
21 An end to shopping around.
22 You will settle when you get tired or bored with seeking. You will give up, give in.
23 As few as you can manage.
24 More of the same for a while

25 Look before you leap—but don't forget to jump.
26 Do not be impatient, because not all new things are good.
27 In retrospect.
28 Winter.
29 You will always be pretty comfortable, never in the catbird seat.
30 You should have traveled when younger and were more welcoming of fun.

3 + 5:

1 Anything where you work mostly on your own.
2 Yes.
3 Off and on. Get used to it.
4 Forget it.
5 No, but you will learn something useful from the disappointment.
6 Yes.
7 How to tap your creativity.
8 A relative who has always cared for you.
9 You have not found your best employment. Keep looking, daring.
10 Your love affair with yourself pushes others aside.
11 Stay away from lawyers. But always get contracts in business.
12 Not at all.
13 No.
14 A fresh start on a once abandoned idea.
15 No.
16 Why do you ask? You don't care, down deep.
17 If you do not you will be bored out of your skull.
18 No, if there is one.
19 Postpone it until you can take more time off.
20 Yes. But don't expect overnight success.
21 Blowing hot and cold.

22 Many different kinds of people are suitable.
23 Two big ones. Try to get over Number One as soon as possible.
24 A realization that it is getting late (whatever time it is) to get seriously started.
25 Work with what you have to get what you want.
26 Never importantly.
27 In variety.
28 Summer.
29 Marry for money if it matters all that much to you to be rich. It's night work.
30 Travel in your imagination.

3 + 6:

1 You are a loner, but business success means you must face being on a team.
2 Your idea of love is someone to lean on—pick a strong support.
3 You tend to get out of scrapes virtually unharmed.
4 Look where you have previously looked too casually.
5 Yes, if you can invent a new gimmick.
6 No, you will change your wish before the present one could work out.
7 Finding a life partner that you won't ever lose.
8 The friend who seems best at running his or her own life.
9 Go where the money is.
10 You don't truly love anyone just now.
11 No.
12 The more you care for a person, the less clear your vision becomes.
13 Maybe. Don't count on it.
14 Next year is a year to get through. The year after next comes the big challenge and opportunity. If you miss out, you'll have to wait years more.

15 You are not expecting any present.
16 This does not apply to you, either.
17 You basically hope not. You want less surprise in your life.
18 The secret is you have no secret.
19 Why not? Next year.
20 In time, you will hit on something good and quite unexpected. Seize it.
21 You might be better unmarried.
22 See 21. Discard that impossible romantic ideal you have been toying with.
23 Not many. Not your style.
24 The unimaginable (to you, anyway). Stay calm; it will be OK.
25 A penny saved is a penny not spent on something you think you deserve.
26 There is no traveler.
27 In feeling invulnerable (if you can manage to be that shortsighted).
28 Spring is always a good time for you.
29 Is that what you think would quell all fears?
30 Stick close to what you know.

4 + 4:

1 Salesmanship, representing others, negotiation.
2 Not likely.
3 Not now.
4 Don't sweat the small things. This is a small thing.
5 Not this time around. Keep trying new ideas, and get advice.
6 Not now.
7 You would feel happiest if protected by several kinds of insurance.
8 Kind relatives.
9 You are going to have to do so, more than once in your career.

10 You are a bit too insincere still to be all that attractive as a lover.
11 Yes.
12 Yes.
13 No.
14 Just another chapter in the continuing saga. The big things come later.
15 No.
16 Maybe, but you may not like what you hear. Don't fret.
17 You tend to try to avoid them. Usually you succeed in doing so.
18 Yes—so what?
19 No.
20 Which ambition? You hold several burning (or smoldering) desires.
21 Loss.
22 The person will be a great listener.
23 Not many. Grab the ring.
24 Too soon to tell. You are in a transitional phase.
25 Nothing is a bargain if you really don't want it.
26 Not until you don't really care anymore.
27 In humbly accepting limitations and fully exploiting strengths.
28 The coming year is not the best for you. Get through it as best you can.
29 No.
30 If you go, go far. That doesn't sound like the real you.

4 + 5:

1 Co-dependence.
2 Happier than single.
3 Not often. Not now.
4 Out of sight.
5 Yes, if not exactly as you expect.
6 See 5.

7 How can people achieve peace with themselves whatever crops up?
8 Your oldest friend, but watch out for a bit of envy, jealousy.
9 If you are that unhappy, why not?
10 You are not in any real love relationship now. Be honest with yourself about that.
11 One hopes not. If you do get involved, it will be bad news for you.
12 Your opinions are often just the teeniest bit off the map.
13 No.
14 Instability. You'll survive.
15 No.
16 No.
17 Nothing special.
18 No.
19 No.
20 Only partly. Brace yourself for disappointment, but don't exaggerate.
21 Not much except social approval.
22 They will choose you.
23 Only one really serious affair. Don't botch it.
24 You are waiting to happen.
25 If wishes were horses, beggars would ride.
26 There is no traveler of real importance to your life.
27 When you lower expectations and raise energy.
28 Winter.
29 Not more than middle income, but you will learn to manage money well.
30 Take short trips only. Put down roots if you can.

4 + 6:

1 Law or anything else where argumentation counts.
2 Love is not your main interest in life. Even sex isn't.
3 Not at this time. Later health may be a problem.

4   There is no missing article worth worrying about.
5   You haven't truly formulated an enterprise yet.
6   Yes, but in future, wish bigger.
7   Professional life.
8   The most learned.
9   You will, whatever advice you are given.
10 Do you care, so long as it doesn't adversely affect your career?
11 Yes.
12 Yes, but you won't admit it, probably. Advice hardens your prejudices.
13 You hope so. Forget it.
14 As with every year, you envision it as a milestone. Keep on traveling forward.
15 No, never.
16 Yes.
17 Yes, but you will take everything in stride.
18 Get two secrets and leak one to put them off the track.
19 Try to do so.
20 You will, or you'll die trying.
21 Social obligations.
22 You can never resist a "good deal."
23 Few. Try to keep the extracurricular from becoming embarrassing.
24 Continual striving.
25 All work and no play make Jack more moolah.
26 You don't care.
27 To travel hopefully is better than to arrive.
28 April 15.
29 You will, or you will know why.
30 All travel to you is business travel.

5 + 5:

1. Learned professions.
2. Too busy.
3. Hardly ever.
4. You don't care.
5. You are sure it will, and you like to think you are seldom wrong.
6. You bet.
7. Me, myself, and I.
8. See 7.
9. Add, but never abandon the basic core. (Lawyer basis is best for you.)
10. Why not?
11. Sometimes.
12. Always.
13. They better pay up.
14. More opportunity for career growth.
15. You certainly hope so.
16. You don't really care, do you?
17. Yes, indeed, if career milestones count.
18. Everyone already knows that I want to be a tremendous success.
19. You will be tempted to postpone it. Go.
20. Industry pays off. Also, you cut a few corners, don't you?
21. Children.
22. Social position.
23. Too busy.
24. The next rung up on the ladder.
25. Pride goeth before a fall—but there is no pride in falling, so climb with care.
26. You don't care.
27. In peer recognition and personal power.

28 Spring.

29 Money comes with power, as well as the reverse.

30 All travel is to the top of the heap or it is wasted effort.

5 + 6:

1 Anything of high prestige. You want to be paid with applause.

2 You will do your best to be so, and overlook some problems.

3 No.

4 It's probably gone for good.

5 Yes.

6 Yes.

7 More success.

8 Anyone not competitive in your field.

9 Never.

10 What makes you ask?

11 No.

12 Almost certainly.

13 Probably not.

14 Here comes another great opportunity, and you are ready.

15 Probably.

16 Probably.

17 Probably.

18 Your secret is that *probably* really annoys you; you love certainties.

19 Not this year if you would lose by absence from duty.

20 You are determined to do so.

21 Family life, hard to balance with career, but you can do it pretty well.

22 You have had a profile in the file since teenage days.

23 As few as necessary; there are more significant things to accomplish.

24 More challenges to be bravely and successfully faced and conquered.

25 What shall it profit a man if he gain the whole world and lose his own soul?

26 You don't care.

27 In making your mark in the world.

28 Winter.

29 Yes, rewards always follow important efforts.

30 Some day the two of you would like to take a relaxing trip around the world but there is always something more important to be addressed.

6 + 6:

1 A person's work ought to benefit the person and all other persons.

2 Family is important but sex is somewhat overrated.

3 No, why would anyone want to harm you?

4 You have more important things to attend to.

5 If the foundations are sound the business can be built on them.

6 If hard work can do it, yes.

7 What to do next if this present scheme succeeds (or fails).

8 Take all men's counsel, but reserve your own.

9 Certainly not. Perhaps you might change your approach somewhat.

10 Of course.

11 Not if you can at all avoid it. Hire lawyers to keep lawyers off you.

12 You consider all your opinions well-founded, and in fact, you have worked on them harder than most people do on their estimates of others.

13 You don't care; the amount is insignificant when time is concerned.

14 More time to do more.

15 You operate on earned recompense, not gifts.

16 Yes.

17 They will be of a business kind mostly.

18 You have no secret but the deep-seated need to prove yourself.

19 Yes, if time permits. When we are young, we have time, but no money; when we are older, we can afford to travel, but have little time to do so.

20 Yes. And your peers will have to admit that you did.

21 A family you can be proud of and to whom you give more than your parents gave you. You feel very lucky to be able to do that.

22 You want a mate as fine as your parent.

23 Romances are for teenagers; love and mutual respect take over when one grows up.

24 More opportunity, more hard work eagerly taken on.

25 Work for the night is coming when you can work no more.

26 What traveler?

27 Right here in work and the respect of my family and fellow professionals.

28 There is no reason why all four seasons should not be good if your health holds up.

29 Certainly. But the man who dies wealthy is disgraced, so when retirement has to be faced a career in managing philanthropy must follow.

30 Every day is a trip.

That oracle has taken a lot of pages. I think readers will find that justified. The nice thing about this is that you get a question answered. The same desire to ask and get a response, any response, sends people to con artists who read palms for money and peddle charms you do not need. This is cheap and at least as good.

As for the method that employs three dice, we can be brief. Throw all three at once; count the spots.

3 Highly unusual and indicative that something unusual is going to happen to you, most likely something unusually good.

4 Get ready to be disappointed, but do not lose heart.

5 A stranger will bring something good.

6 You are going to lose something material, but you can expect a spiritual gain.

7 You are unappreciated, perhaps even slandered, but rise above it.

8 You are on the wrong track; change course.
9 It will all work out all right, especially in the sex department.
10 Good news ahead. Congratulations!
11 Bad news ahead, perhaps related to health.
12 You will be soon confronted with the need to cope with a problem that springs up, so get ready to be decisive.
13 You "know" this is an unlucky number, so prepare for the worst.
14 A new friend will become very important to you.
15 Watch your step, and avoid all something-for-nothing schemes.
16 Prepare to travel, near or far, but certainly for enjoyment and profit.
17 The so-called experts differ on this one, so choose the more optimistic reading, say I: You will hear of something to your advantage.
18 Even better good luck than 3 could bring and with a nearer date.

If you should get the same number twice out of three throws—and for most people a single, silent, non-violent and reverent throw is what is best—that seems to reinforce the message, of course. You have your point! Keep the dice from rolling off the table and try not to have the misfortune of one landing on top of another and staying there. That happens seldom and is extremely bad news.

Remember that these answers, like all advice, need thinking about once you receive them. Consider what they could mean and weigh the consequences of your acting on them. Throwing dice takes no deep thought, but coping with answers you may get requires meditation. Meditation is always good. Talking to yourself can be better than talking at your psychiatrist. (Sorry, therapist, the person who is working on you—or you are "working with.") Do not be discouraged if at first your personal illuminations are only 25-watt. Keep at it. You will get brighter.

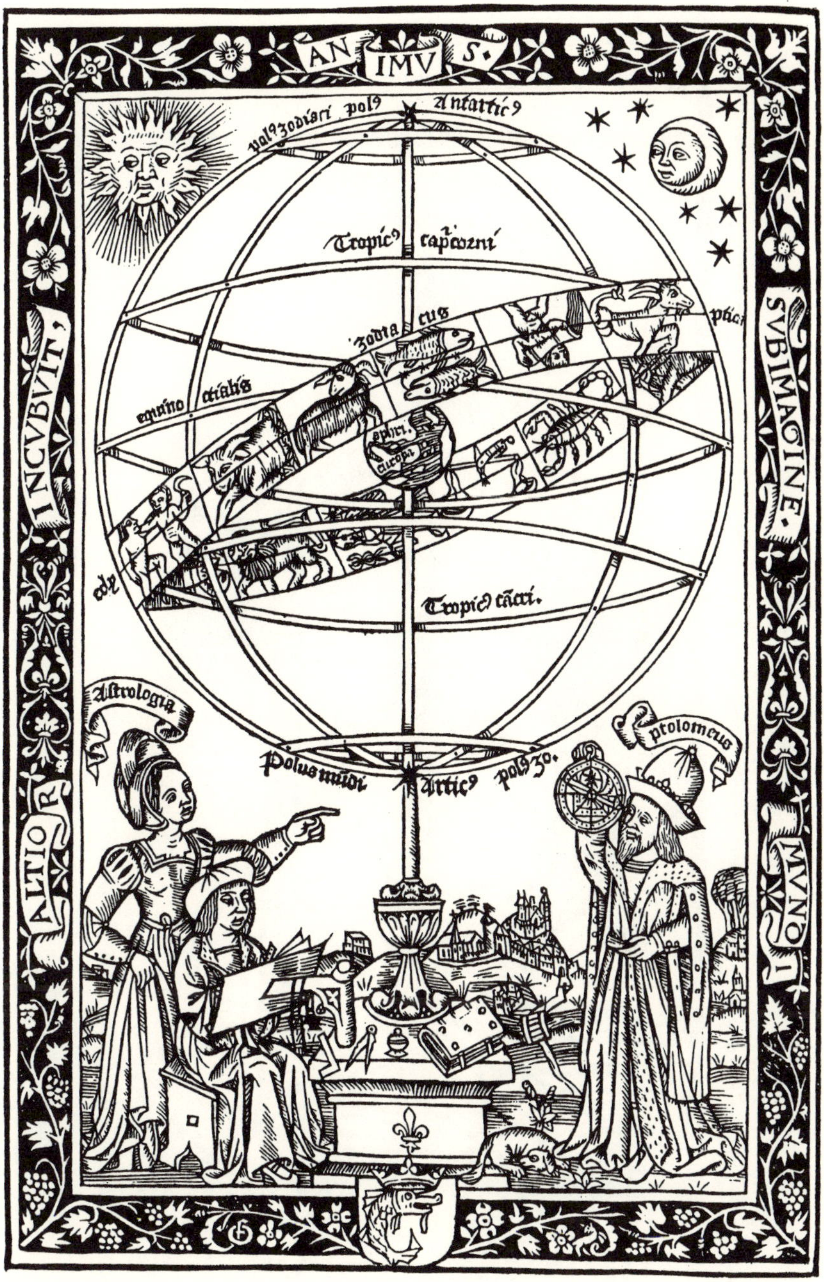
AN IMVS.
INCUBUIT,
SUBIMAGINE.
ALTIOR
MUNDI
Astrologia
ptolomeus

X

LA ROUE DE FORTUNE
THE WHEEL OF FORTUNE

12
How Much Do You Owe?

ל

I put this as section 13. It is rather unlucky to start behind in your psychic life. People say that happens and see it as a good response to the wail of "Why me?" that is raised when you are down.

Buddhists and Hindus, as well as many New Age persons right here in the U.S., among others, have profound faith in reincarnation. They believe that if you are good, if you properly conduct yourself in the great scheme of things, knowing your place and performing your duties fully, each reincarnation brings you closer to perfection, and that in the long run you can break out of the system and not have to go round and round. You gradually learn how insignificant your ego is and in the long, maybe very long, run you escape from it.

Connected to this is the concept of karma. We often use *karma* as equivalent to *fate* or *destiny*; there is more to it than that. Lots more. That, like some other topics in this book, could be a book or a shelf of books on its own, but just think of what you certainly have heard: the expression that "what goes around, comes around." This essentially means that whatever your action, not only is there a reaction but in the long run you reap what you sow, you get what you deserve, your good actions are rewarded, and your bad actions are punished. Sounds fair—unless you think that your fate is set, the script is given for your life, and you just live it. If you have no control over your life then how can you be blamed for what goes wrong any more than you can be congratulated for what goes right?

Karma is about as much debated as (say) whether a 1 + 5 is different from a 2 + 4 or a 3 + 3 that becomes a 6. I would not worry about it to that degree.

Be that as it may, just in case you are in effect responsible for your interpretation of the script or your ad libs or are improvising the whole role, you will certainly want to keep the entries on the good side of the ledger, positive as you go through life. But here's the rub: You may have come into your present existence with a deficit. You may in this life be owing. You may be rewriting the rules to your own satisfaction (which at least leaves you without the burden of guilt, never an easy one to carry).

Your guiding philosophy may be as shallow as that of Amanda in Sir Noël Coward's play, where she says that all she tries to do is to be kind to everyone, give pennies to the occasional beggar woman in the street, and be as gay as possible all the time. At the same time, you may notice that whatever you do you are always, in a sense, facing difficulties. Here's the news: This may be because you have an overdraft at the psychic bank.

Your past, according to the theory or fact of karma, has inscribed some stuff, in a manner of speaking, in red ink. You are not bankrupt, but you are in debt. You may *owe* something because of past life or past lives. Let us hope that your Karmic Kredit Kard is not maxed out! As with credit cards, if you do not pay the minimum, there are penalties. If you do pay the minimum, it will take you an unconscionably long time to clear your debt. Sit down and figure out how long it will take you with your credit card debt to pay back $1000 at the rates they charge. See how much more they get than the $1,000 you thought was involved.

In this section, you will learn exactly how to determine where your psychic account stands. You will be able to find out what your karmic deficit is. This is your psychic financial report. It tells you whether you are in the black (OK) or in the red. Deficits in old ledgers used to be written in red ink, you very well know. And someone or something is keeping the books on you.

First off, let us make it clear that not everyone has a bad balance. That is cheering news. Only some people are so unlucky. Well, you cannot really say "unlucky": They are not unfortunate; they are simply getting what they deserve.

In India they have a way of coping with all the misery one sees around wherever one goes. If you believe that people are simply getting what they deserve, meted out according to some cosmic plan, the blind beggar, the starving child, even the ragged corpse dead in the street does not call upon your compassion and does not give you any twinge of guilt. The sight of suffering may make you uneasy, even frightened. It may make you fear that something bad will happen to you, too, but there is likewise the sneaking joy that at least *that* is not happening to you at the moment, the comforting hope that it never will, and the righteous satisfaction that others are getting no more nor no less than is right and proper and merited and just. Serves them right.

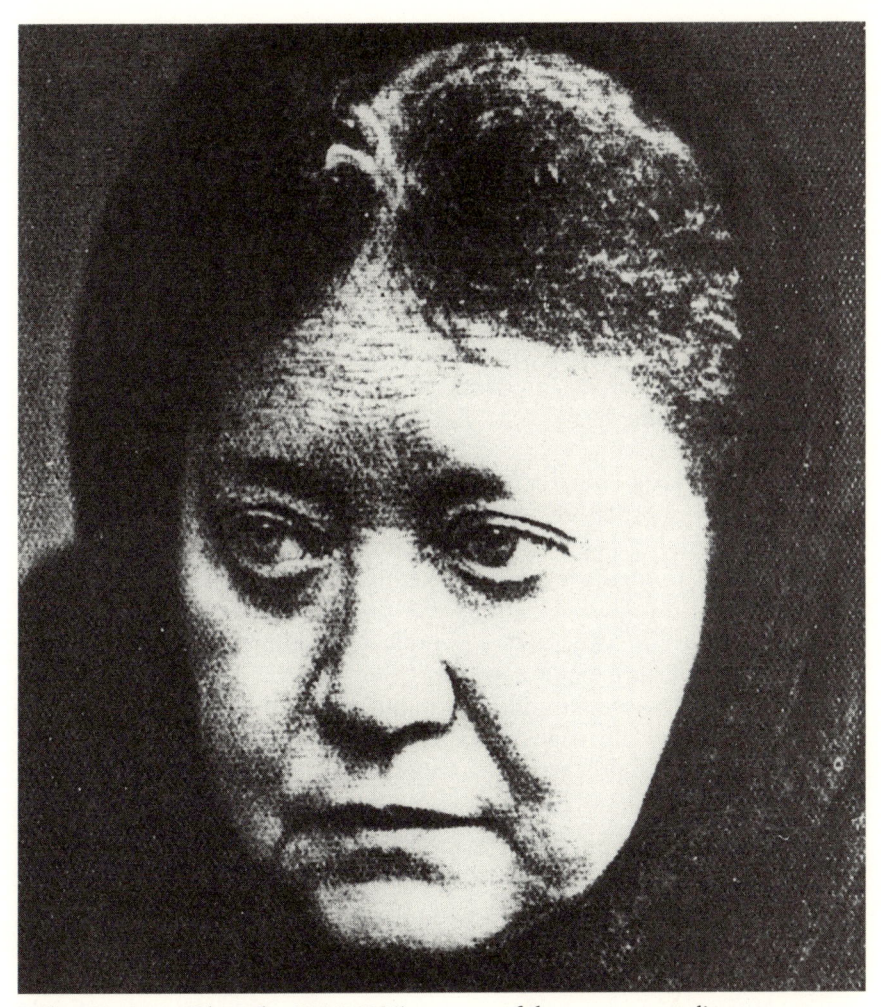

Helena Petrovna Blavatsky (1831-1891) was one of the most extraordinary women in the history of the occult. She and Henry Olcott founded the Theosophical Society in New York in 1877. Theosophy did much to bring eastern ideas such as Karma into Western thought. This was reinforced when Flower Children and others turned to Zen and other forms of Buddhism.

If you are one of those on whom justice is fixed, sorry. Tough luck. This is a debt that tradition says starts on your birthday if you are born on the 13th, 14th, 16th, or 19th of any month. That's any month. It affects individuals whose personal number is 1, 4, 5, or 7. That's a lot of people. If you have determined that your personal number is 2, 3, 6, 8, 9, or (very unlikely) 11 or 22, you are more or less scot free. Feel free to heave a great big sigh of relief. However, do try to feel some sympathy for others less fortunate and do take a look at the (briefer) comments I make on your number. Experts disagree, but I would say that you are not protected against running up a deficit in life (this time around) with 2, 3, 6, 8, or 9. You may not have the thrill of the Screaming Eagle or Cyclone ride this time, but at least you don't start with a bill to pay.

It's a question of actions and results, "checks and balances," says Bruce K. Wilborn in *The Gay Wicca Book* (2002). In that book he says he is gay but may come back as a heterosexual or a lesbian, and presumably he was of various sexual orientations in previous lives. That is if he had any, for we can never tell for certain how long any particular "account" has been running, anymore than we can be certain how many lives it has yet to run—and one must do the best one can now. "Brighten the corner where you are."

On karma, here I shall stress the personality numbers (1, 4, 5, 7) on which the most speculation about karma and the most comment, whether it is wise or not, has been made. If you are one of the other numbers (2, 3, 6, 8, 9), not to mention 11 and 22 who appear to be on some kind of final lap (in the thinking of some speculations on the topic), I suggest you not worry about inherited karma. Simply keep in mind that your actions should be responsible in some way or other. A belief in fairness suggests you will be held to account and you could run up a deficit in this life, in some way or other. Christians, even though we have the occasional *René(e)* or *Renata*, believe they have only one go around. "One Life to Live," as the soap opera says.

Here are the more complicated karma cases on which I undertake to say a few words:

1. Those who are 1s have a karmic deficit that is owed because in a previous life they were selfish, self-centered, sacrificing others to their ambition, misusing power. All they can do now is to try to be more helpful to others, more kind and considerate, less aggressive, more altruistic if only for selfish reasons. At the same time, they must be both more self-effacing and not give in to coasting along. Actually, 1s are going to enjoy very little leisure to be lazy. The life of a 1 who has run up a bill will be extra challenging and pressured, and a 1 is going to have to jump hurdles, occasionally falling flat on their face and getting up, without self-pity, to keep on trying. For people who characteristically love to succeed easily and garner astonished applause, that kind of thing is hard indeed.

2. Twos tend to be quiet and generally avoid worry, so do not worry about your bank balance of karma. Be careful, however, that you do not withdraw too much from the psychic ATM. Remember also that some bad guys fiddle with the ATM machine in order to cheat you of your money in the

How Much Do You Owe? 153

bank. Watch out. Do not be put off caution by fools who tell you that you are paranoid because you worry. It is crazy not to have some worry, the way the world goes. Keep worry under control, and be circumspect. Worry about loneliness, not karma. *You* could get lonely in a crowd.

3. Threes like to be independent and may well feel rather independent of payback for misdeeds in previous existences. They do have to be concerned about the fact that "what goes around, comes around" and watch their behavior right now. Threes tend to believe that everything is OK, and if it is not, they can handle it. It is good to be confident, dangerous to be overconfident. You can generally tell a 3; but you cannot tell a 3 much. They should be more careful of karma. They may come to see it actually working on them.

4. Fours also are going to have a hard time because in a previous existence they goofed off and now, even though it may well go against the grain, 4s have to pull up their socks and apply themselves with unflagging commitment. Worse, with all 4's best intentions (at last) and best efforts, there will likely be a seemingly unending series of setbacks and disappointments. That can make a 4 fearful and threaten to destroy all hope. The 4 will have to get down to focused and unrelenting work and try not to develop blinkers while pulling the load. That load will often threaten to plunge the 4 into despair and waste time and effort by sending 4 off on fruitless attempts to survive by any means than the cruel one step ahead of the other routine that is so galling.

5. While 4s with karmic debts often appear to have little freedom in this life the 5s are burdened now because of exercising too much freedom—or exercising it irregularly and unproductively—in a previous existence. Fives are not always the most realistic judges of situations (and even worse judges of their own abilities and shortcomings). This causes them to waste strength and spirit. Moreover, 5s may get themselves into artistic or professional work where there is a call for self-knowledge and self-discipline; 5s may suffer from deficiencies in both. The creative professions, acting particularly, often somehow attract the people almost uniquely ill suited to coping with the ups and downs inherent in the work. Still, 5s soldier on, secure in their talent whether they have judged it well or not and feeling they will, they will, they will get a big break. That can happen. Fives may be hard working and well meaning and still have to face and cope with one disappointment after another. Load up on David's ammunition (five smooth stones), and do not be afraid to take on Goliath.

6. Sixes can get to feel sorry for themselves and moan about being picked on, but they really have little to complain about when it comes to karma credit records, usually. Sixes seldom, because they are a balanced group, incur large charges in a lifetime. Sixes have in their perfection to worry about the imperfection in their sexual partners or spouses. They are likelier to marry and to marry non-6s than some others. The 6s were the *clerici* of the old English Court of Chancery and were celibate; if they married, they lost their jobs, but then along came Henry VIII, who had a lot of experience with matrimony himself, and he removed that rule by a law of 1533. The rules can change, 6s will discover.

7. What 5s did in another life that put them in their present predicament may be as fuzzy as the plans they tend to make to face their difficulties this time around, but what the 7s did is clear cut. They were sexual predators, and they caused a lot of grief to others they betrayed or used unconscionably last time. This time they themselves may be emotionally betrayed (not necessarily sexually, but just as painfully) and manipulated for material possessions on top of that. In their destruction, not infrequently, 7s themselves may play a part, for they can be villains as well as victims. That is a peculiarly painful business. Most of us can stand almost any punishment, but the realization that we got ourselves into the mess and can blame no one else is insupportable. The life of a 7 will be full of surprises, many of them unfortunate. Mental health may depend upon humble acceptance of this fact plus resiliency and resolve to keep on keeping on.

These painful conditions, which are chronic and last a lifetime, are attached to the significant numbers of our lives and, some optimists believe, if you were to change those numbers, you might be able to escape the burdens. For instance, you could change your personality number by changing your name, another number by changing your address, and so on. It might be worth a try. What do you think? What are the morality and result of running from bill collectors? Can one run from oneself? Sit down and write an essay.

Now, let us look at the last two basic numbers despite the fact that the karmic problem does not play much of a part in their lives.

8. The baptismal font was often constructed with eight sides representing strength. Eights may sometimes be boring, but they are not big spenders of karmic Brownie Points. It takes more imagination than the average 8 possesses to run up a huge karmic bill.

9. When Satan (the Adversary) lost the Mother of All Battles against God, that archangel—his name is Sammael—and his fallen angels fell for 9 days nonstop. Nines do not usually make such gross errors and receive such vast punishments, but (if you stop to think about it) 9s are (and 11s and 22s are even more) in the employ of God. That is the same employment that Satan and his devils and demons have. We all work for God and His Big Plan. (Don't ask!) He wouldn't have it any other way, unless of course He

is not omnipotent and the big battle between good and evil can eventually end up either way, which I doubt. We all most likely cannot but operate as cogs in a great divine machine. We all of us, former gods like the archangels and future residents of heaven (like the elect like you and me—the damned are other people, right?) are all part of God's Great Plan. Really, what could you do that He (or She, if you like) didn't want done, for heaven's sake?

Well, you must do what you can to follow the righteous path as God gives you to see the righteous path—or as you work it out by reason, ethically, for yourself, rather than taking it as handed out, religiously, by some church, synagogue, mosque, or what-have-you—and accomplish what you can. With that, however much or little that may be, God ought to be pleased. If He wanted better results, He could have helped you more, I guess.

What you cannot do perhaps your children can. You can do something about the conceiving and therefore the birth date of each child. You can arrange at least the sign of the Zodiac (if not, these days, the exact date of birth). Aiming at the 15th of the month is promising, but it is perilous. I suggest you try to hit the first or last day or week of the month. I further suggest you exactly determine the latitude and longitude of the Blessed Event and get settled there months in advance of the Blessed Event because the baby may come months early. I did, and so I am undecided as to whether I ought to determine my Zodiacal sign by when I was born by cesarean section or when I ought to have arrived in the usual manner at a later date. If I had not arrived in Miami three months before expected, when my mother was on vacation preparatory to settling down for my arrival, I would not only have been born in quite another "house," but maybe another country.

With babies who insist on being born prematurely—it's a higher percentage than you would credit—there is not a lot you can do. But with so many people who so fully believe in astrology, it is amazing that the Friendly Skies are not full of pregnant women being flown to the "best" places for their babies to be born. The place of birth, if nothing else, can be absolutely determined.

Decide for your children which virtue above all you think will serve them best and do your best to get it for them. By birth date and other means, including naming, get the right personality number.

These are:

1 Self-reliance

2 Harmony

3 Adventurousness

4 Stability
5 Courage
6 Altruism
7 Wisdom
8 Pragmatism
9 Intelligence
11 Missionary zeal
22 Genius

A lot can be done in terms of what the baby is called. That can help a person to cope with karma. That can be accomplished without the expense of travel. True, nicknames cannot be completely avoided, but it is possible to choose forenames that fit in well with surnames and, at the very least, discourage nicknames. It is possible for a grown individual to insist on a certain version of a name (with a good number). Getting a good number is of more use in life than getting a good address, some think.

Here is still one more important personal number, as promised earlier in the discussion of names. You can help by giving the baby the right Cornerstone number. This is said to construct the proper basis for her or his life that can affect the outer and inner selves and the path of life. Calculating it is simplicity itself:

Once again

1	2	3	4	5	6	7	8	9
A	B	C	D	E	F	G	H	I
J	K	L	M	N	O	P	Q	R
S	T	U	V	W	X	Y	Z	

The Cornerstone number is that of the initial of the first name by which you go. Thus

MARK = M = 4. Mark is a 4.

Figure out your Cornerstone number. If you consistently call yourself (say) G. Gordon Liddy, choosing which forename to stress does not matter. But if you are a J. Alfred Prufrock, use **A** = 1 rather than J = 1 (here the same but different for, say, T. Boone Pickens). Check your Cornerstone number against the list above of karmic bank accounts. I really don't see if there is such a thing as karma how you can change your name and, as it were, skip town without paying your bills, but I see you can give a

How Much Do You Owe? 157

child a name that might be good. Of course, you may be predestined to give one that is not good. I cannot help you with everything.

Now that you know what karma is supposed to exact from certain people, perhaps you can do something to ensure that your children do not get born with a deficit other than their share of the U.S. national debt.

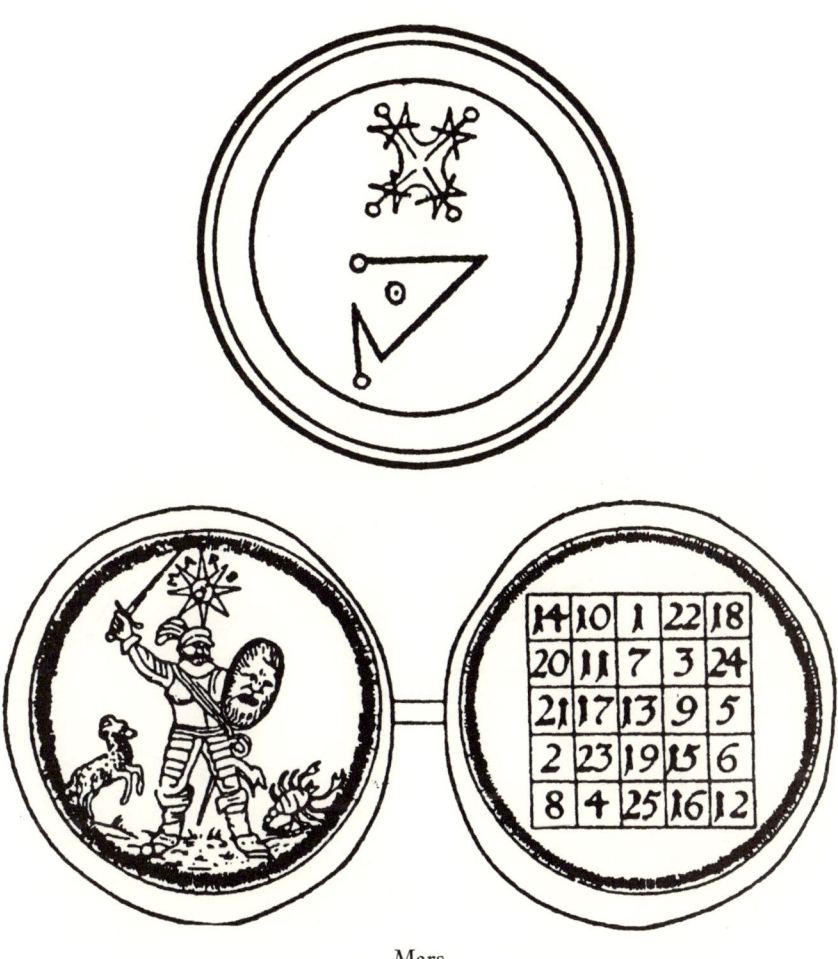

Mars.

TIPHEROTH

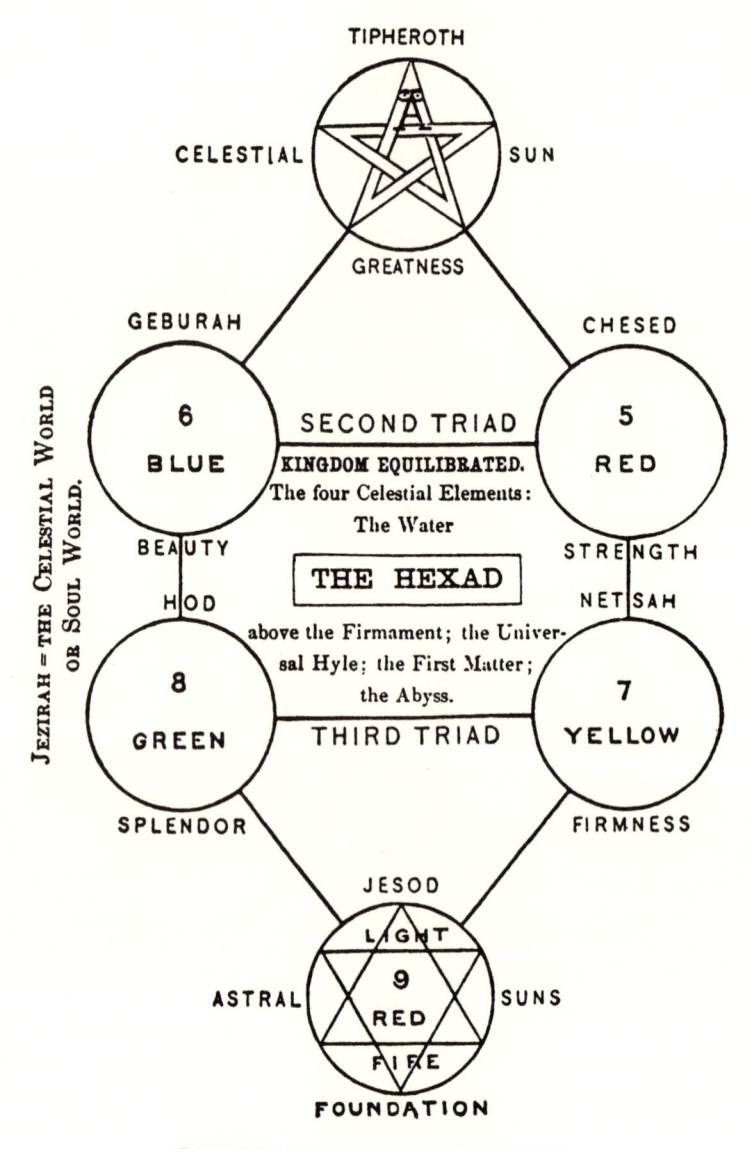

CELESTIAL — SUN

GREATNESS

GEBURAH — CHESED

6 BLUE — SECOND TRIAD — **5 RED**
KINGDOM EQUILIBRATED.
The four Celestial Elements:
The Water

BEAUTY — STRENGTH

HOD — **THE HEXAD** — NETSAH

above the Firmament; the Universal Hyle; the First Matter; the Abyss.

8 GREEN — THIRD TRIAD — **7 YELLOW**

SPLENDOR — FIRMNESS

JESOD

LIGHT
9 RED
FIRE

ASTRAL — SUNS

FOUNDATION

JEZIRAH = THE CELESTIAL WORLD OR SOUL WORLD.

FOURTH TO NINTH SEPHIROTH.

13
Your Color Sense

מ

My studies in the Holy Kabbalah give me one method that may be too arcane to be found very easily elsewhere. It is possible to present a summary of some findings here in a simplified form. These findings are about colors and numbers. Colors can be as important in a person's life as a name. Here in 2003, in New York City, the name Destiny reached the Top Ten, while my surname, Ashley, remained, for the tenth year in a row, the most popular name for girls born in the Big Apple. All those details are reported regarding the 124,023 New York City babies born in 2001, the latest statistics. By the time you read this, new statistics and new names will be available.

If you look at the names given to babies at any place or any time, you can learn important things not simply about fads but about the society in general. Is it growing less traditional, less religious, more diverse? Top Ten names in New York include now not just Michael and Joseph but also Brianna, Kayla, and Justin. Traditional Christianity seems to be losing its grip; standard denominations can no longer impose standard saints' names. Meanwhile, ancient Hebrew names such as Daniel, Michael, and Joseph are no longer thought of as Jewish at all. Kevin is the top name for Asian boys. African-Americans are inventing the most colorful names.

Let us turn now to something ancient and Jewish and very long in its influence, the Hebrew alphabet, a major factor in traditional numerology. The 22 letters of the Hebrew alphabet have been associated in magical lore with the 22 so-called *arcana* (face cards, sort of from O = the Fool to 21 = the World), with the Zodiac and the elements (*aleph* = air, *taw* = Saturn,

&c). Those things you know. Here is something you may never have heard, and it may be useful to you. It associates colors and numbers.

The Hebrew letters traditionally have colors associated:

1 *aleph* pale yellow

2 *beth* yellow

3 *gimel* blue

4 *dalet* emerald green

5 *he* scarlet—the big red 5 in Stuart Davis' painting may possibly recall this!

6 *vau* red-orange

7 *zayin* orange

8 *heth* amber

9 *teth* greenish yellow

10 *yod* yellowish green

11 *kaph* violet

12 *lamed* emerald green

13 *mem* dark blue

14 *nun* greenish blue

15 *samekh* blue *ayin* indigo blue

16 *pe* scarlet

17 *sade* violet

18 *qooph* crimson

19 *resh* orange

20 *shin* orange-red

21 *tau* indigo blue

There are some repetitions. There are some traditions: one is that a 9 person has the associated color violet (1 + 8 = 9).

Those who have assigned gemstones to the signs of the Zodiac (your birthstones) may or may not have taken account of color. I do not, for instance, think that the gem associated with my Sagittarius "house" is the right color according to certain other occult systems. But nobody has ever really attempted to explain why each birth stone is right for its sign. Moreover, I hear that the constellation of Sagittarius is actually being eaten away

Your Color Sense 161

Hebrew letter.	Final form.	Phonetic value.	Hebrew name.	Numerical value.
א		ʾ	Âleph	1
ב		B, BH	Bêth	2
ג		G, GH	Gîmel	3
ד		D, DH	Dâleth	4
ה		H	Hê	5
ו		W	Wâw	6
ז		Z	Zayin	7
ח		CH	Chêth	8
ט		Ṭ	Ṭêth	9
י		Y	Yôdh	10
כ	ך	K, Kh	Kâph	20
ל		L	Lâmedh	30
מ	ם	M	Mêm	40
נ	ן	N	Nûn	50
ס		S	Sâmekh	60
ע		ʿ	ʿAyin	70
פ	ף	P, PH	Pe	80
צ	ץ	Ṣ	Ṣâdhe	90
ק		Ḳ or Q	Ḳôph	100
ר		R	Rêsh	200
ש		S / SH	Sîn / Shîn	300
ת		T, TH	Tâw	400

by the Milky Way; what does one do if one's zodiac sign just ceases to exist? That, like how astrology has been forever altered by the recent discovery of new planets, is simply ignored by the layers of old ideas. Astrology sticks to its old concepts and, similarly, a variety of strange explanations of the powers of gemstones are to be found in old books. Here are ten things you probably never have heard before:

- Beryl, when set in gold and engraved with the image of a frog, makes anyone who touches or is touched by the ring fall for you head over heels.

The name of God with nine letters,	Jehovah Sabboath, יהוה צבאוה		Jehovah Zidkenu, יהוהצרקבו				Elohim Gibor, אלוהים ניפור			In the original world.
Nine quires of angels, Nine angels ruling the heavens,	Seraphim, Merattron,	Cherubim, Ophaniel,	Thrones, Zaphkiel,	Dominations, Zadkiel,	Powers Camael	Virtues, Raphael,	Principalities, Haniel,	Archangels, Michael,	Angels ; Gabriel ;	In the intelligible world.
Nine moveable spheres,	The primum mobile,	The starry heaven,	The sphere of Saturn,	The sphere of Jupiter,	The sphere of Mars,	The sphere of the Sun,	The sphere of Venus,	The sphere of Mercury,	The sphere of the Moon;	In the celestial world.
Nine stones representing the nine quires of angels,	Saphire	Emerald,	Carbuncle,	Beryl,	Onyx,	Chrysolite,	Jasper,	Topaz,	Sardis ;	In the elementary world.
Nine senses, inward and outward together,	Memory,	Cogitative,	Imaginative,	Common sense,	Hearing,	Seeing,	Smelling,	Tasting,	Touching ;	In the lesser world.
Nine orders of devils,	False Spirits,	Spirits of lying,	Vessels of iniquity,	Avengers of wickedness,	Jugglers,	Airy Powers	Furies sowing mischief,	Sifters or triers,	Tempters, or ensnarers;	In the infernal world.

- Chalcedony protects you against lawyers, quarrels, and bad experiences when you travel. From torts to tourism, it is sovereign.
- Crystal necklaces make more milk for the nursing babe.
- Garnet with a lion's image engraved on it protects you during epidemics and while you travel. Good for terrorist times.
- Jacinth with yellowish veins if set in gold prevents conception and cures dropsy. It is good for not coming and not going.
- Jasper can be red or green, but in either case protects against snakebite.
- Pearls make the wearer chaste (as do yellow topazes and emeralds). Pearls can be dissolved in wine for a luxurious drink or crushed and put into milk for a cure for irritability. Crushed and mixed with sugar, pearl is supposed to cure pestilential fever. The expense is not covered by Medicare.
- Pink amethyst prevents drunkenness when worn at the navel set in a silver plaque engraved with the image of a bear. Would you care

to hazard a guess why? Dip this gem in water, and create a drink that cures sterility. Or if the problem is the male's, have him tie 7 knots in a cord and undo one knot each day for a week.

- Moonstone (selenite) with the image of a swallow in flight on it brings good luck and friendship. Some think it is as unlucky as opal.
- Sardonyx set in gold and engraved with the image of an eagle brings good luck. Actually owning any gold is good. In olden days, sailors used to wear one gold earring. If their drowned bodies happened to be found on a beach, the gold of the earring would pay for a burial. Gold is real money and much better priced than diamonds.

Not every stone is good luck, you know. If you have a camel's image engraved on an onyx in a ring, you will suffer bad dreams. Dreams also figure in the lore of the lodestone. You put it under your wife's pillow. If she turns toward you in her sleep, she has been faithful to you. If she has been adulterous, she will soon wake up screaming from a horrible dream. That is unless she has armed herself with some stone that promises calm and pleasant dreams. I know that chrysolite hasn't helped my gout, and I really wouldn't want sapphire to improve my eyesight at the cost of making me chaste. I say with St. Augustine, "Not yet."

I can see little or no connection between these stones and their colors and the powers they are supposed to have. Beryl is frog colored, I guess. Leonardi's *Speculum lapidum* (1590) is a "mirror of [gem]stones" and gives a lot of advice on how to use them, but none on how they function. And nothing is persuasively written on colors as related to powers, not even any very persuasive stuff on red stones and blood. The main way such things work is that they may give the wearer confidence or make the wearer look attractively wealthy.

There are occult connections, somewhat written about, between colors such as scarlet and numbers and magical powers, which are why *Leviticus* says wearing scarlet is forbidden. (It also says you shouldn't eat pork and that if your children disobey, you should kill them. It says a lot of things, many of them ignored today.)

Ritual magic (on which I still by no means consider myself any kind of an expert) was the reason I first became interested in the supposed magical powers of colors. The books of ritual magic always dictate certain colors in the vestments worn for various practices (along with the various elements, metals, incenses, flowers, etc., to be employed). These assignments are presumably something more significant than arbitrary. It is, in fact, the extremely complicated and rigorous rules for ritual or ceremonial magic that have dissuaded most people from ever attempting it. That and fasting, purity of soul, fear of the Devil, and other difficulties, not to say terror of the whole world of the black arts.

In the Christian religion, the colors also bear various significances. Virginity is symbolized by white in the robes of angels and the dress of brides. The chasubles or outer garments of the priests saying Roman Catholic Masses, for example, are gold for great occasions, white for purity, green for hope, violet or black for mourning, red for the feasts of martyrs. Chasubles are worn over long white gowns of white, called albs (the name is from Latin for "white," the alb resembling the basic garments of the time of Christ). In modern times, the black vestments that were used for requiem masses have generally been replaced by more cheerful white ones. Actually, in the West, we used first to wear white for mourning; in more recent centuries we have adopted black for the purpose.

The color of ecclesiastical vestments does not matter magically. It is the statement the color is making. Clothes make various statements, as you know, and custom dictates that certain colors and fashions be worn for certain occasions. The solemn judge wears a black gown, at least in some cultures. The hat that a British judge dons to pass a sentence of death is black. We used to wear black ties and black dresses to funerals. Now people come, if at all, in Hawaiian shirts and jeans, etc. We used to wear black armbands for men and black dresses (after some time changed to gray) in mourning. The grieving Orthodox Jew ritually tears his dark clothes (perhaps as a reminder of older times in which people "rent their garments," ripping them in a frenzy of mourning). In Lent, Roman Catholic churches wrap statues and crucifixes in purple, and they used to wrap them in black. The color does not matter as much as the statement that during the time between Ash Wednesday and Easter, recalling the 40 days of Christ's preparation for His sacrificial death, there ought to be an abstention from church beauty, just as the faithful are required to abstain from what they "give up for Lent" as a gesture of obedience to the religion and the mortification of the self.

What is of relevance here is that colors are given significance. These interpretations develop over centuries and contribute to the iconography, speaking with pictures. A medieval contract for church paintings dictated the symbolic or traditional colors to be used (always blue for the mantle of the Blessed Virgin, for instance) just as there was a tradition that the aura of the blessed would be signified by a halo (round for the dead, square for the living) at the head of a person. Saints carried the symbols by which the faithful recognized their statues or representations in illuminated manuscripts and stained-glass windows. There stood Saint Peter with his keys, Saint Andrew with his saltire (X cross), this saint with her gouged-out eyes on a plate, that one with the stigmata, this one holding the infant Christ, that one with a dog or a dragon, and so on. Saint Jerome had a pet lion.

And some had colors to identify them. What would Saint Patrick be if his bishop's regalia were not green? They even gave him a shamrock to hold, and they started the story that he taught, with the shamrock in hand, the trifold nature of the Blessed Trinity. Actually the shamrock had its original significance in the pagan beliefs that Saint Patrick's mission was to drive along with the snakes out of the Emerald Isle. The old religion was driven out along with the snakes, which was not a real task because Ireland never had any snakes.

Colors can thus be identifiers and deliver messages. They can influence your moods, and also they are sometimes connected to the magical powers of numbers. This is where numerology comes in as it does in what to name the baby and much more. This is where magic is involved.

In the modern world, magic is considered to be something from an earlier time, an age of miracles and an age of necromancy. Still, there are probably more witches, or people who define themselves as witches or wizards, around today than there ever were in the "burning time" of witchcraft persecution. Despite the scare headlines of a decade or two ago, Satanism and black magic are not at all common. What we see is a considerable growth in the modern practice of something that is called Wicca. Wicca is not black magic at all. It is a pagan, nature-worshipping religion.

Wicca is not witchcraft. It more resembles the goddess religions, and its practitioners are very much like the women herbalists of ancient times. A very few Satanists are still around. Most alleged Satanists do not perform the ritual sacrifice of infants that sealing a bond with The Devil is said to require. You would be hard pressed, in my opinion, to find anyone in the U.S. or U.K. today who has a real pact with The Devil, according to the old rules of sacrifice and a contract signed in blood with an evoked demon.

If The Devil appears in person, he is said to dress in black. When he is called a "black man" in old literature that is what is meant, not that he is a person of color. (If you are a Roman Catholic, you have to believe on pain of excommunication that he is a person.) The tradition is that one of the three Magi is a Negro. What I think was intended was to suggest of the three magicians who came to the infant Christ, one was a black magician, a necromancer. But you can have your own ideas, of course. Make up any stories you like, just as the Middle Ages made up names for the Magi. That made them more real, somehow.

Ritual magic is down in popularity from its heyday in France, for instance, in the nineteenth century. We learn that from Lazare de Gérin-Ricard and earlier from the judges who burned thousands upon thousands of witches of the magical groups real and imagined in Paris and the provinces of France, especially in the Basque country. The covens and performers of Black Masses all had their traditions.

The Black Mass is a kind of blasphemy—I don't see how it would work very well for anyone who is not a (lapsed) Roman Catholic or at least an

Anglo-Catholic—in which The Adversary is celebrated by a reversal of a ceremony of the True God. The candles are black, not white. The bread and wine have vile substitutes. There is a great deal of indecency. You would find it very difficult to attend any such travesty these days. Private ritual magic, with magical circles (nine feet in diameter) at the right hours of the day for the magic to be performed are also much too demanding for almost all modern eccentrics.

It is only in ritual magic that certain colors are given crucial importance, although certain colors are thought to have certain powers and are featured in the flags and various other ceremonial objects used in religions such as Voodoo and Santería. Those religions are not as rare as you might expect. There is a lot of Voodoo in Brooklyn, New York, and Santería is also common. The latter is the most popular religion in Cuba.

If someone leaves a voodoo doll on your doorstep, it is most likely to have a red thread or a bit of red wool tied to it, for instance. Red (the color of blood) signifies life. To some people red means bloodsoaked violence. Pianist Glenn Gould had a tantrum when as a child he received a red toy. The voodoo doll threatens to end life if it has a pin stuck in it, most people think, a end to "the blood is the life."

But let us get now specifically to colors and number. To connect the 1 through 9 (and rare 11 and 22) personalities of numerology to colors, we get 1's single-mindedness and strength rather contrasted with the weak pale yellow, 2's femininity connected to yellow (with a touch of the feminine in yellow-green and greenish yellow in other numbers, which Gilbert of Gilbert & Sullivan dismissed as decadent, "greenery-yallery"), 3's brilliance and energy represented by blue (used for boy babies in contrast to pink), 4's squareness somewhat contradicted by the flashiness of emerald green, 5's brashness and extroversion well represented by scarlet, 6's quietness and domesticity challenged by red-orange, 7's intellectuality and strangeness challenged by orange's blatant hue, 8's practical and material character portrayed by amber, and 9's ambivalence and spirituality harmonizing both sexes in greenish yellow. The martyr-prone and definite doer of 11 seems contradicted by violet. The masterful spiritual leader of 22 has indigo, which at least is

First pentacle of the Sun.

thought of as a "deep" color. The cabalistic colors do not (to me) seem altogether to fit the basic characters of numerology very well. There appear to be mismatches. Who or what is responsible for this?

Many traditions in the occult do appear very arbitrary. It may be, some argue, that the reasons are definite, but themselves occult, hidden. There may be, some think, more going on than you know.

Certain things in the realm of the occult have pretty obvious explanations, as when witches dance in a circle widdershins, which is to say in the counterclockwise direction. They are, after all, engaged in perverse, contrarian practices. They are moving against the path of the sun, once worshipped as a god. However, when certain occultists are asked for explanations of some other things, such as what this or that incantation translates or just how the conjunction of Planet X with Planet Y produces bad news for this or that astrological sign, they may take refuge in refusing to respond. The occult is full of secrets.

That is one of its principal attractions for outsider types. The tired old dictum is, "Those who tell don't know, and those who know don't tell." The attraction of the occult is, after all, the promise of *secret* knowledge. If one does not have a secret just keeping the mouth shut when challenged may suggest one does have a secret.

Some color combinations speak a message: "through darkness, through fire, into light" or "the rainbow suggests the diversity of our organization." Some colors have less obvious meanings. If colors and their connections to numbers have to remain secret or just debatable, there is at least one question you can answer for yourself with authority. Whatever your name's numerology or any other hermetic source gives you as a guide to your personality type, life path, etc., you can always ask yourself "What is *my* favorite color?"

Red, blue, and yellow, the basics, all come into the first nine numerological characters as derived from names. Violet seems as unlikely to be anyone's first choice unless perhaps they are homosexual and know that lavender has been adopted as the homosexual color. The gay color used to be green, as in the green carnation and the obscure belief that a male declared his homosexuality to other males by wearing a green tie on Thursdays. Later it was a red tie at any time. But violet goes with being a 22. With your favorite color's number you may have one more clue to what kind of a person you basically are and what general future has been mapped out for you to accept or to face up to or alter by the power of will or the secrets of magic.

Psychological experiments have told us that green is restful and yellow is cheerful. The Chinese have told us "if you paint your room red, you will go crazy within the year." I find that pale blue does not make me as rested as the tests say it should. It makes me feel cooler or colder. I feel that as a Sagittarius I am closer to the blood-red ruby of Capricorn than to the topaz of my own sign though I am not at the end of Sagittarius at all. I like the color of jade (said to be bad for my sign, but lucky for many people), and I do not like opal (said to be unlucky for just about everybody). I like red geraniums though I am told they mean "duplicity." I guess it is my Mars component. I am told "Red should not mate with Orange," so that steers me away—or ought to steer me away—from the Sun signs people. I think that there are certain connections that have been for some reason or another established by tradition such as white for innocence and black for death or solemnity, gray for modesty and yellow for a sunny disposition. However, when you come right down to it, our color preferences are very individual and may not be at all connected to any of our numerological factors. The vibrations of numbers and the vibrations of light that create the appearance of colors do not seem to me to be closely connected. I must admit that some others disagree.

Red is supposed to be in our current society the power color. If in doubt, try that in a dress or a tie. Life Path colors are traditionally something like this (opinions vary, so I try to give the average opinion):

1 red for courage, orange for energy, gold for leadership or wealth, yellowish green for change

2 pink for love, violet for spirituality, gray for attention to detail, pale blue for peace

3 red for attraction, yellow for joy, violet for inspiration, maroon for pleasure

4 dark blue for confidence, orange for energy, brown for security, gray for practicality

5 yellow for communication, yellowish green for change, light blue for freedom, maroon for pleasure

6 pink for love, green for balance, blue for serenity, violet for creativity

7 white for individuality, light blue for analysis, dark blue for intellect, indigo blue for intuition

8 red for ambition, orange for energy, dark blue for self-reliance, black for authority

9 red for idealism, pink for love, purple for spirituality, violet for creativity

"Cheiro" recommends you wear and decorate with the following for best results:

1 brown, yellow, gold

2 green, white, cream

3 mauve, violet, lilac
4 blues, grays, "half shades" not "positive colors"
5 light gray, white, "glistening materials," not dark colors
6 all shades of blue including "electric blue," no red, scarlet, or crimson
7 white, yellow, gold, all pale colors especially pale green
8 dark gray, dark blue, black, purple
9 red, crimson, pink, darker shades of these are best

All of these identifying numbers go back to your full name, and some numerologists insist that the basic You is the full name that appears on your birth certificate whether or not you ever use that full name just that way or not. My mother, for instance had on her birth certificate the forenames Sarah Anne. She was always called Anne. At confirmation, she was given another forename, Constance, which she did not use. She adopted my father's surname on marriage and after my father's death used Anne and her maiden name and her dead husband's name. In the latter part of her life, she was known as Anne Constance Nelligan Ashley. I suppose that, at that point, was her full name. What are your full name, the birth certificate one, and the one you use today? Do you want to base your basic full name on the birth certificate name or the possibly different full name you use today? Would you be interested in finding and thinking of yourself as the number derived from your "short name"? For instance, are you (say) John Fitzgerald Jones in full, but would you introduce yourself as, "Hi, I'm Jack Jones"? The number that can be derived from the "short name" of everyday life may or may not be the same as your "full name." It is derived with the same number-counting as any other name, and some numerologists call it the Minor Expression number. It could possibly change your idea about, for example, the colors right for you.

Fifth pentacle of Mars.

On the Minor Expression number, Hans Decoz's *Numerology: Key to Your Inner Self* (with Toby and Tom Monte, 1994) says of each of the identity numbers in this category some things, and I select a bit for you here about how these "short name" numbers help you:

1 "makes you better equipped for the daily struggle of life"
2 "adds sensitivity and awareness of other people's needs"
3 "increases your capacity to enjoy life"
4 "makes you more practical, orderly, efficient, and dependable"
5 "adds considerable flexibility and versatility to your personality"
6 "adds love, warmth, generosity, and genuine concern for others"
7 "stimulates your desire for knowledge"
8 "provides you with more leadership abilities and business sense"
9 "makes you more concerned with the well-being of others"

That book adds more in each of those categories and even tackles **11** ("increases your sensitivity, intuition, and perceptiveness") and **22** ("increases your ambition, orderliness, and capacity to complete large undertakings significantly"). To tell you the truth, I am a bit dubious about this list, and certainly, when it comes to you personally as opposed to you in society, which this list seems to feature, the main thing I find remarkable is that the Minor Expression number often puts the person on the basis of a "short name" in quite a different color situation especially when compared to the full-name number. Try your long and short names and decide, if the numbers differ, where your intuition suggests to you that you ought to categorize yourself and look for "your" colors of all kinds in gems, dresses, ties, house decoration, and so on. In any case, the colors you wear and the colors in the rooms where you live will undoubtedly have some effect on others and on you yourself.

Days of the week may be important to you numerologically, but I see nothing in the following (apparently arbitrary) list of days and assigned colors. Perhaps you see something and could relate it to some number.

Sunday	Orange
Monday	White
Tuesday	Red
Wednesday	Green
Thursday	Purple
Friday	Light Blue
Saturday	Dark Blue

Numerology and colors are discussed in many books. A recent example is Louise L Hay's *Colors and Numbers: Your Personal Guide to Positive*

Vibrations in Daily Life (2003). Vibrations connect colors to music, too. See William David's *Harmonies of Sound, Color and Vibration* (1984). You might like to investigate synesthesia, maybe stray into Karin Lee Abraham's *Healing Through Numerology* (1985, where diseases are said to have vibrations and numerology is suggested as a way of discovering correct treatments). You may recall that it was Sir Isaac Newton, who studied both Scriptures and mathematics, used the prism to break white light into its components and connected musical notes with colors:

C Red   **F** Green
D Orange   **G** Blue
E Yellow   **A** Indigo
B Violet

That is the basic list. Personally, I think C Major is Royal Blue.

Some people claim to be able to see our auras and to be able to judge by them our health and even our qualities.

Red	Physical passions, sex
Yellow	Love of knowledge, intellect
Green	Holiness, prayerfulness
Light Blue	Spirituality (sometimes violet)
Rosy Yellow	Altruism (with tinges of violet)

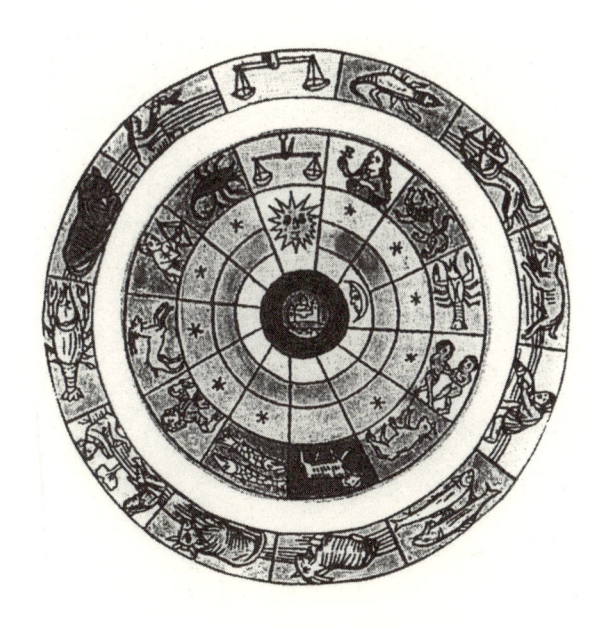

Holy persons are said to have a bright white aura around the head. That is what the halos shown in depictions of saints intend to show. Christ and some other very holy persons are said to have emanated a white light all over the body. It is suggested that the so-called portrait of the dead Christ on the Shroud of Turin was made when a brilliant aura was emitted from the corpse in a flash of soul. Others think the image was created by Leonardo da Vinci.

The colors of your auras can be connected in a roundabout way with the vowels of your name and the numbers thereof. Positive emotions glow brightly; negative emotions darken the aura. Shirley Blackwell Lawrence (1989) goes on about auras and your Inner Guidance number. My deep feeling is that an Inner Guidance number is going too far. But we do emit auras. Colored ones, too. That science can demonstrate, I believe.

There were codes in colors long before terrorist organizations began to signal by changing the colors of icons on certain Web sites. It was natural for colors to carry the traditions of their civilizations and of the numerology of their ways of looking at and describing their worlds.

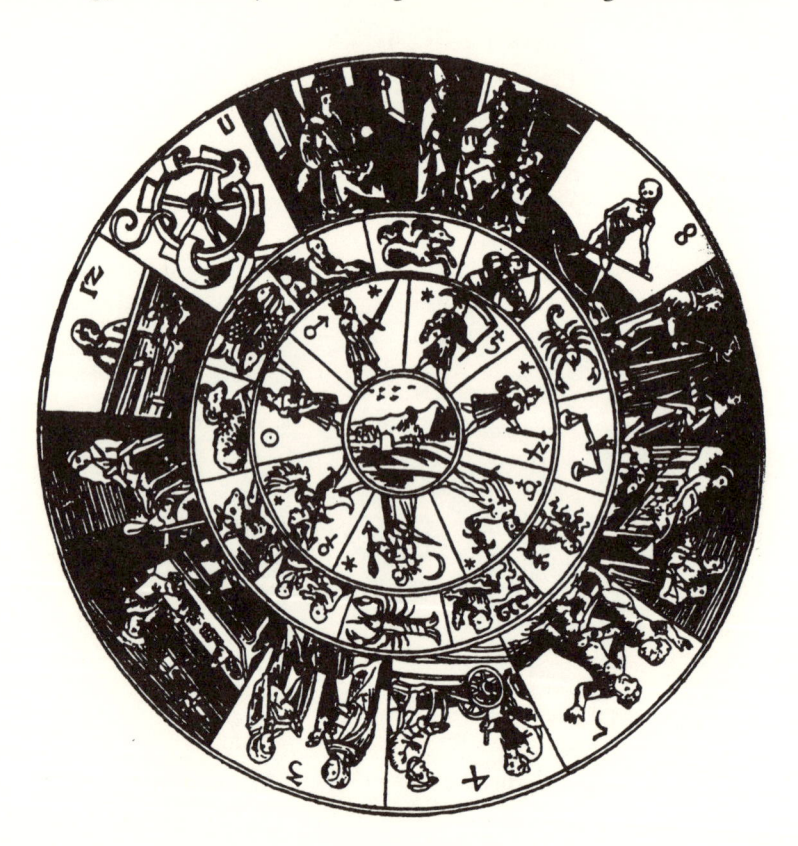

14
Cagliostro Speaks to the Freemasons in Paris

ב

In each of my books on the occult I take some time to talk about one or more leading figures in the field, for the occult has over the centuries attracted some of the most amazing personalities. They have issued stunning prophecies, described their calling up from the dead the likes of Apollonius of Tyana, driven their lovers to madness and suicide, conducted fierce psychic battles, shaped history by their counsel to rulers, founded immensely influential secret societies, said Black Masses or committed multiple murders, or pored over dusty books in private and published the results in obscurity.

A few, such as Nostradamus and Aleister Crowley, are pretty well-known. A few, such as Dr. John Dee and Francis Barrett, are known chiefly to specialists. Major figures include Virgil: He really was not a magician as medieval men like to think, but Virgil's works (like the Bible) were used for bibliomancy. Bibliomancy involves sticking your finger in the text at random to get an oracle. Another person falsely accused of being a magician because of his marvelous talents was Roger Bacon, credited with inventing (bringing from China the ideas about) gunpowder and even the flying machine. Bacon was an early scientist and not a necromancer. One person who did engage in the occult and had a startling reputation will suffice for a biographical vignette here. I want to introduce to you "the Grand Copt" (or "Copht") Cagliostro.

Cagliostro's *Memoirs* (1785) are just another fake in his long history of fraud, and his biography has not been really well written in English since Trowbridge (1910). This note here is by no means an adequate picture of his lurid career. It begins with a plea that some serious scholar industriously research and write the history of his riveting, riotous life, in English. The French have already had a crack at defending him.

The colorful figure known to occult circles as Count Alessandro di Cagliostro was praised as a genius seer and denounced as a quack and mountebank. He was born in Palermo in 1743. His name was Giuseppe Balsamo (unless the few are correct who say that Balsamo and Castiglione were really two different persons, which I do not accept). His father was Joseph Balsamo, about whom the elder Dumas wrote a play, which the younger Dumas produced. Enemies of Cagliostro were later to try to defame the father by calling him a Jew and a bankrupt tradesman. Giuseppi's mother (whose maiden name was Martello) claimed to be descended from Charles "the Hammer" Martel, victor in one of the most important battles in Western history. Charles Martel was one of a number of victors, from Constantine the Great and Charlemagne to some German emperors such as Otto the Great and Frederick Barbarossa, who were said to have owned the "spear of destiny" with which, it is alleged, Longinus pierced the side of the crucified Christ and fulfilled the prophecy of Ezekiel. This sacred relic fascinated Adolf Hitler and the occultists in his inner circle. Hitler finally got his hands on it, but he ended, as you know, in defeat and suicide. Had he been able to contrive it, Hitler would have liked to bring everything down in flames in some gruesome Wagnerian holocaust.

As a boy, the person who was to be known to history as Cagliostro (a name of a branch of his family) was sent to a seminary. Resisting the discipline, he ran away several times. Then he was sent to the monastery of the "Good Brothers" at Caltagirone. There he learned a little about medicine, chemistry, or alchemy among the apothecary monks. Of alchemy, Edward Gibbon (of *The Decline and Fall of the Roman Empire*) says, in part:

> The ancient books of alchymy, so liberally ascribed to Pythagoras, to Solomon, or to Hermes, were pious frauds of more recent adepts. The Greeks were inattentive either to the use or abuse of chemistry. In that immense register [*Natural History*] where Pliny has deposited the discoveries, the arts, and the errors of mankind, there is not the least mention of the transmutations of metals; and the persecution of [the emperor] Diocletian is the first authentic event in the history of alchymy. The conquest of Egypt, by the Arabs, diffused the vain science over the globe. Congenial to the avarice of the human heart, it was studied in China, as in Europe, with equal eagerness and equal success. The darkness of the middle ages ensured a favourable reception to every tale of wonder; and the revival of learning gave new vigour to hope, and suggested more specious arts to deception.

I quote this much to suggest that it may well have been alchemy (which monks did pursue and which eventually the church banned them from attempting) that started Cagliostro on his career of the occult and his path of deception.

Perhaps knowing that the monks were engaging in something of which the church disapproved weakened his faith—or strengthened his contempt. His attitude soon repulsed the monks. Once when he was required to read aloud some religious text, he inserted for the names of saints the names of prostitutes (which the monks ought not to have recognized). He was catapulted out of the contemplative life into one of the most spectacular public careers of his time, perhaps of any time.

By 1769 he had been expelled from the monastery and had taken to the road with a Greek called Althotas. He later claimed that with Althotas and alone he traveled to learn the secrets of Egypt and Asia. He first called himself Count Alessandro di Caligostro when he approached "the Grand Master of the Knights of Malta." Most likely that means the powerful order of knights Hospitaler, also called the Order of Saint John of Jerusalem, dating from the time of the Crusades, not the degree in masonry called the Knights of Malta. He appeared in many European cities. He was jailed in the Bastille in Paris and, on his release, sued the governor for valuables and papers he claimed had been stolen from him in jail. The fraudster was jailed again in the Fleet Prison in London.

Wherever he went, he did so in splendor, and soon he was raising eyebrows by treating the illnesses of the poor rather than the rich (at least publicly) with his nostrums and magic. He resembled the famous John Case (1660–1700—"In this place/Lives Doctor Case"), who announced in a broadsheet that he gave "the Poor, Sick, Sore and Lame advice for nothing and doth also, with great certainty and privacy, resolve all manner of Lawful questions according to the Rules of Christian Astrology."

Cagilostro tried to keep one foot in the church and one in the forbidden pseudosciences. He was rather anticlerical but he recognized the usefulness of ecclesiastic acquaintances in power. He also, like Case, was partly physician and partly quacksalver, it seems, and to please himself or to put up the front needed to inspire confidence and gather the wherewithal to answer the question with which pretenders to occult powers are always confronted, "If you know so much, why aren't you rich?" he engaged in various penny-catching schemes with his wife as honey pot or by perpetrating scams of his own.

When Cagliostro reached Rome, he fell for a fourteen-year-old girl, the beautiful Lorenza Feliciani. Her family wanted her to be a nun. The story is told that he snatched her from church the very moment before she was to take the veil, huddled her into a coach, and fled for the border of Italy. It is true that they eloped and married. It is likewise true that she was very useful to him in flirting with prospects for her con-man husband

and in badger games of blackmailing. Her youth and beauty likewise assisted him in peddling an elixir of eternal youth and a rejuvenating skin cream containing borax, pretty harmless in a time when in Britain a pill for "female strengthening" contained rhubarb and salt of vipers, William Lowther's Medicinal Compound contained powdered human skull, and Frenchman Coy La Blanche's drops for venereal disease, scrofula, etc., contained poisonous mercury (as most promised cures for syphilis did). Cagliostro also dealt love potions and spells. His wife may also have assisted him in sex magic. After a sensational life with Castiglione, she did, in fact, go into a convent. There she died in 1795, still keeping some of Cagliostro's secrets.

Cagliostro's reputation as a physician and as a philosopher constantly grew. He entered Strasbourg in September 1780. There he stayed three years, and Laborde enthusiastically reported 15,000 cures by Cagliostro there in that time. Cagliostro made believers of high church dignitaries and lowly peasants. He convinced Cardinal de Rohan (a prince of the Bourbon line who despite his personal immorality had become a prince of the church) that he could transmute base matter into gold by alchemy (he gave him very large quantities of this), and the cardinal wore an enormous diamond he swore he had seen Cagliostro produce out of thin air. This is the same Cardinal de Rohan to whom Cagliostro prophesied the death of the Empress Maria Theresa five days in advance. This is the same Cardinal de Rohan who is said to have undergone the 40 days of youth-restoring ritual described in Cagliostro's *Egyptian Freemasonry* and thereafter looked half his age. This is the same Cardinal de Rohan whom Cagliostro and the adventuress comtesse de la Motte produced a gigantic scandal that rocked the French court and was the scandal of Europe.

Countess Cagliostro.

Cagilostro's personations and forgeries got this unlikely trio involved in one of French history's most incredible episodes, the affair of the diamond necklace. The jewels intended for Marie Antoinette appear in Alexandre Dumas *père's Le Collier de la reine* (*The Queen's Necklace*). Dumas' literary factory churned out three other works that involved Cagliostro (and even Gérard de Nerval in his work on *Illuminati* grudgingly had to admit that "enthusiasm for the Count di Cagliostro was carried to an extreme that astounded even Paris"): *Joseph Balsamo, Memoirs of a Doctor,* and *The Fall of the Bastille,* as well as *The Queen's Necklace.* But no romancer could have created more extraordinary characters than the real-life Cagliostro, the social-climbing cardinal, or the daring countess.

The countess for her part in the scheme was stripped naked and flogged in public, branded, jailed, escaped to London, and was killed when, dead drunk or attempting to flee creditors (stories differ), she fell from a third-story window. The cardinal was sent to the Bastille, was pardoned, became a hero of the French Revolution, was elected to the Estates General, refused to take the oath to the Constitution of 1789, and returned to his diocese of Strasbourg (continuing his drinking and chasing of women until he died early in the nineteenth century). You may enjoy *The Affair of the Necklace,* a film of 2001 with Jonathan Pryce as Cardinal de Rohan. After the scandalous affair of the diamond necklace, Cagliostro simply swept on to his next exploits.

He had not only luck, but charisma. Baroness d'Oberkirch said he was electrifying, not handsome, but irresistible.

> He was not, strictly speaking, handsome, but never have I seen a more remarkable countenance. His glance was so penetrating that one would be almost tempted to call it supernatural. I could not describe the expression of his eyes, it was, so to say, a mixture of flame and ice. He attracted and repulsed and whilst he terrified, inspired an insurmountable curiosity.

With mesmerism and faith healing, he performed feats that were regarded as miracles. He undoubtedly was a proficient scholar not only of languages but also of psychology. He fed avarice and imagination. It is clear that Cagliostro instructed and impressed many. It is undeniable that he gained a reputation as a sage and a master of alchemy, astral therapy, and black magic.

Rumor followed him everywhere. He encouraged it, keeping his cards close to his chest despite his arrogant and flamboyant manner, knowing that all publicity is good publicity so long as people get the name right. He traveled widely to gain esoteric knowledge in his youth and then grandly toured various countries of Europe, and wherever he went he set up various lodges of alleged Egyptian freemasonry.

It is in connection with an address in Paris in the 1780s to a distinguished group of freemasons there that he earns a place in these pages. At that time, he revealed some of his knowledge of numerology and preternatural foresight (based upon the manipulation of letters that have number significance). On that occasion, he said, with his usual boldness, something striking on the connection between personal names and personal fates. Charms, spells, elixirs, ceremonial magic, imposture, blackmail, and pretense were his trade, and, about them, he could be evasive when it came to what we might call trade secrets. But on the subjects related to numerology, he was outspoken, and riveting.

He obviously did not read his own numbers right (or could do nothing to avoid his fate) because he eventually walked right into trouble with the Holy Inquisition in Rome when he arrived in 1789 (like Julius Formicus Maternus of the fourth century A.D.) with Egyptian secrets of astrology, magic, and divination—or said he did. He and his papers were seized. He was accused of heresy and of attempting to found still another "feeble

The Holy Inquisition torture chamber.

ghost of an Egyptian lodge." His wife confessed their misdeeds. "Éliphas Lévy" says that as Cagliostro sold his wife, so she "sold" (turned in) him, but we have to remember that she was interrogated by the Holy Inquisition in the presence of the rack. She broke under threat of torture. Cagliostro was tortured, signed a confession, and then repudiated it. The Holy Inquisition repressed the manuscripts they had taken from him on his arrest, and Cagliostro's works on the Beatific Vision, the evocation of spirits, "physical and moral degeneration," the elixir, the philosopher's stone, the astrological calculus, and the secret of prolonging life (magi were supposed to enjoy 12 lives in a row, then perish in fire and rise like the phoenix) have all disappeared into the vaults of the Vatican or were burned as heretical. Only his work on Egyptian magic (said to derive in the first instance from God Himself teaching occult systems to the archangels) was published, and that probably belongs, the church might say, on an *index prohibitorum* of spiritually dangerous books. We do have one manuscript he somehow wrote in jail. It is called *Très Sainte Trinosophie*, and it warns a disciple (there called Philocale) "let not a vain desire to shine in the eyes of the world cause your ruin." It is undated, but prophesies his own death "in two years."

Cagliostro was first sentenced to death as a heretic and freemason—the masons were condemned by the papal bull *In Eminenti* of 1738 by Clement XII—and then the sentence was commuted to perpetual imprisonment. Cagliostro was confined for life in a sort of well in a dungeon of the fortress of San Leone, near Urbino. It was rumored that he so infuriated his jailer that he was murdered in his cell in 1795, but he may simply have been starved to death. Thomas Carlyle judged Cagliostro to be one of the most egregious quacks in medicine and faker in the history of alleged black magic. Others have said he had superhuman powers.

We have now to place this extraordinary character in the milieu of secret societies in France in the late eighteenth century. English freemasons had given new impetus to the

Cagliostro.

organization as early as the sixteenth century. The English and the Scots had introduced their beliefs and secret societies into France by the first half of the eighteenth century. As early as 1732, the English Grand Lodge had set up a Masonic lodge in Paris. The so-called Scottish Rite also had adherents in eighteenth-century France, and from there, French masons brought freemasonry to America although earlier, in 1734, Benjamin Franklin (grand master of Pennsylvania) had risen fast in the degrees and himself published *The Constitutions of the Free-Masons*. His was the first book on freemasonry in America. In the U.S. as in France, freemasonry was involved in revolutionary politics. George Washington and many of his associates were all masons of high degrees. As for Masonic symbolism, look at the back of the one-dollar U.S. bill. In politics still, in the U.S. as elsewhere, "men of good will help each other." And always people will fear secret brotherhoods and cry conspiracy.

The French masons were indeed conspiring together. They began, it was alleged, signing their names in blood to contracts that required obedience and secrecy from them on pain of death (throat slit from ear to ear, tongue torn out). Actually Masonic initiations are not so violent: The stabbing the initiate endures is with a knife whose blade collapses into the handle, the procedure more embarrassing than terrifying. The French masons certainly acquired the secrets within secrets characteristic of the various degrees through which initiates passed. By the time Cagliostro arrived in Paris, French freemasons were well organized in their service of the Great Architect, God, and actively sought "the light." Like some in the York Rite in England, they were Jacobins.

The French adepts may have welcomed Cagliostro because he demonstrated knowledge of the symbols, signs, and secrets by which freemasons of the highest degrees recognize their fellows. They acquiesced as he promoted himself from agent of the Grand Copt (the first of which was said to be a biblical prophet) to Grand Copt, period. Now here in Cagliostro, they may have hoped, was an *illuminatus* who might reveal more powerful secrets and lead them to greater illumination. He also had some potentially useful political connections. Perhaps this brother would help.

Count Cagliostro strode to the front of them. He had declared he was one using the power of a god, and he had assumed the title *Ateersata*, setting himself up enthroned in a splendiferous Temple of Isis in Paris' rue de la Sourdière. He reigned decked out in the *nemys* of the Theban sphinx and equipped with all the numerological powers of ancient Egypt (where, some moderns suggest, the pyramids were built to convey information and prognosticate by their measurements).

In his grand mansion in the rue St.-Claude, he enthroned as grand mistress of an Egyptian lodge the princesse de Lamballe, a very close friend of the queen, Marie Antoinette, one of the (too) many children of the

Empress Maria Theresa of Austria. This social connection with the princess did much to draw princes, dukes, and lesser mortals to the fashionable lodge. Cagliostro seemed to have what Anton Mesmer called "animal magnetism," a hypnotic gaze and a commanding presence, and he attracted people (mostly women, as was the case with Rasputin later) to him with his confidence and charm, his gifts of oratory, and his reputation for understanding the mysteries of creation.

Other Parisian freemasons of great importance, nobles, presidents of *parléments*, leaders of society, foreign diplomats, and Frenchmen alike, gathered together to assess Cagliostro's teachings and to ask what freemasonry really was and how it had been created and developed, how it was connected to politics and to the occult sciences, and what its rituals and secrets were or should be and how they could be used to advantage.

Many of them, like masons in England, were revolutionaries, idealistic or opportunistic. They turned to Antoine Court de Gèbelin (1725–1784), distinguished author of *Plan general . . . du monde primatif* (1772) and other famous works; they asked him to debate with Cagliostro the meaning of freemasonry. The history of freemasonry had been confused somewhat with that of the Knights Templar (eradicated in France by a king who accused them of blasphemy, but their sin was really being very rich when His Majesty was in debt), the Rosy Cross, and many other things all the way back to the Temple of Solomon (built, it was said, by demons whom Solomon commanded by the power of a magic ring). Masonic doctrine badly needed straightening out. It needed a plan for the future and some faith that the plan would succeed. It needed someone even more impressive than the Comte de St.-Germain. Cagilostro has sometimes been confused with St.-Germain, who claimed to have the knowledge of centuries because he had kept himself alive for 2,000 years, not as a deathless vampire, but ageless, on a secret elixir, a sort of combination of the fountain of youth and Viagra. Cagliostro peddled such a liquor, as well. In another book, I give a recipe for it but you may not want to make it (it involves a lot of serpents) or take it.

The Count of St.-Germain, like Cagliostro sparkled in the drawing rooms of eighteenth-century Europe and, it is said, like Cagliostro was thrown into a dungeon by the Holy Inquisition. Another story is that he surfaced in California in the twentieth century.

Iain McCalman is the author of a study of Cagliostro called *The Last Alchemist* (2003). McCalman credits Cagliostro with influencing Mozart's freemasonry in *The Magic Flute* and with being a muse of the poet William Blake who was in turn an influence on Allen Ginsberg. Anthony Burgess in a novel referred to "Mozart and the World Gang" and you can follow up at www.math.truman.edu/thammond/history/numerology if you are interested.

At the hush-hush conclave, Gébelin the orientalist was impressed with Cagliostro's detailed knowledge derived from travels in Egypt, Persia, and Greece (to which, tradition says, in the fourth century B.C., an Egyptian king called Nectanebus brought his magic and gift of prophecy). But Gébelin could not get much out of Cagliostro on the subject of freemasonry until Cagliostro was moved to make, with his usual insidious charm and aggressiveness, the following remarks. I take them as reported in James Kirkup and Julian Shaw's translation from the French of "Paul Christian." Using a pseudonym in occult circles was popular in the nineteenth century (another called himself "Papus").

You need to know a little about this source. This "Christian" was born Jean-Baptiste Pitois in 1811. He was also called Dom Marie-Bernard (recalling when he tested his vocation for a time in a Trappist monastery) and Charles Moreau. He was a busy journalist, newspaper editor, and prolific historian of religion and revolution. Through connections, he was given the task of assembling all the duplicate books of other libraries that were assembled in Paris as well as the rich libraries that the French Revolution had taken from churches, monasteries, and convents all over France. He wrote a history of the clergy in France and became a leading French occultist with a bit of an anticlerical bias. He had a strong Roman Catholic faith but still clung to a fascination with astrology and onomantic divination (using names) as a way of getting to the prenestine fates. He had a strong disapproval of all things Masonic. His major book resulted from small-*c* catholic reading in the "black books" of the occult, and his standard book here quoted was *Histoire de Magie, du Monde surnaturel et de la fatalité—traverse les temps et les peuples* (*History of Magic and the World of the Supernatural and of Fate across Times and Peoples*, 1870).

Cagliostro speaks:

> "Gentlemen," he said, "in accepting the invitation with which you have now honoured me, I did not foresee as clearly as I do now the seriousness of such an interview. If I am not mistaken, you believe that Freemasonry should possess the key to the occult sciences, and, not having been able to discover this key at your lodge meetings, you came here in the hope that I would be able to cast some light on your researches. Well, gentlemen, honesty compels me to tell you that you can learn nothing from Freemasonry."

Cagliostro Speaks to the Freemasons in Paris

After that startling announcement, he went into a discussion of the Rosy Cross we associate with the Rosicrucians, but he said that it was "a symbolic expression of the divine idea" and sixty centuries old, going back to the magi (magicians) of Egypt. Of freemasonry's allegedly farcical ideas, he continued:

> "Gentlemen, how could such stupid nonsense be accepted by intelligent Frenchmen? If you wish to revive among you the majesty of the doctrines which illuminated the ancient world and rekindle on the heights of human intelligence the beacon of divine radiance, you must first of all destroy the doctrine of Hiram [supposed founder of freemasonry] and your meaningless rituals."

Gébelin questioned if it was necessary "to destroy everything in order to prove one's superiority." He demanded proof that Cagliostro was "the inheritor of the ancient Magic." Making everyone present swear to secrecy (which they did and which made them feel, very likely, privileged and more ready to entertain his opinions), Cagliostro went on:

> "Gentlemen," continued the Sicilian with a magnetic look, "when a child is born, something has already preceded its entry into life. That something is its *Name*. The name completes the birth, for, before naming, a king's child and a peasant's are no more than small pieces of organised matter, just as the corpse of the most powerful ruler in the world, shorn of the brilliance of funeral pomps, has nothing to distinguish it from the remains of the lowest slave.
>
> "In modern society there are three sorts of names; the family, the Christian and the surnames. The family name is the common impress of race which is handed down, transmitted from one being to another. The Christian name is the sign that characterises the person and distinguishes the sex. The surname is a secondary qualification, applied to any individual in a family in particular cases. The family name [he means the surname] is imposed by civil requirements; the Christian name is chosen by the affectionate intentions of the father and mother [and is traditionally intended to place the bearer under the protection of a saint]. The surname is an accidental title, sometimes used only in one lifetime, sometimes hereditary. There is finally the social title, such as prince, count, duke. Now I can read in the ensemble of these personal designations the most outstanding features of any destiny; the more numerous these designations are, the more clearly does the oracle within them speak."

At this point the English translation of "Paul Christian"'s book inserts the "Alphabet of the Magi," which Cagliostro showed his auditors and which looks like this:

184 *The Complete Book of Numerology*

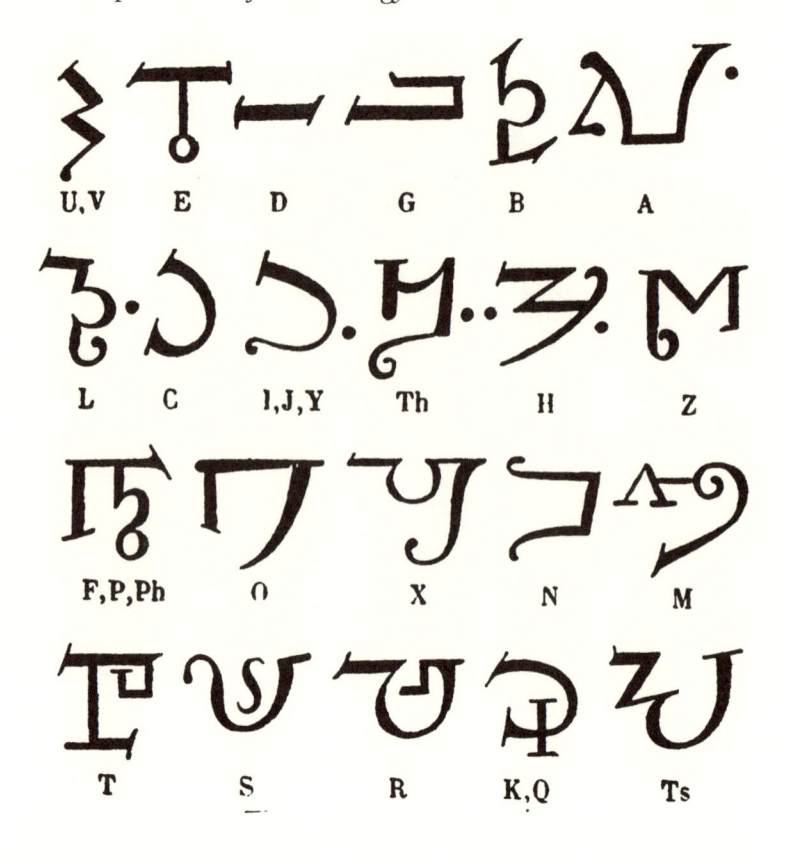

U,V	E	D	G	B	A

L	C	I,J,Y	Th	H	Z

F,P,Ph	O	X	N	M

T	S	R	K,Q	Ts

"Do not smile, gentlemen. My conviction in this respect cannot falter, for it is based on fairly numerous experiments and on proofs too striking to be ignored. Yes, each one of us is named in the heavens at the same time as on earth, that is, predestinated, bound, by the occult laws of increate Wisdom, to a series of more or less fatal ordeals before he has made the first step towards his unknown future. Do not tell me that such certainty, if it existed, would be the certainty of despair . . . All your protests will not prevent Predestination from being a fact and the Name a sign to be feared. The highest wisdom of the ancients believed in this mysterious connection of the name and the being who holds it as if it were a divine or infernal talisman that could either illuminate his passage through life or destroy it in flames. The Magi of Egypt confided this secret to Pythagoras, who transmitted it to the Greeks. In the sacred alphabet of Magism each letter is linked to a number; each number corresponds with an Arcanum [icon as in the Tarot]; each Arcanum is the sign of an occult power. The 22 letters [corresponding to the 22 major *arcana* or face cards of the Tarot, which adds them to the cards of the regular playing card pack] of which the keyboard of the language is composed form all the names which, according to the agreement or disagreement of the secret forces symbolised by the letters, destine the man so named to the vicissitudes which we define by the vulgar terms of *luck* or *misfortune*."

So Cagliostro places crucial importance on names and numbers. He goes on to state that from the start, they set the course of our lives—much as the stars are alleged to do by their position at the exact time and place of our birth. They give us our basic characters (numerology generally says 9 or 11, Geoffrey Hodson says only 7, astrology claims 12) from the person wrapped up in himself to the great humanitarian. Cagliostro goes on to say that we can "seek and discover the secrets of the future" in a literal statement of the event that has just taken place or in a definition of a person by the names, titles, and deeds that constitute his individuality. Cagliostro says, breaking into learned Latin (though his detractors say he pronounced that and all other languages besides the Sicilian dialect of Italian very badly):

Tacentes Casus Denunitat Nomen;
Decreta Dei Per Numeros Præfantur.

(The Name announces the events that still remain in the silence of the future; And divine decrees are predicted in numbers.)

But numerology takes into account not only names from birth, but also names and numbers that are adopted by or attached to the individual in later life. If everything is predestined, including all the honors and titles we acquire, how can we change our personalities or our circumstances by altering our names and numbers? Can we take action by name and numbers to alter "divine decrees" and change our futures, or does not predestination prevent any such change? Or, if an effort is made and names and numbers changed, was that predestined?

A huge problem that confronts those who would change the future lies in the assumption that in the Mind of God, the past, the present, and the future all exist, simultaneously and immutably. You have been faced with this conundrum before this. What good is it, even if we can predict the future, if we cannot alter the future? We always ask that. What use is there in fiddling with numerology if all it can do is tell us what is or what must be, not what can be if we make efforts?

True magic lies in transformations. Superstition accepts mysteries. Magic takes matters in hand to change things, whether it is Christ performing His first miracle of changing water into wine or Moses changing his staff into a serpent to confound the lesser magicians of Pharaoh. Magic goes into action to lay a curse. Magic is the magician risking his life (and soul), the necromancer raising the dead or a table-rapper or medium making the departed speak to the living. (You may not think séances are black magic, but they are at least attempts at black magic and so a sin.) Magic usually progresses from minor (water into wine, the lame made to walk) to the major (the blind are made to see, the dead are raised from the dead and called out of the tomb). Magic is the transubstantiation of the Mass, and magic is the conveying of ecclesiastical power (the Apostolic Succession) by the laying on of hands, and magic is the sinner born again, "washed in the blood of the Lamb," cleansed to purity. Magic is casting a spell, calling up or driving out a demon, much more.

Always, Magick (as Crowley called it, to distinguish it from an entertainer's prestidigitation) is dangerous hands-on work. It can infect one with the infernal that one touches, to speak in spiritual terms, and it can bring personal disaster and even death from political enemies and jealous rivals, to speak in mundane terms. Magic may kill the soul and the body. It can fail and drive to despair. If magic does not work, it is a fatal deed, for in Christianity, intention can be a mortal sin.

In the East, it is said, a person confronted with a problem asks, "How can I accept this, bow to its inevitability?" In the West, confronted with a problem, we tend to ask, "What action can I take to get rid of this problem, to evade an unwanted outcome?" We often look to instant results in "voodoo economics" and magical politics. What do we want? Change! When do we want it? Now!

Cagliostro, to return to him, lived in a time wanting, expecting major change, and Cagliostro had big news about change. Later to that same audience, he made a dire prediction on the basis of this sentence: "*Reine de France, et si jeune encore, je mourrai par hache—la tête tranché dans nid de son*" that Marie Antoinette "Queen of France, and still so young, shall die by the axe—the head severed into a nest of bran." He said he got that sentence from the letters of the name and title *Marie-Antoinette-Joséphine-Jeanne de Lorraine, archiduchesse d'Autriche, reine de France*. He said the letters by the intuition of the seer could be rearranged to make that prophecy that revolution would decapitate her by what Cagliostro called "an apparatus frequently employed in Florence whose mechanism makes the victim's head fall into a basket filled with bran to absorb the blood." For the leftover (or "mute") letters (*IIIH*), Cagliostro supplied Latin words as an extra: *Inermis Immolor—Inexpiabilis Hostia* [I am immolated, unarmed—inexpiable victim]. Really bad news.

This prognostication may well have been rather attractive, good news to most of his listeners, for, in France at that time, freemasonry was hop-

Cagliostro Speaks to the Freemasons in Paris 187

ing for the end of the monarchy and a new liberty, fraternity, and equality in the land. Freemasons, like the Jesuits, have often been accused of working politically behind the scenes. Soldiers of reason, soldiers of the faith. Was the legend not that the king of Tara had three sons, a warrior, a poet, and a mason? And did not the legend say that the warrior was killed in battle, the poet told lies, and the mason lived to build the world?

Gébelin, perhaps more pious than political, was shocked. He expostulated:

"M. le Comte, you have just prophesied unbelievable catastrophes with unexampled daring. The benefits of the most laudable of revolutions are as nothing, if paid for at such a price! But as a man of good will, if convinced you are right can you not think of some means of warning the victims? For if God is pleased to let us see into the future, doubtless it is to remind us that He is its sovereign and that our prayers may influence Him . . ."

If we do fear what names and numbers tell us about what is to come, can we take some action (such as petitioning God to let the chalice of suffering pass from us), or is what is to come just going to come?

Can we read the future? If so, knowing what it promises, is there anything good that can come of that?

Cagliostro some years before the event thus predicted the French Revolution would begin in 1789 when the Third Estate rose up against the First Estate (nobles) and the Second Estate (clergy).

*Révolution faite en mil sept cent quatre-vingt-neuf, par le
Tiers-État contre Louis seize, roi de France?*

(Will there be a revolution of the Third Estate [people] in 1789 against Louis XVI, King of France?)

Rearranged to:

La Démocratic sanglante tue Roi et Reine prisonniers en tour et étouffe leur fils en captivité.

(Bloody democracy kills the King and Queen imprisoned in the tower and suffocates their captive son.)

From the leftover letters (*VCQTZ*), Cagliostro made *Vastatio, Cruor, Querelæ, Terror, Zonatim* in Latin, or in English "a circle of devastation, blood, groans, and terror" plus one puzzle. Isn't that a perfectly accurate description of the reign of terror that marked the blood-soaked birth of the first of France's republics?

Cagliostro predicted at the same time that the mistress of his own Temple of Isis, the princesse de Lamballe (widow of the son of the duc de

188 *The Complete Book of Numerology*

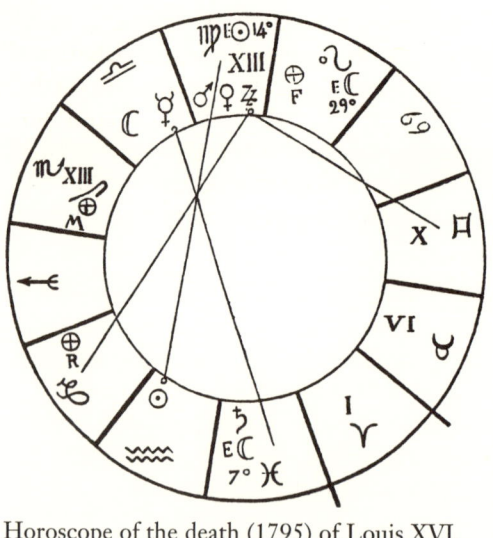

Horoscope of the death (1795) of Louis XVI.

Penthiève), would be "murdered by evil-doers" at the height of the revolution. He added she would certainly die in the rue des Ballets. Had he informed her of that? No. What good would that do? What he secretly told the assembled freemasons that day (unless the whole story was made up after history had had its say) was exactly what happened some few years after the session with Cagliostro that I have described. When the revolution broke out, the princesse de Lamballe was jailed, but she was released—and guess what happened as she made her way to the corner of the rue des Ballets.

Did some people who knew the prophecy act to fulfill it? Are some prophecies effective because we work to make them work? Was Cagliostro prescient? Did he understand the future, or did he simply understand human nature and what people would do? Are some prophecies merely shrewd guesses, and do not prophecies work very much like other aspects of superstition, in which we ignore the evidence of misses and play up too much the evidence of hits? Was the basic story that she would die in the revolution, which would be highly likely for a woman of her rank at that time, elaborated after she died on that street corner, adding the detail that nails down the forecast? I cannot answer these questions.

Here is a nagging question for you: If the future is fixed, in what cases is it of any real use to have any sort of marvelous ability to read it now? And there is another thing to consider, if "David Conway" in his "occult primer," *Ritual Magic* (1972) is correct in stating that

Coat of arms of Count Cagliostro.

"the future is filled only with an unknown potential which cannot be realized until acted upon by the steadily advancing present. . . . [so that] we face an amorphous future whose eventual form depends on a series of forthcoming presents. For that reason, the future, being formless, should not be foreseeable."

So there you have a glimpse of the colorful count who astounded with his cures and his comments. He was perhaps the most colorful in the history of France next to Sade. (The so-called marquis de Sade was only a count, really.) And there you have something to think about in connection with "reading" words and numbers to tell the future.

I cannot predict what conclusions you will form. All liquid takes the shape of the vessel into which it is poured.

ÉDIT DU ROI,

POUR la punition de différens crimes, notamment des Empoisonneurs, ceux qui se disent Devins, Magiciens & Enchanteurs; & portant reglement pour les Épiciers & Apothicaires.

Donné à Versailles, au mois de Juillet 1682.

Registré en Parlement le 31 Août audit an.

LOUIS, par la grace de Dieu, Roi de France & de Navarre : A tous présens & à venir, SALUT. L'exécution des Ordonnances des Rois nos prédécesseurs, contre ceux qui se disent Devins, Magiciens & Enchanteurs, ayant été négligée depuis long-temps, & ce relâchement ayant attiré des Pays étrangers dans notre Royaume, plusieurs de ces Imposteurs, il seroit arrivé que sous prétexte d'horoscope & de divination, & par le moyen des prestiges des opérations des prétendues magies & autres illusions semblables dont cette sorte de gens ont accoutumé de se servir, ils auroient surpris diverses personnes ignorantes ou crédules, qui s'étoient insensiblement engagées avec eux, en passant des vaines curiosités aux

Beginning of Louis XIV's edict against "diviners, magiciens & enchanters" (1682).

15
Seventh-Inning Stretch

ס

I hope that by this point you will agree you have learned interesting things from this book. At this point, we take something of a breather. It is our seventh-inning stretch, from baseball. The Cincinnati Red Stockings were the first professional baseball team, and the manager, Henry Wright, wrote in 1869 about this custom:

> The spectators here all arise between halves of the seventh, extend their legs and arms, and sometimes walk about. In so doing they enjoy the relief afforded by relaxation from a long posture on hard benches.

Take a breather. Relax for a chattier and easier-than-usual section, and then we shall go on with the more challenging material. A writer has to give his readers a break now and then, in case you "can't put it down" rather than have been getting it in small doses.

The occult topics deserve a popular audience for whom a vast body of information can be condensed and made instant; just add interest and stir. Modern readers need to have solid research professionally collected, attractively arranged, and commented upon for them. This is especially true, perhaps, when it comes to anything to do with the occult, whether it be the black arts or (say) bumps on the cranium (described by J. G. Spurzheim in *Phrenology; or, The Doctrine of Mental Phenomenon*, which had reached a third edition by 1833). Phrenology and necromancy, once popular but now rejected pseudosciences, have done much to blacken the reputation of the occult, to cause people to regard it as "stuff." Gypsies in tearooms have given way to television-advertised psychics.

"That stuff," as some of my academic colleagues call it, may have some good stuff in it, and if nothing else, like UFO matter or mania, it is important in the understanding of mass psychology, governmental information management, and other topics.

Numerology has held up where phrenology has not, even though phrenology seemed to have in anatomy a sounder basis in fact. My book *What's in a Name?* undertook to introduce the whole field of onomastics (personal names, nicknames, and aliases, character names in literature, place names worldwide, naming systems in various cultures, everything from what to name the baby to what to name the dog) but the section on numerology proved to be one of its most attractive and applauded features.

This is a whole book on numerology, of course. In it, I do not trouble the reader with French, German, Swedish, or other such references. The public seems to demand, or publishers want to invest in, simple approaches. English is all you need. Librarians approved lots of book lists in some earlier books of the series, but I do not think librarians will stock up on numerological treatises, and I would be glad if they would just buy this one.

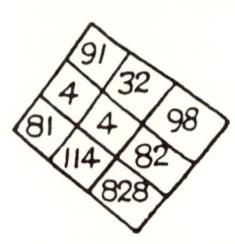

I addressed in the first volume in my series of occult books, *The Complete Book of Superstition, Prophecy, and Luck*, the same basics that I address in this book. That is to say, I continue to write about people's superstitious beliefs, this time about numbers. I am interested in the way they think numbers have directed their lives and can be discovered to predict their future. I am interested in the way that numerology relates, or that many believe that it relates, to their ideas about fate, fortune.

The occult books I have written, on superstition, magic, witchcraft, prophecy, the interpretation of dreams, and other subjects, range from Wiccans and warlocks to werewolves, from such undead topics as vampires to such old-fashioned ones as gemology, though crystals had a vogue among hippies. In all of them, I have naturally included chiefly the long histories of Europe and Asia, as well as the shorter histories of the Americas. It seems to me, however, that although our experience here in the U.S. may be much influenced by the beliefs of older continents, there is something quintessentially American about our fascination with numbers. It is quintessentially American to want to change the world, and our belief in the power of the will to change things to our advantage and how vital the importance of luck is obvious everywhere in our everyday lives.

The very foundation of our country meant trusting that luck—or God, but about Him the deists were not so sure—would favor our optimistic experiment "in the presence of this continent." We started out as a nation of people ready to take their chances in a new world. Along the way, we produced such typically American folk heroes as John Gates and William "Bill" Gates. Bill Gates of Microsoft you know; he dropped out of Harvard and took an informed risk on his great idea, which paid off handsomely. Maybe you never heard of John Gates. John Gates was nicknamed "Bet-a-Million." He was a gambler (he made a lot of money in the Wild West in the nineteenth century with his barbed wire) who once bet a large sum on how many raindrops would hit the windowpane (or which of two drops would hit the windowsill first, because the story varies).

Betting and numbers must go back a long way before nineteenth-century gamblers, as far back as the first humanoid who calculated that there were more or fewer of something than he (or she) had noticed before and wondered if there was some way of getting more of the good things, if the gods could be talked into contriving that. At a more advanced stage came the numbers and writing systems, the first of which we have record was used to tally things, to keep track of grain stored, debts owed. People started to punch symbols and numbers onto clay tablets not a long time after they started to paint murals in caves. The cuneiform writers were the first accountants.

The Romans used to count on their fingers. You can see the 3 in III, the thumb and four fingers separated in V, the crossed hands in X, the cupped hand in C for 100, two cupped hands together in M for 1,000. Perhaps you never thought of that origin of Roman numerals. This book on numbers wants to bring to your attention a number of new perceptions, some simple and some more complicated. It wants to have you consider that, for thousands of years, there has persisted an idea that there is a magic in numbers of all kinds, that numbers are the key to the universe. That's the crux.

Today people who believe in the power of numbers may regard themselves as New Age. Actually they are following an extremely ancient tradition. This book is for them and for others who want to know what those people find so gripping, so magical, in numbers. By this point in the book, you may share their enthusiasm.

I might have written about astrology, but there is so much on that in print already. Every publishing season brings a stack of new astrology books. I considered that the subject would be difficult to deal with in the reader-friendly style that I prefer even for the most abstruse and arcane topics and that a lot of what astrology provides or says it provides can also be found in numerology. That is not to say astrology is unworthy of attention or will go out of favor. Will Durant offered the opinion that "astrology antedated—and perhaps will survive—astronomy; simple souls are more interested in telling futures than in telling time."

194 *The Complete Book of Numerology*

Another skeptic has suggested amusing new Love Signs (a little too vulgar for my taste) and here is a list of Southern Astrology Signs:

Okra (22 Dec. – 20 Jan.). This person is all gooey on the inside.

Chitlings (20 Jan. – 19 Feb.). Humble beginnings. Good with gut feelings.

Boll Weevil (20 Feb. – 20 Mar.). A great bore. Choose the lesser of two weevils.

Moon Pie (21 Mar. – 20 Apr.). Likely to spend a lot of time mooning around.

Possum (21 Apr. – 21 May.). Tends to be withdrawn. Plays dead in bed.

Crawfish (22 May – 21 Jun.). This is a water sign. Will bite your head off when angry.

Collard Greens (22 Jun. – 23 Jul.). Fits in well in the melting pot.

Catfish (24 Jul. – 23 Aug.). Prefers muddy bottoms.

Boiled Peanuts (24 Aug. – 23 Sept.). Salty personality to which some may be allergic.

Rebel Yell (24 Sept. – 23 Oct.). Boisterous and unreconstructible.

Butter Bean (24 Oct. – 22 Nov.). Prospers on the vine of life.

Alligator (23 Nov. – 21 Dec.). Rip-roaring individualist. Snappy dresser.

Numerology undertakes, like astrology, to explain what kind of person you are and to predict what will happen to you. There is no numerology column in your local newspaper or popular periodical the way there is something devoted to astrology. So here we have a simple and straightforward book, for the general reader, as diverting as it can be, on the magic of numbers and the numbers in magic, and you can construct your own personality check and fortune. With this book, you do not need a daily astrology "reading." With this book, you can use numerology for yourself, whether as a hobby or a kind of religion.

200	6	90	40
89	41	199	7
32	92	4	198
5	197	33	91

Musawwir (He Who Fashioneth = God)
M (40) + S (90) + W (6) + R (200) = 336.

Religions such as Christianity, following Judaism and the religions that preceded that, link numbers and other ideas in much the same way if not with the same directness. When medieval theologians put together 3 (the number of the Trinity) and 4 (the number of

Seventh-Inning Stretch 195

the body), they got 7. So medieval theology reveled in the Name of God "which only 7 elect know," 7 days of the week, 7 books of Lactantius' *Divinarum Institutionem*, Seven Deadly Sins, 7 gifts of the Holy Spirit, 7 petitions in the *Pater Noster* (Lord's Prayer), Seven Virtues (3 theological + four cardinal ones), 7 planets and 7 "administrators" influencing mankind, 7 voices (7 vowels), 7 ages of man, 7 sacraments, 7 last words of Christ (which Saint Albert the Great connected with the 7 gifts of the spirit), the 7 churches (which Durandus says is not right, but they "are called 7"). Consecrating a cathedral one asperges 7 altars. There are 7 sorrows of Mary, the 7 years of torture of St. George, 7 devils of Mary Magdalene, 7 devils derived from the Babylonian Pleiades and/or the Egyptian Hathors (you fight them by tying 7 knots in a handkerchief, in case you ever need to know), 7 thrones (Ursa Major), 7 Pillars of the World (Enoch, Noah, Abraham, Isaac, Jacob, Moses, and Jesus), and much more. Folklore spoke of the Seven Sleepers of Ephesus, 7 pillars of the House of Wisdom, 7 seals of Solomon, 7 as "crucial" (this from the Pythagoreans who thought anything divisive by 7 was critical), and of course the 7 dwarfs with Snow White, Seven Wonders of the World, sailing the 7 seas, and the 7 heads of the hydra, not to go on and on about this until we are all at 6s and 7s. Seven is universal and is regarded as the number of universality (according to Saint Thomas Aquinas). I think it is a wonder that there were not 7 degrees of angels or 7 commandments (7 deal with our relation to other humans, 3 with our relation to God) or even 7 apostles.

The number 7 figures prominently in many religions other than Christianity. In Islam, the Divine Word of Creation was written in Arabic with 7 letters. The 7th prophet will mark an end. The Druze have 7 commandments. Seven figures are equally prominently in Vedic writing. The sun god's chariot is pulled through the heavens by 7 steeds. The baby Buddha took 7 steps to indicate that this would be his last reincarnation. The Japanese believe 7 deities bring good luck.

There are a lot of 7 superstitions. You know that breaking a mirror brings you 7 years bad luck. The seventh son of a seventh son is credited with the powers of a seer. That one is a superstition you may never have encountered in these modern times of smaller families. How many superstitions involving 7s can you think of?

The Seventh Heaven comes from the Hindus. Hindus believe in 7 heavens, one above the other. There are three times as many hells: 21 in all, three groups of 7, each one of all the hells divided into 7 sections. We modern Christians are not the only people who like to call 7 our lucky number—and maybe we are three times as likely to wind up in hell instead of in any heaven. I don't know.

There are two very important questions. First, when 7 is reported as fact in various religious texts, there may be the suspicion that what we are reading is literature rather than revelation. Second, what is the fact: Is there anything in this ancient and widespread belief in 7? You can see why our fingers got us counting in 10s, and maybe it has occurred to you that counting in 20s (scores, because recorded with notches on a stick) came from counting on fingers and toes. But where did 7 get the beliefs that cluster around it?

Where did we get our ideas about 13? Moritz Jagendorf (rightly thinking that folklore concentrated too much on the rustic poor and neglected the tales of the wealthy urbanites) wrote something on 13 in "The Rich Lore of the Plaza [Hotel in New York City] in *New York Folklore Quarterly* (1953). Here is one of the stories he collected from a bellman (Romeo Giannini):

> One day a man, a golden stick-pin with the number 13 in his tie asked for a room number thirteen—any floor. Romeo Giannini thinks his name was Chapman. On being told there was no room with such [a] number, he asked for a room on the thirteenth floor and explained that he was a member of the Thirteen Club; he always began his business deals on the thirteenth day, and he always had thirteen people at his dinner table. It was his good-luck number.
>
> A room on the thirteenth floor was assigned to him. He occupied it for exactly thirteen days, when he took ill and died.

I think that is one of the phoniest stories I have ever heard. Notwithstanding, what interests me is not that such tales give rise to the idea of 13 as an unlucky number, but that the reputation of 13 as an unlucky number gives rise to such supposed explanations or examples. There *could* have been a Thirteen Club. I do not for a moment believe there was one. What there was, and seems ever shall be, is a superstition about numbers and a desire to show that the superstition is based on fact, even if one has to fabricate the facts. The folk make up the stories to support the superstitions they cling to.

If you take ill, you might be well advised to move into a room at the Plaza (on its 13th floor or not), I think, and use room service and the hotel doctor and visiting physicians. The Plaza is expensive, but it is more comfortable, much healthier, and much less expensive than New York hospitals, and its bills do not have the dishonest extra charges that hospitals tack on. Practically all hospital bills get the numbers wrong, and mistakes in hospital bills by a very large margin favor not the patient, but the hospital. In a hotel, you can always hire outside round-the-clock nursing services just for you. If you do not like the hotel food, which may not be up to the luxurious surroundings, you can send your nurse out to nearby places for takeout or ask for an outside line and put in your order for delivery. If you can pay the bills, lucky you!

One could go on and on about the history of numbers other than 7 and 13. People have done so.

However many books have been written and folktales told, do we want to believe in 7s and 13s and other numbers? What truth is there in Scripture and in folk belief? Is numerology something we want to give a certain amount of credence to, something like astrology, pooh-poohed by many persons, but regularly turned to with at least interest if not full acceptance?

9	8	18	1
8	18	1	9
1	9	8	18
18	1	9	8

Renaissance scholar Pico della Mirandola studied magic and the Holy Kabbalah. He delved into the tradition of the Jews of Alexandria in ancient times under the influence of the Pythagoreans, who stated that numbers were the explanation of everything if only you can decipher what they say. But Pico balked at believing in astrology. Bellanti of Siena got angry at that. He cast Pico's horoscope and predicted Pico's early death. Pico died at age thirty-three. Voodoo suggestion? Astrological accuracy? Who knows? The full explication of any single event involves an extremely complex tissue of factors. Maybe numerology and such things appeal because they offer simple explanations. Maybe these explanations appeal because they are mysterious.

Are numerology's explanations sound? When it comes to Lucky 7 or Unlucky 13 or any other number's significance, is occult belief well founded or just foolishness? Most people would sheepishly say they "sort of" believe.

Let us look for a moment at astrology, with which to some degree or other you are more familiar than you are with numerology. ("What's your sign?") Why, in astrology for instance, have we thought we could get something of a grip on secrets of the universe? Astrology, as we know it today, first arose, as far as we know, from the Chaldeans and Assyrians. The Chaldeans were obsessed with prediction. They lived by omens. They believed omens revealed what had to happen. It is worth emphasizing that these ancient peoples who wanted to know the future believed that all human events are predetermined. They were sure that everything on earth was dictated by the movements of the stars and planets and that these were set in their courses. People did not think they could change things.

Still they were desperately curious. Curiosity led the Magi to follow a star to Bethlehem because in their view only an extremely important new person arriving on earth would warrant a new star appearing in the heavens to herald the great event. You may have noticed that *magi* is where we got *magic*.

Magicians like privileged information, whether they are the proponents of black magic who jealously guard their secrets or entertainers who conceal the way the trick works. Stage magicians want to fool you. They want to astonish. Black magicians think that if they know, they can alter anything. They want power.

Are we being duped when we are led to believe that fortunes can be altered? It is worth underlining the fact that ancient belief in astrology as a means of fortune-telling always struggled with the conviction that even if you know what is coming, there is nothing you can do to change the future. The whole thing is foreordained. The Muslims say "it is written," meaning that Allah (God) has authored the script for the universal performance, that each person has a determined fate, a leading role or more likely a bit part or at best a cameo. If the future is already all set, there is no use going "back to the future." You cannot alter fate. You cannot beat cause and effect.

Modern astrologers fudge the facts, if that is what to call them, because moderns like to believe in free will. We do not relish the idea of having no control whatever over our lives. We would hate to accept fully the idea that the decisions we make are really all just handed to us. We like to say "be whatever you want to be." We like to believe in metamorphosis, drastic change through magic, or if magic doesn't bring us supernatural assistance, then taking the bull by the horns and doing something on our own to effect personal change or to change the world. We are DIY, can-do people, or we like to think we are.

Divinatory systems, from astrology to palmistry to drinking all but a teaspoon of your tea and turning the cup upside down and turning it three times in a counterclockwise direction with the left hand—all this lefty stuff ought to register *sinister* with you!—declare your fate is basically out of your hands (or in the case of palmistry, written right there on your hands). Short life line? Regrettably, you will be leaving us soon. No way out, just out. A black disk of tea leaves? An eclipse of your good fortune. Sorry. There is no independence offered by the likes of that. That bump on your head? Sorry, little imagination. What is, is; what will be, will be. Your life is all marked out. That rhinoceros in the teacup (if that is what you see) means "a gross and cruel nature." That ax means you will somehow get the chop. That being so, it won't do you a lot of good to be able to read it, will it?

You certainly don't want to get a bad fortune presented in the lines in your hand or the details of your horoscope or the leaves in your teacup or even the bumps on your head that a fellow had the gall (he was named Gall) to promote into a pseudoscience.

There is less in phrenology than in graphology (analysis of handwriting) or even physiognomy (your facial appearance). Lambroso said there were criminal ears. Come on! That seems to me not far from the idea of putting a lit candle in a shoe in a sick room and chanting three times

Go away death, go away death!
Life from the flame, give new breath!

Or (as some Orthodox Jews do) changing the name of a sick person so that the Angel of Death will not be able to locate her or him. You think the Angel of Death is so easy to fool? From so much experience, he is still stupid already?

The funny thing is that you seldom do get bad news from any of the pseudosciences. One of the most interesting aspects of divination is that bad fortunes are rare. Why is that? I think it is because nobody wants one.

Whether one uses the Tarot or the horoscope or the coins of the *I Ching*, the oracle is usually rejected if the message is unwelcome. As Bill Hopkins said to Colin Wilson (author of "the ultimate book for those who would walk with the Gods," *The Occult*) about the *I Ching*, "If it gives good judgement, I'll believe in it. If it doesn't, I won't."

Well, thus far in the book from which for a few pages I have been taking a sort of vacation in order to chat even more personally than usual with you, we have been seeing what numerology can or would like to be able to do about things. Things (once called the 10,000 things) have names, but all names can be made into numbers, so that is what you can work with.

Cornelius Agrippa of Nettesheim (1486–1535) was a professor of theology at a very young age and a mage of the Renaissance. He was the author of the revisionist *De occulta philosophia*. He put huge emphasis on words and especially words in Hebrew, which some people thought must be the native language of God and all the powers, dominions, principalities, and other residents of heaven. Agrippa dealt with numbers for letters of the (Hebrew) alphabet and connected to astrology's 7 planets. For all his reputation in the occult, he liked to think of himself as a pragmatic and unsuperstitious man and said that the wonders of numerology need not be thought of as involving miracles any more than the great cathedral of his native Cologne or "heaps of rocks such as I saw in Britain" [Stonehenge?] or any other masterwork of man had to be attributed to the work of demons or the help of The Devil.

Somewhere in this book, you see a reference to the passes that magicians make with their hands. Agrippa said that the idea that these were waving at demons was ridiculous; they were, he said, references to the power in numbers, numbers that contained ideas, perhaps divine ideas, and thus were realities. He was willing, though, to attract the power of planets by the use of magic squares. The fact of the matter is that, as a scientist, he was naturally working with both facts and speculations, and in his time, science and superstition were very much mingled. I bring up Cornelius Agrippa as an example of the common occurrence in all discussions of numerology of the argument that it is a practical science founded in reality and at the same time a part of occult philosophy.

To get back to specifics before I end this section, let me tell you about some basic ideas of this Cornelius Agrippa I have introduced into the

Portrait and magical seal of Cornelius Agrippa.

conversation. I shall now give you his "Hebrew" system of numerology. It differs from the more recent systems, which do not hesitate to include the 3x3 "divine" number 9, which Cornelius Agrippa in his superstition would not touch:

A, I, Q, J, Y are 1

B, K, R are 2

C, G, L, S are 3

D, M, T are 4

E, H, N are 5

U, V, W, X are 6

O, Z are 7

F, P are 8

Now you can get to work to change things, if you wish. Why not stop right here and if you have not already tried this block-print your full name and write the number under each letter and get out your calculator and add up the numbers using this unusual "Hebrew" system of Agrippa's?

That's *you*. Not the lines in your palm or the shape of your fingernails, not your stars, not the shape of your cranium or your nose, but the entire *you*, and the same goes for people and things you encounter in this life, the facts of the present and the realities of the future. That is what numerology claims. They say, you know, your date of birth is you, but you cannot change that. You can *lie* about your age, of course. Case in point, the late, great, Katharine Hepburn. Katharine Hepburn was the subject of an article entitled "What Her Birth Date Means to Her" in *Picturegoer* in 1934 in which the star was described as "strongly individual, very uncompromising, critical and judicial in a clear decisive fashion" as dictated by a birth date of 8 November 1909. The problem is that Ms. Hepburn lied about her age. She was born 12 May 1907. (In fact, most people are born in December.) The date in 1909 was that of her brother, Thomas, whose suicide, when young, haunted Ms. Hepburn.

If you like what you find when you do numerology, great. If you don't, consider changing your name (or just the spelling of it, the way that Dionne Warwick said she made great improvement) or altering any numbers you can. That may make you feel better. Making yourself feel better, you will have to admit, is metamorphosis, the very stuff of magic. You may be stuck as a Pisces and stuck with your Social Security Number, but there is a lot you can do with some other things. In the Tarot, even if the Tower Hit by Lightning or the Hanged Man turns up, you are not doomed.

202 The Complete Book of Numerology

If you flip a coin to make a yes-or-no decision and don't feel pleased with the heads (or tails), why not flip again?

Or try something with some leeway in it like the *I Ching*. Have you consulted the *I Ching* by this time? It used to be more popular a generation or two ago with the hippies, but it goes back thousands of years before tie-dyes. It keeps coming back into style, like platform soles. It goes back to throwing stones or other objects and reading a fortune in the way they lay or plucking a daisy ("he loves me, he loves me not") for an answer.

I keep making reference to the *I Ching* because it can be said to be somewhat more closely related to numerological prediction than most other divinatory (fortune-telling) systems. All such systems tend to require some reading of the answers they provide to the seeker's questions, except the likes of daisy consultation.

The *I Ching* deals with numbers in that you throw down coins several times, having first formulated a clear-cut question on which you want the oracle to decide. If you get more heads than tails in a throw, write down an unbroken line, and if you get more tails than heads, write down a broken line. Each set looks something like the figures in the corner of the flag of Korea (if that helps).

Then consult the *I Ching* list. If you got (reading from the top line down, BROKEN, SOLID, SOLID, BROKEN, SOLID, SOLID, then you have Diagram #58,) and that, you will find as you consult the book (although I know operators who have all the information down pat, as do the best of the Tarot readers), comes out as Joyous Lake, Judgment, Joyousness, Success, Persistence Pays Off (or something like that). Any help? This is where intuition enters in. But in the long run, you are dealing with BROKEN, SOLID, SOLID, BROKEN, SOLID, SOLID. That's it.

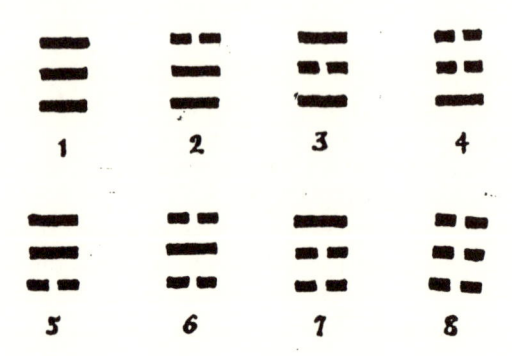

Maybe you liked the dice better. For the Changes of the *I Ching*'s more than 60 oracles you need more details than I can give here. If you want to try it, get another book. With such a book you can check your fate and with numerology you can change (say) from an 8 to a 9, alter your fate, more or less. That's encouraging. That is where the magic comes in, and magic is taking matters into your own hands and *doing something about it.*

If you have got this far and still have not got a number or numbers with which you are content, now is the time to act to improve your life or at least the way you look at it. There is more you can do. Change some numbers if you think that will make you happier.

And now we have had our little chat and go on with the rest of the book.

A German Jew (with garlic for food, a purse for money-lending and the yellow circle he was made to wear.) From Mark Zum Lamm (1544–1606)'s *Thesaurus pictuarum*.

16
Hebrew Letters

ע

I have composed this book in 21 sections, one for each letter of the Hebrew alphabet. That is so important in the occult, from the major *Arcana* of the Tarot to the very basic idea that letters are numbers and numbers are letters, the fundamental Hebrew idea. The number at the head of each section is preceded by the letter of that place in the Hebrew alphabet. I did not wish to bother you before with the information that comes now, but by this point, you may have been wondering what was up all along, and at this time, you may be interested to hear something about Hebrew letters and numbers.

An alphabet is a series of items representing sounds. The move from picture writing to connecting first pictures and then symbols to sounds was a major advance. So was our Western idea of having symbols for the vowels where the Semitic languages wrote only the consonants. One vowel can have more than one sound, as you see in *ache, man, father,* etc., and even when a letter represents one sound that can be various in the mouths of users (pronunciation, intonation, stress).

Before the invention of numerals, letters of the alphabet marked 1,

Earliest known inscription in Greek letters (from Thera).

2, 3, 4, 5, 6, 7, 8, 9. There was for a long time no zero, and the Babylonians worked on a basis of 60, not 100. Our word *alphabet* comes from the two first letters of the Greek alphabet, the Greeks having adopted the Hebrew system (beginning with *aleph* and *beth* and suiting it to the sounds of Greek, adding, as everyone who adopts alphabets does, letters to represent sounds peculiar to the language).

The letters of the Hebrew alphabet appear to have developed from pictorial writing similar to the Egyptian representations in hieroglyphics (which could represent both what is pictured and sounds) and the Chinese ideographs, which designate whole ideas or words (the sounds given may differ widely from one language or dialect to another using the same characters). Words used to be written (no spaces between them in old manuscripts), and Hebrew words are written from right to left. This, some say, is because Creation mirrors the Creator. One of the very oldest inscriptions in Latin reads from left to right. The letters were originally pictures. See G. R. Driver, *Semitic Writing from Pictograph to Alphabet* (1948).

The first letter of the Hebrew alphabet *aleph*, was originally a picture of the head of one ox. Lawrence sees in this symbol (a circle with curved horns) a representation of the uterus, but I think this is too fanciful.

The second letter of the Hebrew alphabet, *beth*, originally depicted a house. The word you may know is *bethel* (house of God). It no longer looks like that as Chinese ideograms may or may not be distinguishable: Their symbols for "one" and "man" is clear, "horse" is a bit more difficult to see, and some are hardly to be guessed.

The third letter of the Hebrew alphabet, *gimel*, was originally the neck of a camel.

The fourth letter of the Hebrew alphabet, *daleth*, looks nothing like its original, which means "door." A feminist might read *daleth* as "womb," from which life issues.

The fifth letter of the Hebrew alphabet, *he*, is of uncertain origin. I think it means "lattice window." It is somehow related to Arabic and appears in "generation," a long time of indefinite years, but the letter stands for 5.

The sixth letter of the Hebrew alphabet, *waw*, means "hook" or "peg." Once again, the original form has been changed out of recognition.

The seventh letter of the Hebrew alphabet is a 7 and seems to have something to do with "sacrifice" or "scattering." Value of 7.

The eighth letter of the Hebrew alphabet is *heth*, and it is hard to imagine what the origin was, though it relates to a guttural sound in Akkadian and in Arabic. Some say it may be "fence" or "barrier" or "boundary." Value of 8.

The ninth letter of the Hebrew alphabet has a *t* sound, but its origin is obscure. It could be "winding." It is *teth*, its value 9.

אין סוף
THE ENDLESS

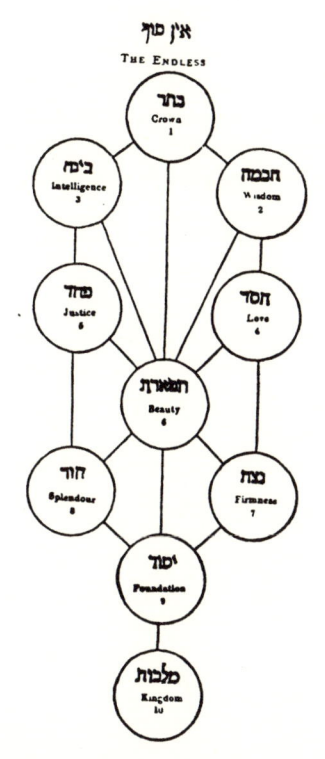

כתר
Crown
1

בינה
Intelligence
3

חכמה
Wisdom
2

גדולה
Justice
5

חסד
Love
4

תפארת
Beauty
6

הוד
Splendour
8

נצח
Firmness
7

יסוד
Foundation
9

מלכות
Kingdom
10

THE TREE OF THE HOLY KABBALAH The Hebrew letters at the top (*En Sôph*) are perhaps to be translated as "The First Cause" or "The Everlasting" and below come the 10 "emanations" from that First Cause, so that the *Karma* of cause and effect is related to the following:

1. KETHER, *i.e.* the Crown, or Supreme Emanation.
   (DA'ATH), *i.e.* the link between Wisdom and Understanding.
2. CHOCHMAH = Wisdom (theoretical).
3. BÎNÂH = Understanding (practical).
4. GEDULLAH = Greatness = Love, Mercy, Pity (Var. HESED = Mercy).
5. GEBHÛRAH = Strength (Var. PAHAD = Justice).
6. TIPHERETH = Majesty, Sovereignty, Beauty.
7. NESAKH = Conquest, Victory, Permanence.
8. HÔD = Fame, Glory, Spendour.
9. YESÔD = Foundation, Base.
10. MALKÛTH = Kingship, Kingdom.

I choose here to copy one scholar's spelling where he renders Gedullah also as Hesed; it is often found as Chesed, the male (Gebhûrah or Geborah is the female). The basic 10 "emanations," however, have not varied down the centuries.

The tenth letter of the Hebrew alphabet, *yod*, related to "hand," the symbol of perfection in the old numerology. Value of 10.

The eleventh letter of the Hebrew alphabet, *kaph*, is "hollow of the hand." In Hebrew thought, it is a 20 and as a final letter (somewhat resembling the sixth letter) the value is 500.

The twelfth letter of the Hebrew alphabet, *lamed*, means "rod" (such as would be used by a teacher to punish) and was presumably originally a goad.

The thirteenth letter of the Hebrew alphabet, *mem*, is supposed to come from "water," and its original form was intended to suggest waves. It has a value of 40 and 600.

The fourteenth letter of the Hebrew alphabet, *nun*, means "fish." Its values are 50 and 700 in the final form.

The fifteenth letter of the Hebrew alphabet, *samekh*, comes from "support" or "fulcrum." Its value is 60.

The sixteenth letter of the Hebrew alphabet, *ayin*, is "eye," which was the original form. Its value is 70.

The seventeenth letter of the Hebrew alphabet, *pe*, probably used to resemble a mouth. Its values are 80 and 800.

The eighteenth letter of the Hebrew alphabet, *tzade*, comes from "fish hook." Its values are 90 and 900.

The nineteenth letter of the Hebrew alphabet, *koph* or *qooph*, means "eye of a needle." Its value is 100.

The twentieth letter of the Hebrew alphabet, *resh*, has a name from Aramaic (the language Jesus spoke), and it means "head." One value is 200.

The twenty-first letter of the Hebrew alphabet, *shin*, does not look much like the original, which signified "tooth." One value is 300.

The twenty-second and last letter of the Hebrew alphabet, *tav* or *taw*, means "sign." One value is 400.

With these letters, ancient Hebrew wrote, counted, and performed numerology in three ways. The first has been called gematria, and it sought hidden meanings in the shapes of letters and in the numerological content of letters, words, and phrases. Words with the same numerical value could be substituted for others to conceal sacred truths. The second is called temurah and sought meaning in possible anagrams. *Ephesians* 6: 17 says "the *sword* of the spirit is the *word(s)* of God." This can, I suggest, get way out of hand when persons try to find words that add up to (say) 5 or 9 to define the characters of people whose personal numbers are 5 and 9. The third is notariqon, and it works with the initial letters of words (see what I say earlier about the *M* of *Mark*) and plays with abbreviations to seek secret meanings.

The Jews worshipping the Golden Calf. This example of Swedish folk art dresses the ancients in modern clothes, as did medieval and Renaissance artists. The idea of the *biblia pauperum* (bible of the poor) was to emphasize the modern relevance of the old stories. With numerology it is interesting to know the history but what is really important is what you can do with numerology here and now.

In Hebrew, the "secrets" of the powerful vowels (connected to the planets) were hidden: Ordinarily in writing Hebrew, one did not insert the vowels, which introduced a certain amount of guesswork when reading.

The guesswork extended into connections between words and realities (though general semantics stresses today that the map is not the territory and the word is not the thing), and the fact that letters and numbers were so connected led to reading numerologically for the secrets that The Almighty, credited with giving the writing system—the Jews might be annoyed to hear that some authorities say they got their alphabet from the Philistines!—had hidden in His gift. What the Jews called the *sephiroth* (cypher) and *elohim* (divinities) were letters, sounds, and meanings all proceeding, they said, from the Creator. Certainly they came from human reason, which few dispute is a gift from the Creator if not a natural development out of whatever (a Big Bang? I always ask what it was that exploded) started the universes. As John put it, in the old Hebrew tradition and

210 *The Complete Book of Numerology*

much influenced by Greek philosophy, "In the beginning was the Word, and the Word was with God, and the Word was God."

The word of God in the Bible has been often said to be a code. On the basis of such codes predictions are made. For instance, the great Los Angeles earthquake is supposed to come in 2010 and in 2012 a hugely destructive comet or asteroid is supposed to strike the earth.

The Torah or Five Books of Moses are written in 248 columns, said to reflect the 248 positive laws that orthodox Jews must follow (or an alleged 248 bones in the human skeleton). There are also said to be 356 things listed in The Torah that Jews should never do. Note that The Torah is written in Hebrew letters with no spaces or punctuation and that each letter has, as you know, a numerical equivalent, so it is said that if you add up the values of all the letters—a computer would come in handy here but it was attempted "by hand" even before computers came along—you might get the Sacred Name/Number of God. There is still another "code" said to be in the scriptures. Common "codes" are sought by counting every fifth or tenth letter, etc. Will you find words of prophecy? Might you get in close proximity such combinations as OSWALD/RUBY, KENNEDY/ASSASSINATED/DALLAS, R. F. KENNEDY/S. SIRHAN, or NEWTON/GRAVITY? Or is this like taking the English translation of Psalm 46 and counting 46 words from the start (SHAKE) and 46 words from the back (SPEAR) to "prove" that Shakespeare signed a translation he himself did?

The Greeks and Romans (the latter saying that *omnia in numeris sita sunt*, "everything is veiled in numbers" and *nomen est omen*, "the name is the fate") picked up the cabalistic readings of the Hebrews and gave us Western numerology as we know it today. Whether the Phoenicians, great traders who spread their alphabetical knowledge and may have been innovators, put numerological meanings on their letters, I do not know. Surely, however, from the earliest times of pictographs, there was considered to be some mysterious connection between realities and their depictions, vaguely related to the still current superstition among some peoples that a picture or photograph of a person may "steal the soul" of that person. Magic works with depictions and photographs and poppets (dolls) to cast spells on individuals to this day.

As I have said previously, despite the fact that there is a "Hebrew" system of numerological values in which the 9 is missing and the Roman alphabet is distributed according to a different system than the one with which we are familiar in English, you do not need Hebrew to do modern numerology. You need neither the ancient concept of the secrets nor any mysteries of the initiate.

You can easily learn the modern system, and it will give you what you expect from numerology. The Hebrew system may do us all some good if we stop to think that making too much of secrecy in a text inhibits the very purpose of modern writing, which is communication. Do not look for too much to be hidden, and do not hide from yourself or others what you find.

If I were you, I would pay little attention to the *Sepher Yetzirah* (Book of Formation) of the cabalists. Whether you believe in an anthropomorphic God or just a creative force, that hermetic book is right that "by the Word of the Lord were made the heavens; all the host of them by the breath of His mouth," and the metaphor is there for you to interpret as you interpret all poetry. Pay less attention still to the tradition that that book was written by Abraham. As far as I know, Abraham, revered in Jewish, Christian, and Islamic cultures, has never been established as a historic person.

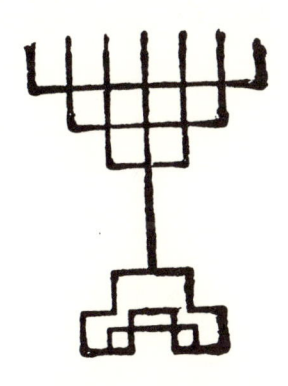

The "fish hook" that should catch you is the possible usefulness of numerology to you here and now. Open your hand to a *kaph*, receive the gift.

By this point, you have probably "done" your birth date number, the numbers of your names, your names' vowels, and your name's consonants, even perhaps other things, such as the names of friends and relatives.

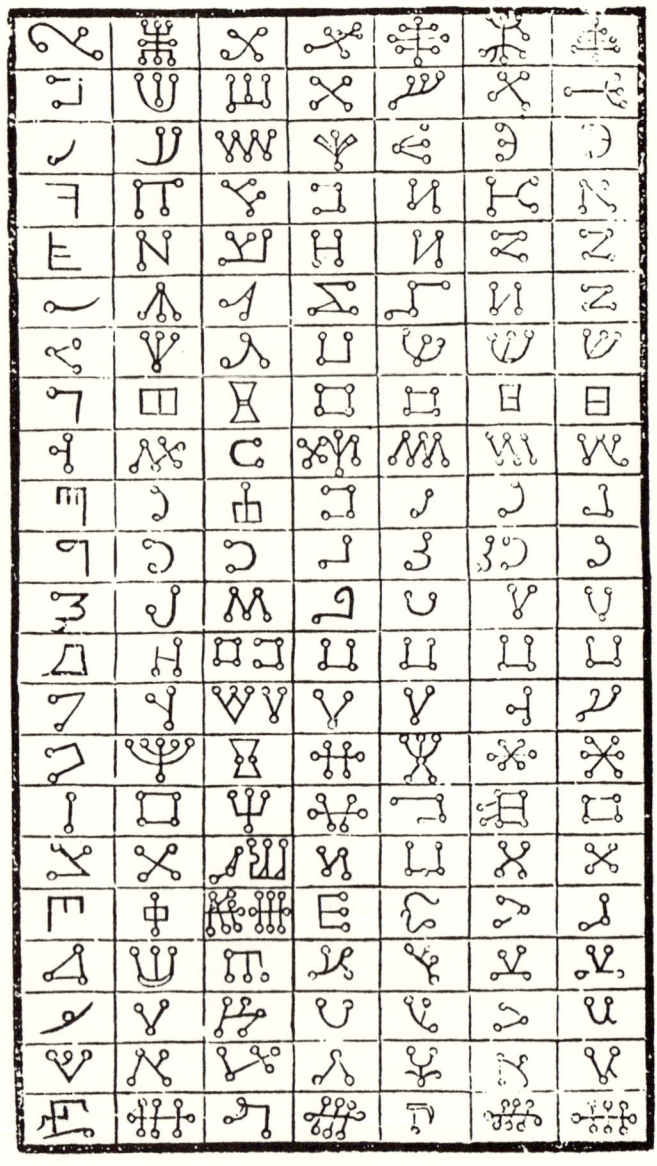

Hermetic scripts (based on Hebrew) from Bartolozzi's *Biblioteca magna rabbinica* (1675).

I suggest that at this point you see what you can do with some famous names and consider what numerology tells you about them as compared to what you have read about them in histories and biographies.

Try CHRISTOPHER COLUMBUS and CRISTOBAL COLÓN.

What is the difference between NAPOLEON BUONAPARTE (born in Corsica before the French acquired it) and the more Frenchified version: NAPOLEON BONAPARTE, which he later adopted?

Try JAMES EARL CARTER and JIMMY CARTER and JIMMY CARTER, PRESIDENT OF THE UNITED STATES.

Try BILL CLINTON and WILLIAM JEFFERSON CLINTON and WILLIAM JEFFERSON CLINTON, PRESIDENT OF THE UNITED STATES.

Try the names of some movie or music stars (and their real names, if different). Try the numerological value of a name you want to give to your new business or your country house.

Play with numerology. Do not be overwhelmed by Hebrew letters or by the extremely subjective and complex details that some numerologists writing books seem to put in to show how intuitive and even inventive, how sensitive and scholarly they are.

Always ask how reasonable they are. There can be no harm in doing that.

One of the designs Leland drew to illustrate one of his books on gypsies and with the circular caveat that you should take numerology no more and no less seriously than you would take a gypsy reading your teacup.

בָּרוּךְ אַתָּה, יְיָ אֱלֹהֵינוּ, מֶלֶךְ הָעוֹלָם, שֶׁהֶחֱיָנוּ וְקִיְּמָנוּ וְהִגִּיעָנוּ לַזְּמַן הַזֶּה.

Baruch Atah Adonai Elohenu Melech ha'olam shehecheyanu vekiyemanu vehigianu lazeman hazeh.

Blessed is the Lord our God, Ruler of the universe, for giving us life, for sustaining us, and for enabling us to reach this season.

This elaborate Turkish amulet is made up of the individual names of the Seven Sleepers and (in the center) the name of their dog.

17
Superstitions About Numbers

ב

You have heard about 13 as an unlucky number. Maybe too often. The ides of March, which the Romans feared, were usually 15 March, but could occasionally be 13 March. It is nice to know that 13 can sometimes be a fortunate number: the *Great Magical Papyrus* of Paris, fourth century A.D., tells you how to make someone love you by fashioning a poppet or figurine of them and sticking 13 pins in it, although sticking pins in such representations of a person were usually expected to bring them pain in the part in which the pin was stuck. (Those who recommend this method tell me pins with colored heads are best; they seem to like red, but a homosexual told me he uses lavender.) This is said to be better than burning candles of various colors you get in bodegas or grocery stores in poor neighborhoods.

In Sardinia, they still petition Saint Anthony to help them by lighting 13 lamps before his statue. There are many other superstitions regarding numbers, and I love to write about them, although I do not enjoy the advantage of Saint Fillan (whose right arm glowed when necessary so that he could write in the dark). With all my research and writing, I am still in the dark about the origin of some superstitions, but I find them illuminating evidence of the way our minds work, "for," as David Hume observed, "custom is the great guide to human life." I like, for instance, the old English tradition of Saint Distaff's Day (there was no such saint) on which one should "neither work nor play." It was just a day of fun before getting back to spinning wool after the Twelve Days of Christmas that you know from the carol.

216 The Complete Book of Numerology

In my books I resist repeating information I have written before but I cannot count on any reader reading all or even many of my books, and so here I commence this section with a repeat of something I do not want you to miss from the first of the series, *The Complete Book of Superstition, Prophecy, and Luck*. Translated from the Latin of the old Sarum (Salisbury) Missal, the old verses about evil days go like this:

January. Of this first month, the opening day
    And seventh like a sword will slay.

February. The fourth will bringeth down to death,
    The third will stop a strong man's breath.

March. The first the greedy glutton slays;
    The fourth cuts down the drunkard's days.

April. The tenth, and the eleventh too,
    Are ready death's fell work to do.

May. The third to slay poor man hath power;
    The seventh destroyeth in an hour.

June. The tenth a pallid visage shows;
    Nor faith nor truth the fifteenth knows.

July. The thirteenth is a fatal day;
    The tenth alike will mortals slay.

August. The first kills strong ones at a blow;
    The second lays a cohort low.

September. The third day of the month September,
    And tenth, bring evil to each member.

October. The third and tenth, with poisoned breath,
    To man are foes as foul as death.

November. The fifth bears scorpion-sting of deadly pain;
    The third is tinctured with destruction's train.

December. The seventh's a fatal day to human life;
    The tenth is with a serpent's venom rife.

L'ASTROLOGUE.

Je suis le Maître Spectateur
Du temps et de son bonheur.

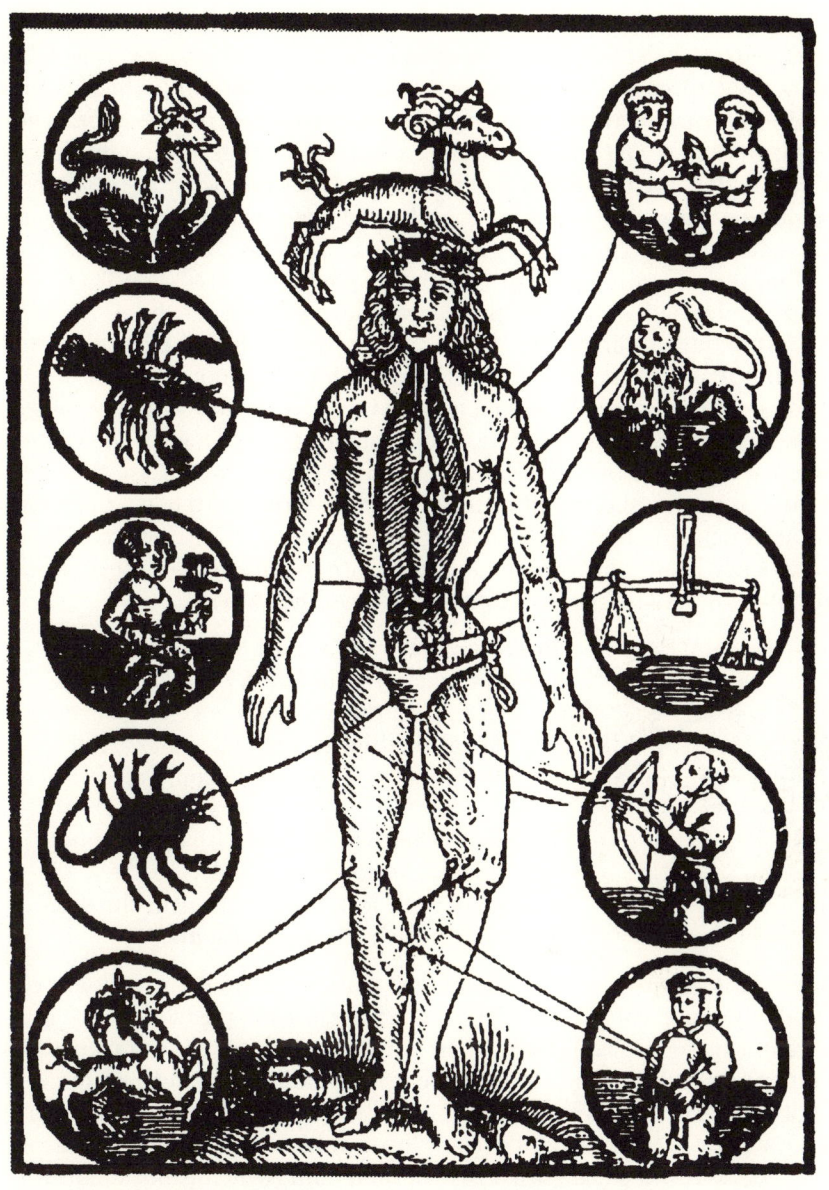

From the *Kalendarius teütsch* (Augsberg, 1512) by Johannes Müller (1436–1476), called Regiomontanus. His *Ephemerides 1475–1506* (1473) was of great use to Christopher Columbus. Regiomontanus died in Rome, to which he had been commanded by Pope Sixtus IV to assist in reforming the calendar.

Do you see any pattern in these numbers? They are presented without explanation. They are presented in verse, for mnemonic reasons: folklore knows verse makes things easier to keep in memory (which is one reason that early plays were in rhymed couplets, easier on the actor, if not the playwright). The fact is that verse often seems to lead thought, but as these couplets are translated and the numbers do not occur in the rhyme, the numbers are clearly not dictated by the need to find a rhyme. In any case, balance or rhyme leading thought is not always a bad idea. Think of the Buddhist coming up with "be at home where you are" (good) and following up immediately with "then learn to be at home nowhere" (better).

As for the warnings, two days a month may seem to be bad news for men, but women may think two bad days a month is not so awful.

There are other bad days (such as 2 October, as you will note below) and some that continue pagan customs such as May Day (in the church calendar the Feast of Saint Philip and Saint James), which are times for license. Some number significance may derive from word plays and some, like so much superstition, from mere coincidence. The best example of coincidence I can think of is in Quentin Cooper and Paul Sullivan's chockfull folklore book, *Maypoles, Martyrs & Mayhem* (1994):

> On December 5 1664, a ship foundered and sank off the coast of north Wales. Eighty-one passengers died, the only survivor being a man called **Hugh Williams**. On December 5 1785, another ship went down—60 people died and there was just one survivor, a man called Hugh Williams. When a third ship with a December 5 problem went down in this day in 1860, 25 passengers were lost, and once again the sole survivor was a Mr **Hugh Williams**.

Hugh Williams is, granted, a fairly common name, but still you can see what people would think. These are the same people who do not realize that a string of (say) heads when you toss a coin does not make heads coming up the next time either more or less likely. In an infinite number of tosses, heads and tails would be equally frequent, but each toss heads has (only) a 50/50 chance of turning up—unless someone is very sneaky and undertakes to cheat with a two-headed coin (which is not unknown).

There are mathematical tricks that some think magical, and there are more striking numbers in proverbs and even nursery rhymes (why 24? "Four-and-twenty blackbirds/Baked in a pie"?), and old expressions are always warning us to avoid x of these or y of those.

There are plenty of other numbers lucky and unlucky according to folk tradition, or religion, or superstition. Here are some of them (and once again Schimmel is studded with examples, and I can add many more):

Superstitions About Numbers 219

Day	SUN.	MON.	TUES.	WED.	THURS.	FRI.	SAT.
Governing Planet	SUN ☉	MOON ☾	MARS ♂	MERCURY ☿	JUPITER ♃	VENUS ♀	SATURN ♄
Hours							
12.00—13.00	☉	☾	♂	☿	♃	♀	♄
13.00—14.00	♀	♄	☉	☾	♂	☿	♃
14.00—15.00	☿	♃	♀	♄	☉	☾	♂
15.00—16.00	☾	♂	☿	♃	♀	♄	☉
16.00—17.00	♄	☉	☾	♂	☿	♃	♀
17.00—18.00	♃	♀	♄	☉	☾	♂	☿
18.00—19.00	♂	☿	♃	♀	♄	☉	☾
19.00—20.00	☉	☾	♂	☿	♃	♀	♄
20.00—21.00	♀	♄	☉	☾	♂	☿	♃
21.00—22.00	☿	♃	♀	♄	☉	☾	♂
22.00—23.00	☾	♂	☿	♃	♀	♄	☉
23.00—24.00	♄	☉	☾	♂	☿	♃	♀
24.00— 1.00	♃	♀	♄	☉	☾	♂	☿
1.00— 2.00	♂	☿	♃	♀	♄	☉	☾
2.00— 3.00	☉	☾	♂	☿	♃	♀	♄
3.00— 4.00	♀	♄	☉	☾	♂	☿	♃
4.00— 5.00	☿	♃	♀	♄	☉	☾	♂
5.00— 6.00	☾	♂	☿	♃	♀	♄	☉
6.00— 7.00	♄	☉	☾	♂	☿	♃	♀
7.00— 8.00	♃	♀	♄	☉	☾	♂	☿
8.00— 9.00	♂	☿	♃	♀	♄	☉	☾
9.00—10.00	☉	☾	♂	☿	♃	♀	♄
10.00—11.00	♀	♄	☉	☾	♂	☿	♃
11.00—12.00	☿	♃	♀	♄	☉	☾	♂

Magic requires that making talismans be done at appropriate times. The talisman of the Sun can be begun between noon and 1 P.M. on a Sunday and work may continue that day (engraving a disc of pure gold) between 1900 hours and 2000 hours and between 2 and 3 A.M. and 900 and 1000 hours. Amulets and talismans are frequently engraved with Hebrew letters and sometimes numbers.

1 the "mother" of all other numbers, the monad, the sign of the one true God, **becoming** one with God, husband and wife are "one flesh," the first heaven is of fire, the second heaven the *Primum Mobile* (first Motion), and so on

2 a mixture of two things is not kosher; a Jew must not pass between 2 women, pigs, or dogs, nor 2 men together pass by 2 of those; twins have special powers, duality special dangers, 2 October (the Feast of Saint Leger) planting might make the crop "light" (which is the French meaning of his name)

3 signs of the cross (marked in prayers and magical incantations with 3 Maltese crosses), making the sign of the cross with three fingers, saying the beginning of the Athanasian Creed (*Quincunque vult*) three times over a woman in labor was a medieval way of ensuring a less painful delivery, there are 3 divisions of the year (hot, cold, temperate), 3 forms of water (liquid, snow, ice—forget steam, the #-seekers ignored that traditionally), sons of Noah, 3 friends of Job, Samuel called 3 times and Peter denying Christ 3 times, Samson deceived Delilah 3 times before she discovered the secret of his strength in his hair (his faith, not cutting was a religious dictum of his sect), the triple tiara of the pope, the tripod of the oracle at Delphi, the symbol of the triangle, innumerable examples of what is done or said thrice being regarded as more magically effective, to dig herbs one should try to get them up in 3 stabs after dancing around them 3 times (and if you are going to use them in magic pick them in 3s or other odd numbers and always with the left hand if you touch them at all)—heaven, earth, hell (leave out limbo—the Roman Catholics have given it up)

Three angel trumpeters announce the Apocalypse.

4 number of the basic elements of creation, of the humours, of the seasons, of the cardinal points of the compass or the points of crosses, of the evangelists and creatures in the vision of Ezekiel, of the corners of the (flat) earth, of the horsemen of the Apocalypse, and it is the number considered powerful because 4 numbers (1, 2, 3, 4) add up to the perfect 10 of Pythagoras, 4 archangels who direct the 4 heavens (Michael, Raphael, Gabriel, Uriel), gold rings on the Ark of the Covenant

5 the quintessence, Aristotle's 5th element (ether), the Seal of Solomon, a number connected to the *E* in the alphabets of the Egyptians, Phoenicians, Greeks, Romans, and others; the 5 Ancient Ones of Confucian belief (masters of East, West, North, South, Center), there are senses and many another grouping of 5 (such as the fingers of a hand), in "*Les mois en Franche-Comté*" (the months in that department of France) in *Revue des Traditions Populaires* 14 (1889) the folklorist Beauquier speaks of the time of encouraging crops by planting crosses in the fields and reciting 5 Lord's Prayers and 5 Hail Marys (an unusual number for such prayers)

6 the female marriage number (according to *De Nuptiis philologiæ et mercurii* of Martianius Mineus Felix), and at this point I suppose we need one sample of the rap erudite specialists can get into when they warm up, so here goes the very learned Michael J. B. Allan in *Nuptial Arithmetic* (1994). His is a book entirely devoted to the commentary of Marsilio Ficino (1433–1499), the Italian Platonist, on the so-called "Fatal Number" that

The Four Horsemen of the Apocalypse. Spanish miniature from Beatus of Liebana's *Commentary on the Apocalypse*.

Plato mentions in Book VIII of his *Republic*. I must quote a bit more than convention usually permits in order to present a sensible sample. Here is a comparatively short passage (with its footnotes):

SIX is called by the Pythagoreans the "spousal number" because "in its conception a male number joins with a female" (4.41–42).[67] As 3x2 it is thus the first product of the first even number and the first odd (given the 1's unique status). However, as the first of the perfect numbers, the first to equal the sum of its factors, and as the higher of the first two purely circular numbers (as 6–36–216), it is also a symbol of divine generation and "contains the circuit itself of divine generation" (17.3–17).[68] This refers, I take it, to the six days of Creation, to the six intervals between the seven planetary spheres,[69] and to the "circuit of the firmament," that is, to the revolution of the sphere of the fixed stars above the fifth region of the planets which is in turn above the four elementary regions. Working with the Platonic order of the planets (or rather with its Porphyrian variation),[70] Ficino uses 6 to plot certain critical astronomical durations or distances in the sense of spans. Thus in six steps from the firmament we reach Venus, from Saturn we reach the Sun, and from the Moon we reach Jupiter. Since these are the three "vivific" planets, the 6 is therefore associated with propitious periods in our lives, particularly the sixth month of gestation, and, even more importantly still the sixth, the jovian, year and its multiples.[71] The 6 is the key number to be taken into account when determining the opportune time for marrying and begetting and for embarking on any kind of project, material or intellectual. Even so, the 6 pertains more to the class of the "divine" than to that of the human; for, like the divine, the 6 is neither wanting (deficient) nor overflowing (abundant) and as such it is tempered equally and consists in, in the literal Latin sense of stands firm in, its parts and powers (17.57–62). Finally, it is the key to the ratios governing the Platonic lambda, being the first of the geometric means.[72]

67. Cf. Theon, *Expositio* 2.45 (ed. Hiller, p. 102.4–6); and the *Theologumena* 43.5–9, "it is also called 'marriage' in the strict sense that it arises not by addition, as the pentad does [i.e., 5=3+2], but by multiplication" (trans. Waterfield, p. 75). In his *Timaeus* Commentary 12 (*Opera*, p. 1443.2) Ficino observes that Pythagoras had agreed with Moses "probans senarium numerum genesi nuptiisque accommodari, unde et Gamon appellat propterea quod partes suae iuxta positae ipsum gignant similemque reddant genitum genitori." Six is also the mean between the prime square numbers 4 and 9.
68. On the perfection of the hexad, see the *Theologumena* 42.19–43.3 (and, in general, 42.18–54.9), and Augustine, *City of God* 11.30, and *De Genesi ad Litteram* passim (the most authoritative for Ficino of many hexaemeral commentaries).
69. Cf. the *Theologumena* 48.10–14, 50.5–6.
70. The Porphyrian order goes: Moon, Sun, Venus, Mercury, Mars, Jupiter, Saturn, whereas the strictly Platonic order reverses the positions of Venus and Mercury. See my *Platonism*, pp. 118–119, n. 17, for further references.

Superstitions About Numbers 223

71. And we should recall the importance of the cube of 6 in determining the period between reincarnations. See Chapter 1, n. 82 above.
72. See n. 6 above. An Orphic verse familiar to Ficino from Plato's *Philebus* 66C reads, "With the sixth generation ceases the glory of my song" (ed. O. Kern, *Fragmenta Orphicorum* [Berlin, 1922], frg. 14; cf. Plutarch, *De E apud Delphos* 15 [*Moralia* 391D], and Proclus, *In Rempublicam* 2.100.23). He cites this verse in his *Philebus* Commentary 1.27, 2.2, and summa 65 (ed. Allen, pp. 257, 405, 518), in the first instance quoting the Greek and arguing that "Nature's progress stops at this, the sixth link of the golden chain introduced by Homer." In summa 65 he entertains the possibility that Plato's reference to the Orphic "sixth generation" may be to the Good Itself; for, he concludes, "Orpheus orders the hymns to end at the sixth generation, at the ineffable [Good] as it were. We see that the number 6 is celebrated by Orpheus as the end, as it was by Moses. For in the first ten numbers, this is the perfect number, being compounded from its parts disposed in order, that is from 1, 2, and 3." These comments point not only to Ficino's subtle sense of Platonic play but also, given the summa's heading which reads "Jupiter is the savior of the sixth grade or level," to his early association of Jove with 6; and this is despite the fact that in his ontology he identifies Jove with Soul (or with Soul in Mind), not with the Absolute Good that is the One. See my *Platonism*, pp. 125–128, 238–240, 244–245, 250–251, 252; and Chapter 4 below.

We should also recall that Ficino saw Plato as the sixth, and therefore as the most perfect, in the line of the six ancient theologians, the *prisci theologi*: Zoroaster, Hermes Trismegistus, Orpheus, Aglaophemus, Pythagoras, Plato. See, for example, his *Philebus* Commentary 1.17, 26 (ed. Allen, pp. 181, 247), and his *Platonic Theology* 6.1 (ed. Marcel, 1:224).

7 parts of the Mass, sacraments, 7 ages of man, 7 Pillars of Wisdom, 7 gates to the Babylonian underworld, number of Limbo (7 parts, like the 7 hills of Rome, ruled by 7 kings), 7 archangels who rule the earth (Michael, Raphael, Gabriel, Raguel, Suriel, Uriel, and Yerachmiel—following, I think, on the Babylonian idea of 7 planets and the powers that rule them and that exert influence on us), plus many other 7 beliefs that are mentioned in our Seventh Inning Stretch—Chapter 15. Also, elsewhere you read that the 7th son of a 7th son as seer, the 7th son of such a man has the powers doubled (which indeed he may need to deal with so many relatives), in rabbinical commentary we read that the Hebrew for *Samuel* is 7 in numerology and that his mother (Hannah) gave thanks that "the barren hath brought fourth the seventh," at Jericho 7 priests bore 7 trumpets 7 days, Queen Esther had 7 attendants, Naaman was to be dipped 7 times in the River Jordan, Nebuchadnezzar ate grass in his insanity 7 years, 7 champions of Christendom, 7 "against Thebes," Ahasuerus had 7 chamberlains, Joseph mourned Jacob 7 days, Hezekiah cleansed the temple by offering a sacrifice of 7 bullocks and 7 rams and 7 he-goats, in Holy Scripture there are 7 resurrections, in the *Apocalypse* 7 gold candlesticks and 7 stars, 7 lamps (7 spirits of God) and the book with 7 seals, and among a long list of 7s, here is one that looks very unusual: the U.K. Seven Whistlers (who come to warn of imminent death, like the banshee, the Grey Lady,

Talismans for the days of the week. From *Les Secrets merveilleux de la magie et cabalistique du Petit Albert* (1722).

and other folklore figures, although a single magpie, or owl, or raven, etc., may bring similar bad news), 7 gifts of the spirit (wisdom, understanding, counsel, power or fortitude, knowledge, righteousness, and fear of God—you see here a little padding to make 7, which occurs in many instances), and if you want to play some more consider what 3 + 1 + 3 (all the "male" numbers) can yield to the industrious artisan

8 parts of paradise (garden) and angels of the throne of Allah, Jewish circumcision on the 8th day after birth, the 8th day will be the end of the world (next step after the 7 days of creation), the 8 beatitudes and 8 rules for Sufis and 8-petal lotus of Buddhism and 8 precious items of Confucianism—always an auspicious number, the first cube (2x2x2), justice (Pythagorean view), and much more

9 triply divine (3x3), the symbol of the Aztec underworld, novenas, 9 rivers of the Chinese underworld, number of lives of a cat, number of compartments of a magic square going back to Ishtar (adds up to 15 every way), the number of symbols of power among the Mongols, gathering red honeysuckle (for an eyewash) Anglo-Saxons were told to forget the old pagan incantations and to substitute 9 Our Fathers and 9 Hail Marys and finish for good measure with the Creed (a lot of pagan numerology came over into Christianity), among the Celts 9 people were required before an assault could be called an attack and 9 appears elsewhere in some Celtic laws, Orgendus (king of the Danes) "cast lots every day for three days to see who should die," and 9 figures prominently in Scandinavian superstitions (many of which came there from Germany) and are 3x3, Arnold van Gennep wrote that in Savoy the christening cap was kept on the baby's head "for nine days and nights, or nine days for a boy and three days for a girl" (changing the clothes of infants at all was, like cutting their nails, considered very bad luck) "Flashpoint" and "Pastor Daniel L. Brow, PhD" edited and expanded upon "Occult Numerology and the Number 9" at www.logoresource.epages.org/nine.

10 according to Aristotle "the total of all things," embracing the entire world, basis of the decimal system (the Maya used a basis of 20), Ten Commandments, candlesticks in the Temple of the Jews, Levites in the Temple

11 Petrus Bungus declared 11 "has no connection with divine things . . . nor any merit," 11 stars make obeisance to Jacob in his dream (a 12th sign of the Zodiac always being behind the sun), the 11th (almost last) hour, the 11th sense (of balance or equilibrium), Saint Ursula and her 11,000 virgins (that being one supposes just "very many," as in *1001 Nights* or "hundreds and thousands"), one more than 10 for confused thinkers such as those who wanted in the U.S. "a more perfect" union when "more nearly perfect" is what was intended

12 the material related to the spiritual (4x3), the tribes of Israel, the apostles, the hours of the day and of the night, the signs of the Zodiac, 12 days of Christmas, 12 joys of Mary in the old English carol, and 12 is a featured number in *The Faerie Queene* and other works, the 12th *imam* of the Shi'ites, a dozen, the gross (12x12), an ancient cure for epilepsy was

> He'd found a hotel in King's Cross, opposite the station. Room 12a (between 12 and 14) was on the second floor. . . . Here my father died.
>
> —Jacob Beaver, "Diary," London Review of Books
> 3 April 2003.

to wear (fourth finger, left hand) a ring made of 12 bits of silver obtained (without telling people what you were doing) from 12 people (must be of the opposite sex), 12 gods of the Greeks, 12 spokes of the Hindu wheel

13 On a Friday the 13th the Knights Templar were suppressed by Philip le Bel of France. Thousands were arrested, 54 burned at the stake, many imprisoned for life. Before he died the Grand Master (Jacques de Molay) cursed the royal house of France

14 number of pieces into which Osiris was cut up, 14 sun letters and 14 moon letters make up the alphabet of Arabic

15 number of items in German *Mandel* (Little Moon), generations between Abraham and Solomon and between Solomon and Zedekiah, the 15 Os of Saint Bridget

16 in India "the complete human consists of 16 parts" and 16 is seen in 16 ana = 1 rupee, Rosicrucian perfection (4x4), the path to individualism

17 the Flood began on the 17th day and ended 5 months later on the 17th day, in Ireland farmers believed that the potato crop would be best if the first planting of a row was done on Saint Patrick's Day (17 March), and I think this was a pre-Christian ceremony and that the saint's day (like much of his teaching) might well have incorporated the new with the old (prayers before planting are mentioned in both pagan authors such as Virgil and in Christian tradition)

18 the Hebrew prayer *Shomoneh-Esreh* (Eighteen) speaks of 18 blessings

19 number of parts of the human body (each with its own god) in the Egyptian *Book of the Dead*.
Rashad Khalifa, author of *Number 19: A Numerical Miracle in the Koran* (1972), can serve as a fine example of someone carried away with a single number. His obsession was 19. The Koran has 114 *sutras* (chapters) , and that 114 is 6 x 19. The Koran has 6346 verses, and that is 19 x 334. The

CHAPTER II

THE INITIAL RITES AND CEREMONIES

§ 1. *Concerning the Virtues of the Planets.*

The "Key of Solomon the King" is the only Magical Ritual which regulates the operations of Magical Art in accordance with a formal attribution of certain hours in the day and night to the rule and influence of certain planets, and the Book of "True Black Magic" is the only Goetic Grimoire which follows the Clavicle closely in this as in other respects.[1] The directions given are, however, exceedingly confused. The common attribution of the seven days to the seven planets obtains in both cases, and is set out in the Grimoire as follows.[2]

Solday	= Saturn	= ♄	= Saturday.
Zedex	= Jupiter	= ♃	= Thursday.
Madime	= Mars	= ♂	= Tuesday.
Zemen	= Sol	= ☉	= Sunday.
Hogos	= Venus	= ♀	= Friday.
Cocao	= Mercury	= ☿	= Wednesday.
Zeveac	= Moon	= ☽	= Monday.

But as there is inequality in the length of the days, says the Grimoire, that is to say, the comparative dura-

[1] It should be observed, however, that favourable days and hours are occasionally mentioned, but there is no attempt at a systematic salutation of the times and seasons suitable to different operations.

[2] The apparently barbarous names given in the table are corruptions of Hebrew words, and the English editor of "The Key of Solomon" has restored their proper orthography, as follows: —Shabbathai, Tzedek, Madim, Shemesh, Nogah, Cochab, Lebanah.

145

A page on *The Key of Solomon the King* from *The Book of Black Magic.*

Koran, he tells us, has 329,156 letters, and that is 19 x 17,324. (Actually The Koran has some odd letters at the start of some chapters of which I can see no explanation at all, but I guess that is another matter. They do not add up to 19 or any multiples of 19, however.) Sometimes in The Koran the first word of something is *bism* and that occurs 19 times. The word for God (Allah) occurs 2698 times, and that is 19 x 142. The sum of all the verses that mentions Allah, Khalifa alleges, is 118,123, and that is 19 x 6217. There is much more of this kind of thing—although some critics have faulted Khalifa's arithmetic, but let that pass—but I can mention one more thing. (I won't try for 19 things.) In The Koran 30 numbers are mentioned and they add up to 162,146, and that is 19 x 6534. Now, what are we to make of all this 19 business? Perform 1 + 9 and call it 10, perfection, or go on to 1 = 0 = 1, the One Book, or what? What do we have here? Accident or design? Coincidence or mystical power, secret or nonsense? There could be 19 guesses and none of them right. What seems likely is that what we have is not science, which deals in at least *provisional* fact, something that no reasonable person would refuse to credit, at least until some better explanation comes along

20 a score, the basis of Mayan counting (in which the glyph for 20 is a human being)

21 coming of age, perfection (sacred number 3 x sacred number 7)

22 number of prayers in the *Avesta* of the Zoroastrians and the letters of the Hebrew alphabet and the major *arcana* of the Tarot (by which I distinguish the sections of this present book), 22 is the fewest number of letters (or parts of names) of which the Ineffable Name of God is made up, and Valentinus says that there are other Names of Power with 42 and 72 syllables, but does not explain why power resides in these numbers. Once a year the High Priest pronounced the Name(s) of God in the secrecy of the innermost past of the Temple while the servants of the Temple shouted to drown out the speech so no one could hear it but the Deity. Valentinus says pronouncing the Name made the earth shake

24 elders in *Revelations*

25 the sum of the magical male, odd numbers 1 + 3 + 5 + 7 + 9

30 years of the divine Christ (3) preparing to teach perfection (10) to humanity

31 paths of wisdom

32 said to be "the master number of spiritual giving," 32 is the 10 of the *sephiroth* (translate as "spheres" or "influences" or "powers" or however you think best) + the 22 letters of the Hebrew alphabet so that 32 is "perfection," the sum of all possible worlds

33 years Jesus Christ was on earth, years of the reign of the Antichrist, years it took to build the first temple, years of David's reign, number of times God is mentioned in *Genesis* I (counting not the numbers in a name or other reference, but the number of times it occurs is a neglected aspect of numerology of texts)

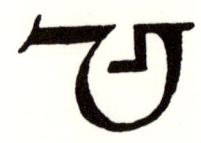

35 halfway through a human life span that the Bible promises, the Divine Pageant of Dante's *Divine Comedy* involves 35, the number of the books of the Old and New Testaments

36 thought to have some magic because it is the first quadrangular (6x6) and rectangular (9x4) number as well as the first of three successive cubes (1, 8, 27), *Horoscopi* of the Babylonians

40 a round number of some magnitude (Hebrew, possibly from the rainy season of the Babylonians and meant vaguely, not literally) meant literally—but once you say the Bible is not inerrant in every word, the problems of how to interpret what is there face you in frightening numbers, 40 is important in Orthodox rituals and beliefs, the Greek *liokra* (a Greek amulet) is made of the skin of a horned snake, washed in 40 waves of the sea, and blessed (to add Christian power to the old pagan rite) by "40 liturgies" of the Greek Orthodox Church, 40 days of Lent, 40 years' reign of David and Solomon

42 number of magical books Hermes Trismegistus (Thrice-Powerful Hermes, most likely identical with the Egyptian god Thoth) is supposed to have written

43 "the master who solves the material needs of the world" (just a spiritual 7, in my opinion)

49 Orphism's sacred number (7x7)

50 According to the parish register of Brailes (Warwickshire), a plague in 1603 is said to have killed 50 people after the bad omen of a flock of 50 ravens flew around the church steeple, 50 is a nice round, sometimes magical number in Old Irish

54 the treatises of the Muslim Brethern of Purity are 51 (17x17) because the initial letters of *Muhammad* (40), *'Ali* (70), *Salman* (50) = 170 = 17 x 10 (perfection). "But I do not understand this—and that is true for a number of such 'explanations'"

55 sum of the numbers 1 through 10, supposed to be "the number of intelligence"

60 the basic Babylonian unit, whence 60 seconds and 360 degrees

66 Nostradamus is alleged to have predicted the Great Fire of London with "twenty-three the sixes"

70 generations of mankind, length of a human life, number of the Sanhedrin, a possibly vague number meaning "a lot" as with the 70 children of Jacob and of Gideon

80 number of secondary signs of the Buddha

91 numerical values of both *amen* and *Jahweh Adonai* (Lord I Am)

99 number of the names of Allah (there is one more, but you are not to know it), which are really more virtues He has rather than names in the usual sense, more like the long lists of "names" of The Virgin in litanies, etc.

100 completion, perfection, numbers of cantos (chapters) of Dante's *Divine Comedy*, Philo Iudæus says *Sara* became *Sarra* because Greek ρ (*rho* = *r*) was 100, the equivalent of "may you live 100 years" is a nice Italian toast

120 ideal number of years in a human life (Old Testament) as a "great 100"

150 "thrice 50" figures in Irish tales of heroes such as Bran, Cuchullin, and Loeg

300 maybe a vague (lucky?) number in some Hebrew texts as when the Gideon's army is 300, 300 trumpets, 300 lamps, 300 pitchers

318 number of the name of Abraham's only named servant, Eliezer

354 days of a lunar year (which required a 13th month now and then to fit with the solar year; this was a month the Chinese called the "Lord of Distress")—bad periods exist in many cultures: August is said to be very bad in Brazil

358 numerical value of *Messiah* and of *Genesis* 14: 10's "Shiloh shall come"

365 days in the year, numerical value of the name of the god *Abraxas* from which, I think, we got the magical phrase *abracadabra*

777 Aleister Crowley has some writing with this title, but I always hesitate to recommend his work because (though there is something very good in it on occasion, and at least as often there is something dangerous to susceptible intellects) if you can understand what Crowley is truly saying, you do not need him, and if he baffles you, it can be bad for your mental health—someone once dramatically said that after you have read a great poem you will never be the same, that it inflicts a wound that never heals, so be warned that with Crowley, something of a dealer in metaphor and a brilliant if flawed man, you may be dealt a serious and permanent blow

801 Christ as "the dove" in the figuring of the Gnostics

888 Jesus (according to Tertullian, one of the Fathers of the Church)

A Table shewing the names of the Angels governing the 7 days of the week with their Sigils, Planets, Signs, &c.

Sunday	Monday	Tuesday	Wednesday	Thursday	Friday	Saturday
Michael	Gabriel	Camael	Raphael	Sachiel	Anael	Caffiel
☉ ♌	☽ ♋	♂ ♈ ♏	☿ ♊ ♍	♃ ♐ ♓	♀ ♉ ♎	♄ ♒ ♑
name of the 4th Heaven	name of the 1st Heaven	name of the Heaven	name of ...	... the 6 Heaven	name of the 3 Heaven	As Angels ruling above the 6th Heaven
Machen.	Shamain.	Machon.	Raquie.	Zebul.	Sagun.	

A specimen of the Book of Spirits to be made of virgin Vellum.

From Francis Barrett, author of *The Magus*; or, *Celestial Intelligencer* (1801). He is most notable for his watercolors of the faces of demons, allegedly drawn from life. He was a key to the English magical group that involved Bulwer-Lytton. Éliphas Lévy visited and showed them a few tricks.

998 Islam associates this (because of letter values) with the divine name *Hafiz* (Preserver)

1000 a very big round number, Anne of a Thousand Days, the first 1,000 days of a U.S. presidency, as M (from Roman numerals) symbol of Mary and of the eagle, the Irish greeting "1,000 welcomes"

1001 very many but not exactly counted: *1,001 Curious Missouri Place Names, 1,001 Nights*

7000 years of the world (though Archbishop Ussher once worked out a much lower number—and, as far as I recall, it used to be believed that the Creation began on a Wednesday morning less than 5,000 years ago, though archeology and geology have since made the learned Irish bishop and such believers look pretty silly—better (I think) to read the Bible as poetry than as history and to regard the "days" of creation as epochs (but you do as you think best) and also to be aware that while archeology, for instance, may or may not find the history in the Bible (some of it in *Numbers*, the fourth book of the Torah) accurate, science has not much to say about faith (and often does not silence argument: witness the Creationists and the Darwinians) or even superstition (which deals in cause and effect with no rational or factual relation between effect and supposed cause)

10,000 Chinese number for immortality

18,000 number of Islamic worlds

144,000 from the gospel of *John*: "And I heard of them that were sealed [elect]: and there were sealed a hundred and forty four thousand of all the tribes of the children of Israel," the number of persons in heaven (according to Saint Augustine)

432,000 years before the Flood

You can count up, if you like, numbers described (or the number of superstitions recounted) or add up all the numbers referenced and see what you can make of the result. You can speculate all you wish on why I wrote as much (or as little) as I did on the vast trove of number superstitions. I caution you not to be too ingenious in handling numbers or too credulous. Some numerologists will take a bunch of words that happen to add up numerologically to some number they wish to promote—but you can always find contradictory words that have the same numerical values. What Lawrence makes of 88 or 99 or such, I think you could easily demolish, maybe with some much ruder words, if you put your mind to it. In trying to make sense of numerology, I strongly urge you not to lose sight of common sense. The intuition and intelligence that may bring you some enlightenment from playing with numbers should warn you when you are getting ridiculous. Learn to stop when it is sensible to do so.

The Alchemist.

Some people have gone very far to try to show that certain measurements in the pyramids of Egypt predict great events of modern times, imagining a kind of Nostradamus of numbers. Martin Gardner debunks that in "The Great Pyramid," pp. 173-185 in his *In the Name of Science* (1952) but things like pyramidology have a very long half-life, however harebrained they may be.

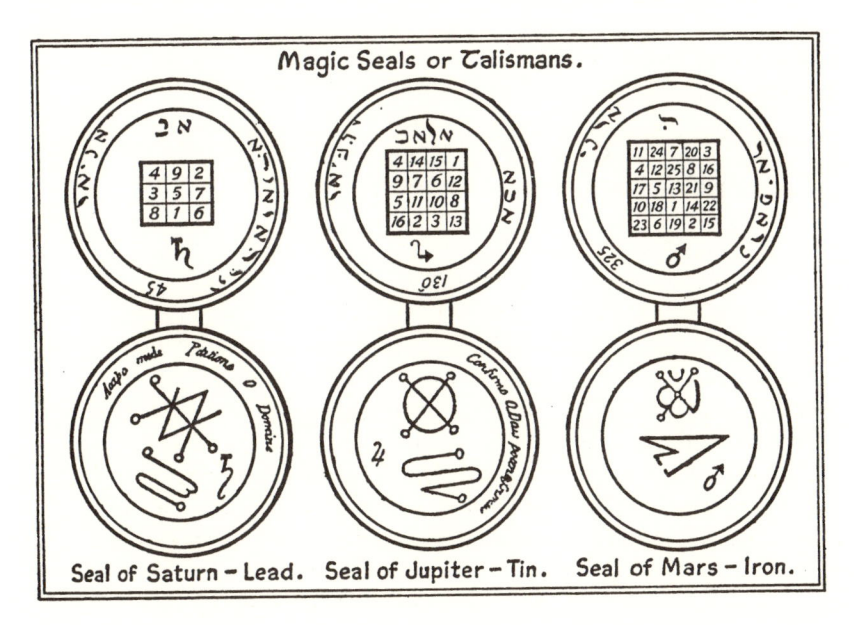

Magic Seals or Talismans.

Seal of Saturn – Lead.   Seal of Jupiter – Tin.   Seal of Mars – Iron.

I should like to mention as I stop here that the book by Schimmel (page 279) concludes:

We cannot lose ourselves in such speculations, nor can we offer any recipe for successful number magic. Humans have tried to solve the mystery of numbers for millennia, using and misusing them, and yet, the fascination remains. As the architect Le Corbusier tells us: "Behind the wall, the gods play. They play with numbers, of which the Universe is made up."

Bill Ellis' *Lucifer Ascending* (2003) was mocked by Michael Shermer, the publisher of the useful *Skeptic* magazine, who refers to "Mr. 666" and notes that Ellis' book has a subtitle of 36 letters (6x6), William Ellis has 12 letters (6x2), the Ouija board has 6 symbols in it, and Chapter 6 is about death. "Obvious, isn't it?," says Shermer.

18
"Cheiro"

In section 14 we had a brief biography of Cagliostro. In this section the focus is not so much on a fascinating life of the person but on writings of a mysterious man. He wrote under the pseudonym "Cheiro," which he called a *nom de guerre*. He was Count Louis Hamon. His right hand had what they call "a double line of head" and he remarked that he led two lives, one as "Cheiro" (whom the public knew) and one as Count Louis Hamon (in society, where he mingled with royalty and celebrities, British generals, stars such as Sarah Bernhardt and Nellie Melba, nobles and merchant princes, "Mark Twain" and a murderer). Here we concentrate on "Cheiro"'s book on numerology, a classic.

I shall be much briefer than "Cheiro" deserves because I hope to encourage the serious reader who wishes to go on in the study of numerology to read that classic text next for herself or himself. Copies are available in some libraries. The copy I read was graciously loaned to Brooklyn College Library for me by the Bartle Library of the State University of New York at Binghamton. This classic book ought to be reprinted still again; there is nothing as good in print today. Meanwhile readers still go about their business and seem in telling fortunes to rely more upon rigmarole or clever reading of the client's age and appearance, facial expressions and body language than on any traditions or principles of cheiromancy.

"Cheiro" is most famous for his work on palmistry, which is standard. We associate that science (or pseudoscience) with the gypsies. Such writers as Benham and D'Arpentigny learned their palmistry from the Romani, or Roma, as they prefer to be called, though they are not at all connected to Rome. In Italian, Roma.

Charles Godfrey Leland comes into the picture. He was really an American named Hans Breitmann, 1825–1903. After graduating from Princeton (1845) he studied abroad as wealthy Americans did in those days (Heidelberg, Munich, and Paris). Then he returned to the U.S. and was admitted to the bar in his native Philadelphia (1851). Later he went back to Europe and mingled with the gypsies in Italy and England and published four fine books on them 1873–1891. In introducing his *Gypsy Sorcery and Fortune-Telling*, he writes that gypsies "have done more than any other race or class on the face of the earth to disseminate among the multitude a belief in fortune-telling, magical and sympathetic cures, amulets and such small sorceries as now find a place in Folk-lore" [*sic*, the spelling underlining the fact that the modern science of folklore was just beginning to appear, a departure from antiquarianism, a harbinger of the very popular study of popular culture of today].

I do not know to what extent "Cheiro," whose pseudonym suggests he thought of himself as a wandering scholar, learned his secrets from the traveling people. I do not know whether he thought of himself as a student of popular culture. It is more likely he believed in ancient traditions of the people, found all over the world. He himself traveled widely, including in the U.S., and for decades he was a huge success on the lecture circuit as well as conducting private readings for a long succession of the great and near-great. "Mark Twain" had a reading and afterwards wrote in "Cheiro"'s visitors' book that he (a) didn't believe in palmistry and (b) was amazed at how well "Cheiro" had read his inner self and told him all his faults, about which he was ashamed to admit the seer was completely right.

"Cheiro" was chiefly known as a student of the hand. "Cheiro"'s palmistry appears in his *Language of the Hand*, *Book of the Hand*, *Guide to the Hand*, *Palmistry for All*, *Complete Palmistry*, etc., and translations such as *Que disent les mains*. He is the master, the basic writer, on the subject, as his many books and many reprints of those books amply testify.

Here we speak of his *Book of Numbers*. It has appeared in thirty editions or more so far and is often reprinted. One fairly recent publisher of it is called Timeless Books. It really is a book for all time.

I am going to have a look at the yellowing pages of the 1977 sixth printing of *Cheiro's Book of Numbers* from Arco Publishers, New York. As I write it costs more than $50 secondhand, and a recent (2003) edition out of India in paperback is surprisingly offered at the same high price. Much of what "Cheiro" says in this book, I, and many other writers on numerology, have already written after him, but here are just a few almost randomly selected things which he has and which neither I nor most other numerology authors have in print. I give also a general outline of the treasures you will find in the book.

"Cheiro" starts by examining history and the planetary numbers of the months and moves on to the single or "root" numbers (**1, 2, 3, 4, 5, 6, 7, 8, 9**) with examples from the lives of the famous of earlier times and his own time, the later nineteenth and early twentieth centuries. Then he addresses the compound numbers in their occult and spiritual significance, touching on the Tarot, the 52 weeks of the year and cards in the usual pack of playing cards, and more. He considers the birth number as the most important. He says this unalterable, fadic number is the easiest to find and the one most to be studied. He believes that the day and hour are more significant than the month and year but that all birth dates create something powerful that "has influence on our lives from the cradle to the grave." He gives examples of how numbers recur in our lives. He relates that Edward VII always referred to him as the seer who "would not let me live past 69" (because 6 and 9 in the king's life would be "fatal" when they joined). "Cheiro" was right. Edward VII died in his 69th year. "Cheiro" tells more of his conversations and readings with Edward VII in his book *Confessions: Memoirs of a Modern Seer*. It is astounding.

"Cheiro" has a brief chapter on "The Dread of the '13' Unfounded." He mentions 13 recurring in some cases. Then he moves on to numbers in the lives of two kings of France to comment on the book *Research into the Efficacy of Dates and Names in the Annals of Nations*. This leads him in the next chapter to periodicity in dates as illustrated in French history. He tells you how to find lucky days, how to concentrate on using your personal number as much as possible and recognizing that, for instance, a **1** is wasting time trying to dominate a **3** without considering the way to hit on that number's weaknesses. Anyone but a **4** or an **8** is well advised to know and repeatedly use his or her own number to the fullest. Those latter two persons are told to "avoid all numbers making an 8 or a 4 as much as possible, not to live in houses that have such numbers, and not to choose dates that make them." He adds "More Information About Persons Born under the Numbers 4 and 8" because out of every 100 authors of letters he received, he says, "fully eighty write testifying to the accuracy of my system of numbers, especially as regards the hard luck that appears to pursue persons who have the combination of 4 and 8 continually cropping up in their lives." He says "due probably to some law of magnetic vibration, 4 and 8 people generally attract one another," but that is not lucky. Eights seem to be "the children of fate" more than other persons, in his opinion. You 4s and 8s, listen up.

He continues on colors associated with numbers, music and numbers, disease and numbers, numbers and the best places to live. He cites, among many others, New York 1, Los Angeles 2, Moscow 3, Montreal 4, Chicago 5 (but 5s can harmonize with any other number so in their case a 5 place such as Vienna or Cork is not necessary for them), Paris 6, Hollywood 7, Bombay 8, Berlin 9. He deals in "Horse-Racing and Numbers," the numerological aspects of the names of George Washington, Abraham Lincoln, Grover Cleveland, Warren G. Harding, Theodore Roosevelt, Woodrow Wilson, Calvin Coolidge, Herbert Hoover, and Franklin Delano Roosevelt (a **22** "but not so fortunate *personally*").

His chapter on "The Bible and Numbers" every preacher should read. He is better than E. W. Bullinger (*Number in Scripture*, 2004) and other such writers on the numerology of the Bible. He detects design in The Bible on the basis of numbers that is as intriguing as it is intricate.

In his conclusion "Cheiro" states: "We feel there is Design in all things—but it is only in looking back on the past that the wonders of 'the pattern' become manifest." He finally says that in his occult studies, "I have tried to explain . . . in no matter how small a degree, to call attention to those hidden laws of life that illustrate the Divine Design. . . ."

This is the man who predicted the date of Queen Victoria's death and, as you read, that of her son, Edward VII. This is the man who warned well in advance of the "grim destiny" of Czar Nicholas II, of the assassination of King Umberto of Italy, and twenty-two years before the event he told Lord Kitchener the year of his death and that it would not be the sort of death a soldier might expect but would involve water. Kitchener died with the sinking of HMS *Hampshire* when Kitchener was sixty-five, just as "Cheiro" had foretold.

It is only fair to point out that while "Cheiro" is the modern master of the tradition there are those who depart from his teachings. One I choose to mention more because he is so articulate rather than so followed is John King. King is the author of *The Modern Numerology* (1996). That book declares that "[t]he venerable and ancient science of numerology has often received bad press—mostly well deserved" and that the use of the English alphabet of 26 letters and the digit-simplification system is all wrong, "hooey." If you have read thus far in my book you probably will not agree with his dismissing out of hand the system we have been examining. However, you may be curious as to what he proposes to replace it with and you may even wish to seek out *The Modern Numerology* and struggle through King's search in mathematical oddities for special meaning in The Tarot (such as 19 for "strength" and 30 for "sun"), the so-called "weird numbers" (70, 836, 4030, 5830, and 7192), and the numbers assigned to great persons of history (such as 259 for Hitler, 677 for Shakespeare, and 1480 for Christ). My personal feeling is that King's work partakes too much of mathematical manipulations and coincidences such as that which in the King James Version of The Bible presents a translation of Psalm 46. I say often that in that psalm, when you count 46 words from the start and 46 words from the end, you get the elements of the name *Shakespeare*. People are always looking for coded messages in the works of The Bard. One of those who famously did that happened to be named Looney. Looking for codes in Elizabethan literature, as if the text were nothing more than a cover for secret messages, is, I think, to use the surname of one of the nineteenth-century persons who tried is not to bring home the Bacon.

I suggest you stick with the English alphabet and the system that makes (say) 1978 into $1 + 9 + 7 + 8 = 25 = 2 + 5 = 7$, and that puts "Cheiro" centrally in modern numerology. From our point of view, "Cheiro" is of compelling interest not as a prognosticator nor as a palmist but as a numerologist of fifty years' experience in the occult who was able to cram his immense expertise into a small book and make it readable in the "language understood by the people" because "the truth contained in this study appeals to all classes and conditions of people."

The clear-cut system of "Cheiro" comprises and culminates the long tradition of Pythagoras. To Pythagoras, Bertrand Russell, towering mathematician and philosopher, opined (as King reminds us) that we owe our "whole conception of an eternal world, revealed to the intellect but not the senses," a world that without the ancient Greek genius "Christians would not have thought of Christ as the Word."

It is worth noting that "Cheiro" dealt with persons whose hands he personally read. It was not a matter of constructing horoscopes of the famous dead whose careers were well documented and on which astrology could play an "I told you so" game. The casting of horoscopes for important individuals of the past has long gone on, hoping thereby to build confidence in astrology for use among the living. It goes on today. There have been astrologers who worked out the horoscopes of people they never met, such as Louis XVI, Napoleon, and Jesus Christ. The horoscopes of Jesus Christ usually take the year AD 0 as the date of his birth, which has been determined by experts to be several years off the mark. People say that His birthday was 25 December. The fact is that the early church chose 25 December because it was the traditional date for the Roman orgy holiday of the Saturnalia. A birth date in December seems highly unlikely, according to Christian scriptures. At that time of the year the shepherds were not "abiding in the fields" because it was too cold. The exact date of the birth of Jesus Christ is of far less interest, to me, than what He was. In my view, the current debates about whether He survived the Crucifixion or not are nothing compared to what He was and is to mankind, whether you happen to hail Him as a savior or simply rank him as a mere mortal who has had unequaled influence over the last two millennia.

Of course everyone wants to know or should want to know the truth about Jesus Christ. There is an abiding interest in that. Palmistry and astrology and reading fortunes in the lines and bumps of the hand all give indisputable evidence of—if of nothing else—the abiding interest of human beings to know the secrets of their own characters and what the fates hold in store for them. These fates were represented by three women who spun, made a thread, and cut it, the thread representing human life. They can be related to the three Weird Sisters of Shakespeare's *Macbeth*. Weird is the right word here.

In modern times, we are discovering more and more about how genes control our personal characteristics and the length, barring accident, of our individual lives. So far no connection has been made by science between genes and the marks on an individual's hands. Scientists have determined that a small part of the brain is a bit larger in homosexuals than in heterosexuals and experts speak of genes which may explain alcoholism, among other differences with which people are born.

Careful astrologers always recognize that there are important differences between people, even those born in the same place at exactly the same time, and careful astrologers state that the planetary configurations and stellar constellations under which we are born and live impel but do not compel. Astrology even suggests that by knowing what is on the way—forewarned is forearmed—we can avoid problems, but of course if fate is set there is nothing to be done along those lines. "We live and learn" in that case means we find out what happens to us, pre-ordained, as we go along. There are some people who think salvation or damnation is preset. There are some people who say of the stories of our lives that "it is written," we blindly play a script.

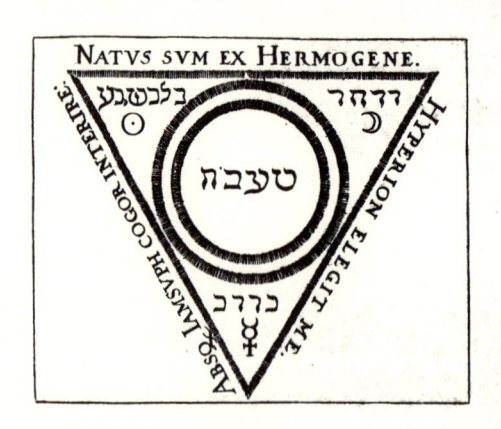

Those who read hands undertake to read possibilities or even a script. These observers start with the left hand as the "subjective" one, paying special attention to the basic character as indicated by the shape of and lines of the thumb. They usually have some connection to astrology—the bumps or mounts on the hands have been given the names of planets, such as the Mount of Jupiter and the Mount of Luna (Moon), though there is the non-planetary mount of Apollo, and there is a ring of Saturn, a ring of Venus. Palmists are most attracted to the idea of a script from which

"Whatever happens make the best of the future." Hie[ronymus] Car[denus] = Jerome Cardan (1501–1576), author of more than 100 books on mathematics and physics, medicine and natural history, dialectics and rhetoric, history and music, and astronomy and astrology.

derivation is impossible, a book of what will happen rather than what might happen in our universe or even in parallel universes.

As for the question of whether the Greek gods are real and have or ever have had any influence on human life other than mere superstition granted to them, you probably are as atheist as was Anaxagoras. Long before Christ, Anaxagoras (who lived from about 500 to about 428 B.C.) scanned the skies—he was the first to discuss eclipses—and he witnessed a devastating meteorite which struck Greece from which he concluded that the Greek divinities did not exist (rather than that they were not always on the side of the Greeks). Nonetheless he did believe in a *nous* or divine power that created and controls everything, causing all changes that occur in nature, which includes you and me.

Today the gods and goddesses of Greece survive only in such names as we find on some of our months, and on our hands, among other things. As with much else in the occult, we tend to deal in poetic ways of discussing practical things of a complexity beyond our understanding.

Palmists offer an explanation of all aspects of hands, even the so-called rings at your wrist (which perhaps might better be referred to as bracelets), saying that *this* means *that* without ever explaining how they know. Is it by experience? Is it by intuition? Is it blink, by revelation? They do not bother to say. As always in the true occult, we have assertion rather than proof. We are told that big hands mean, counter-intuitively, that one will be better at detail than people with small hands. We are told that certain lines can tell us of our love life. Other lines and signs are said to show future health or illness, even the very dates on which important events will occur in our lives. We are told many things. Never do we get to hear how so. Exactly *why* does a conch-like birthmark on the palm indicate that a baby is the reincarnation of the Dalai Lama?

Sticking your pinkie out when you hold a cup is supposed to be a sign not of delicacy but of showing off. That could be learned or unlearned. The size of your hands is inherited; extending fingers is learned and can be altered. Ill health can cause the nails to be ridged, but how can we connect the shape of nails to artistic or inartistic temperaments?

In palmistry the right hand is regarded as full of life information. The right hand is supposed to give knowledge of how far the script written on the left hand is followed by the subject. Now, you certainly want to know that, right? As we go through life, lines on the hand may change. Repeated clenching of the hands may alter lines running across them, for example, or gaining weight, or severe illness, may cause some lines to disappear. Are they "still there" anyway? Keep a close eye on your lifeline. Is it getting longer or shorter? How far along it are you now? Does it have "islands" or hatchings or crosses on it, and do these mark times of special problems of health? Does the lifeline run deep or shallow, and how does it end? Is there a bifurcation near the end? Could some choice at that point change your time limit here on earth? What does it mean when someone with a long, firm lifeline gets killed young in an automobile crash or a war? Is there some force working against the designer's plan for you? Try to be imperturbable. (This is easy if your Saturn is connected to the upper part of your Mars.)

The followers of the ancient art or science of palmistry, like the followers of numerology to a somewhat lesser extent, continue with old prejudices. One says that if a line descends from your line of heart to your line of head it marks the occasion on which you, having contemplated marriage, think better of it and call the whole thing off. Tell the partner you break off with, "It's not you, it's fate." Maybe you have a chain-like Via Lascivia (Way of Lust) and are not suited for settling down with one sex partner, or perhaps you discover that the potential spouse has an "island" or "islands" on the Line of Affection, indicating a proclivity for infidelity. Turning to numbers, maybe her or his name adds up to the wrong number for you or numerology otherwise informs you that your fate with that person would be unfortunate. We can graze the buffet of occult systems, including numerology, and we can put together our own idea of what they may all together say about our fates.

The followers of Islam have that interesting expression regarding our fates: "It is written." Whether it is written on our hands for the talented to read is a question open to debate, as is all of numerology.

As for telling the future, I don't know. You will presumably have to be content to voyage to the past if and when physicists figure out a way to use what they call wormholes, and even then you will have to be content to wind up back at some date determined by where the wormhole terminates. At this point in time, many physicists think that the firewall of what used to be called "chronology protection" may be breached and that some day—don't ask me, indeed right now don't ask anyone, when—humanity may be able to time-travel back in history. Meanwhile, if you want to time-travel forward you may wish to play with prognosticators and believe that your future is in your own hands. Or your numbers.

Oswald Croll's title page to his *Basilica chymica oder alchymistisch königlich Kleynod* published at Frankfurt-am-Main in 1629 shows leading occultists.

19
Publications on Numerology

ק

Dr. Samuel Johnson, who compiled the great English dictionary in the eighteenth century, said that a man would turn over half a library (some say a whole library) to write one book. *Ecclesiastes* says that of the making of books, there is no end. I keep quoting those words—in the books I keep on writing.

Here is still another book. This book was written only after an examination of a great many of the books on numerology now in print were examined to determine that, indeed, a new, better book was needed, as my preface said. My late friend "Monty" urged me to look into this matter and I found he was right: There ought to be a better book, in several aspects, and I hope this book of mine fills the bill. My book offers to be a considerable improvement over the hundreds of such books now in print, as well as drawing on and surpassing a lot of older books. It is not satirical, like my recent *Art Attack: Essays in Satire*, although Jonathan Swift did wonders with his cute and cutting *Predictions for the Year 1708* (as by "Isaac Bickerstaff, Esq., Written to Prevent the People of England from Being Imposed upon by Vulgar Almanac Makers") and *The Wonder of all the Wonders that Ever the World Wondered At* (1722, demolishing astrologers). This book is direct, short, and sensible. It is my first and only book on numerology with no recycled material such as one is apt to find in Lisa Robin (*The Little Big Book of Numerology*, 1998 and *All about Numerology*, 2001) or Dusty (*Numerology and Your Future*, 1980 and with Victoria Knowles, *Birthday Numerology*, 1982 and earlier with Faith Javane

Numerology: The Divine Triangle, 1978), not to mention Sonia Ducie (*Do It Yourself Numerology*, 1998, *The Complete Illustrated Guide to Numerology*, 1999, and *Numerology*, 2001, etc.).

In my series on the occult I do not mean to make light of any other author's industry or anyone's beliefs. Still I am sure I will get carping critics who say they have heard a lot of this stuff before (hey, not making this up, you know!), and so far in my occult series, I have not outraged Catholics, Protestants, or Jews, but have not been able to avoid (say) the eight-page screed from someone who says he is not a Satanist but is furious because I was not as polite as he thought I ought to be to the Church of Satan. Worse, I (not deliberately, errors do occur no matter how well we edit or proofread) misspelled the middle name of Mr. LaVey of San Francisco and former leader of that group. One gothic group thought my style was too flip for serious matters. Fortunately, thousands like it. To write at all on these subjects is to challenge opprobrium from a few. Either you take the matter too seriously or you do not, and either way you may prompt angry reactions. I just stick a pin or a *mot* in a critic doll and move on, trying to do my best.

In other books I find that the basics are sometimes mangled, and often the subject of numerology is combined (or confused) with books on various kinds of divination, astrology, the Tarot, the Kabbalah, the *I Ching*, and so on. Those are separate entities, which even in this book concentrating on numerology, I have often not been able to escape taking into some account. I particularly regret astrology. I realize that the planets have influence on us (ask any woman any month), but, as I told you, I do not know *why* (for instance, as I write this sentence) Jupiter coming back into prominence—it has been retrograde in my sign for far too long—means that I need to do some mental housecleaning or watch out for people who whine. Won't someone at least try to explain how astrology works if they really think it does? And do a better job of connecting it up to date with fortune-telling (compare Sydney Omar on *Thought Dial*, 1972), the Tantra, the Tarot, and so on?

2	7	6
9	5	1
4	3	8

On the oldest of the great Chinese classics, I can recommend Thomas Cleary's translation of Chi-hsiu Oui's brilliant textbook, *The Buddhist I Ching* (1987). Alfred Huang has a nice recent book on *The Numerology of the I Ching* (2000), so I need not tackle that topic. For those who want one of the lite approaches, how about Roderic and Amy Max Sorrell's *The I Ching Made*

Easy (1994)? It was picked up by HarperCollins after having been published, as most similar works are, by a small press. I could recommend a long list of other sources, because from Arnold Schoenberg the composer (see Colin C. Stern, *c.* 1993) to Paul Maslow the psychologist on intuition (*Intuition Versus Intellect*, 1957) there is much of related interest.

Newspaper and periodical indexes in any library can lead the researcher into numerology material, and do not forget magazines (see "The Number Game," *Skeptic* 8:2, 2000, 101, and so on).

Numerology these days is not the subject of as many books as astrology or other fortune-telling methods. Cagliostro is pretty much forgotten, and Nostradamus is all over the place. I predict that the remainder tables of bookstores will be seeing Nostradamus for the rest of our lifetimes. I cannot say to the Day of Doom because, according to Nostradamus, that has already come and gone. I must have been out of town and did not get the word.

Numerology is, however, still around as science or superstition. Books tout it as a way to understand oneself or others, as a key to the cosmos, as a guide to choosing sex partners or how to succeed in business without really trying, and so on. Huge claims are made for it. Authorities are seldom quoted: Each book tends to pretend that it is the first and only way to approach "the science of numbers," and some authors, many of whom think to sell best if in the so-called nonfiction field, one must offer something a little sensational or innovative, promise to reveal "the secrets" of numbers for the very first time. Secrets are big now even in fiction. Have you heard of *The DaVinci Code*? Although vast publishing success has recently greeted books designed for "dummies" or even "complete idiots," among writers on the occult a few make matters so complicated that they leave you with the sneaking feeling that either you are dimwitted or they are insane. This can work, if only among the truly stupid. "He must be terrifically brilliant because I didn't understand a word."

As for general content and to evaluate how little has basically changed in writing about numerology, take a look at C. Hogenraad's *Names and Numbers* (1910) and compare it with "Numéro"'s *The Power of Numbers* (*c.* 1936) and then with *Numerology: The Romance in Your Name* (1979) by that grand old lady of numerology, the late Juno Jordan (who missed living to 100 by a very short time). Note also that "professional" psychics and astrologers write a lot of books, but "professional" numerologists do not. Most new books are by other ladies not nearly so talented. Indeed, we do not need a pretended "professional" to do numerology for us. We just need someone to interest us in the subject and tell us straightforwardly how to do numerology ourselves.

To accomplish that a writer does not have to tell you everything. Some authors promise you everything you always wanted to know but were afraid

248 *The Complete Book of Numerology*

to ask and then, despite that *complete* business, recycle their notes to produce book after book on the subject. No book can be complete.

On a personal note: One of the figures in the small but intense world of would-be vampirologists I mentioned without what he considered sufficient respect in *The Complete Book of Vampires*. Subsequently, in a journal I was renounced as a "self-styled occultist" and my book as "incomplete" (although nobody bothered to detail what had been left out). Take, if you will, both *complete* and *numerology* in the title here with grains of salt. Take it to mean that the author is going to give you all he thinks you need to know, not all that could be said. Be reasonable. The main things are: Did you enjoy reading this book and does it give you what you were looking for? Do you think the author knows whereof he speaks? You do not have to agree with any expert. I don't.

Not one of the many authors of works on numerology today, however much they have written, can actually claim to be experts the way some of us writing about vampires or demonology may claim. One writer on numerology, "Anna Riva," for instance, has dabbled in so many aspects of the occult that her little books, actually pamphlets, can be said to add up to some kind of library. I myself have published so extensively in so many aspects of the occult field that I, too, can stake some claim to authority as the author of a virtual encyclopedia of the occult in many volumes. I do not self-style the way some bishops and archbishops of non-mainline churches have done (as if episcopacy and erudition went together these days), and I do not set myself up as a practitioner of magic and witchcraft or as a psychic or "reader." I have published, unlike "Anna Riva," real books, not pamphlets, and I have published all over the occult field, unlike the vampirologists or the ceremonial magicians or the Wiccans or the Satanists. "Self-styled occultist"?

50	10	400	40
40	50	10	400
400	40	50	10
10	400	40	50

The true test of any author is not specialization but what you as the reader get that is useful to you from some specific publication. It is up to you readers to judge us writers and to say if the information we give you is adequate for your purposes, and readable, or not. The likes of Ballantine Books' *The Hidden Truth of Your Name: A Complete Guide to First Names and What They Say about You* (1999), I can tell you as a name expert of long standing and author of books on names of all sorts, is *not* complete. One has to be a fool to expect otherwise.

The name field or the numerology field tries to gain readers of all sorts and conditions, fools and wise men (and women). There have been numerology annuals, lucky-number books, books on numbers in dreams and their interpretations, books promising to map out your destiny, all sorts of claims. Books on numerology in the Scriptures continue (witness R. D.

Johnston's *The Arithmetic of Heaven; or, Scripture Numbers: Their Spiritual Significances* and the like), but most numerology books of the latest generation belong to the fad for personal improvement in life and love. Almost every author promises to make the secret known, the complicated simple, and the results sure. History and theory of numerology as opposed to workbooks are hard to come by.

I do not intend, as I have said before, to contribute lengthy bibliographies to this book, but I must offer a sampling. Here are quite a few samples. I do not list similar books in languages other than English, though those are plentiful. The books I do list are seldom from leading publishers in the U.S. and the U.K.; most come from small presses. Small or niche publishers more often than not offer a number of undistinguished and indistinguishable books on the topic, although in publishing, big is not always better, and some niche publishers certainly know their job and give excellent value for the money. The only problem with books from niche publishers is that they tend to exclude the non-believers. Difficult as it is to do so, I think one must speak to everyone at once. I try that.

I list one book per author; some have written more than one. Here we go, starting with a Madame Arcati (in case you are a fan of Sir Noël Coward):

❊

Krystyna Arcati, *Numerology* (1999)
Margaret Arnold, *Love Numbers: How to Use Numerology to Make Love Count* (1998)
Leonard R. N. Ashley, *What's in a Name?* (1989, revised edition 1995)
Kevin Quinn Avery, *The Numbers of Life* (revised, 1977)
Geri Bauer, *Numerology for Beginners* (2000)
Robert M. Baer, *The Digital Villain: Notes on the Numerology, Parapsychology, and Metaphysics of the Computer* (1972)
Rodford Barratt, *The Elements of Numerology* (1994)
Colin Baker, *Numerology* (2003)
Clifford W. Cheasley, *Numerology at a Glance* (1996)
William Colville, *The Kabalistic Significance of Numbers* (1997)
D. Jason Cooper, *Understanding Numerology: The Power to Know* (1990)
S. Crawford & G. Sullivan, *The Power of Birthdays. . . .* (1998)
Richard Craze, *Numerology Decoder* (2001)
Hans Decoz, *Numerology* (2001)
Sylvia DiPietro, *Live Your Life by the Numbers* (1991)
Doris C. Doane, Blending Numerology, Astrology and Tarot (1997)

900	10	80	8
7	81	9	901
12	902	6	78
79	5	903	11

Ruth A. Drayer, *Numerology: The Power in Numbers* (2001)
Underwood Dudley, *Numerology, or What Pythagoras Wrought* (c. 1997)
Julie Gale, *Soul Numerology* (1999)
Stephen Gibbs, *Kabalistic Numerology* (1993)
Walter B. Gibson, *The Science of Numerology* (1995)
Maurice Goodman, *Modern Numerology* (1978)
Uma & Marlow Gray, *Numerology for Newlyweds* (vol. 1, 1997)
Louise L. Hay, *Colors and Numbers* (2003)
Corinne Heline, *The Sacred Science of Numbers* (2003)
Holly Johnson, *The Hidden Truth of Your Name* (1999)
Juno Jordan, *Your Right Action Numbers* (2003)
Linda Joyce, *The Day You Were Born* (1997)
Joyce and Jack Keller, *The Complete Book of Numerology* (2001)
John Robert King, *The Modern Numerology* (1996)
Dawne Kovan, *Secrets of Numerology* (2001)
Kay Lagerquist & Lisa Lenard-Cook, *The Complete Idiot's Guide to Numerology 2* (2004)
Shirley Blackwell Lawrence, *Behind Numerology: Complete Details on the Hidden Meanings of Letters and Numbers* (1989)
Alana Lotharius, *Numerology* (1992)
Malcolm Madison, *Numerology* (1985)
Glynis Kathleen McCants, et al., *Glynis Has Your Number* (1997)
Rose Murray, *Astro-Numerology* (astrology and numerology) (1991)
W. Mykian, *Numerology Made Easy* (1979)
Derrick Niederman, *What the Numbers Say* (2004)
Alan Oken, *Numerology Demystified* (2001)
George Oliver, *The Pythagorean Triangle, or The Science of Numbers* (1984)
Susan Osborn, *What's in a Name?* (1999)
Alex Owen, *The Place of Enchantment* (2004)
Lynne Palmer, *Your Lucky Days and Numbers* (1998)
Steven Scott Pither, *The Complete Book of Numbers* (2002)
Anna Riva, *Your Lucky Number Forever* (1993)
Paul Rodrigo, *The Numerology Workbook* (1996)
Michael Rowan-Robinson, *The Nine Numbers of the Cosmos* (1999)
Greg Russell, *Numerology* (1998)
Atul Seghal, *The Secrets of Numerology* (1998)
Damian Sharp, *Simple Numerology* (2001)
Norman Shine, *Numerology: Your Character and Fortune* (1994)
Jean Simpson, *Hot Numbers* (2002)
S. C. Singh, *Let the Numbers Guide You* (2004)
Sandra Kovacs Stein, el al., *Instant Numerology* (1986)
Leeya Brooke Thompson, *Basic Chaldean Numerology: An Ancient Map for Modern Times* (1999)

Roy P. Walton, *Names, Dates and Numbers* (1996)
Richard Webster, *Chinese Numerology* (1999)
W. Westcott, *Occult Powers of Numbers* (1999)
Hazel Whitaker, *Numerology: A Mystical Magical Guide* (1998)
Hazel Wilson, *A Guide to Cosmic Numbers* (1982)

❋

There are many others, old and new. With so many (most of what I list above are in print), why still another, why mine? I hope that if you compare it to other both general and specialized books, you will see the reason and use of mine. If nothing else, this list makes a point: There is always room for one more on the topic!

6	32	3	34	35	1
7	11	27	28	8	30
19	14	16	15	23	24
18	20	22	21	17	13
25	29	10	9	26	12
36	5	33	4	2	31

The bibliographies on the Internet these days make it possible to identify the whole picture. The writers of books on numerology, I am glad to say, usually give their works good titles by which to locate them, not the allusive, zany ones too often encountered in the field of the occult where, for example, a book on the Talmud is titled *The Bones of Joseph* and a fradulent *grimoire* is the *Necronomicon*.

Numerology occurs naturally in the great encyclopedists of the occult such as J.-A.-S. Collin de Plancy (*Dictionnaire des sciences occultes*, 1846–1848) and M.-C. Poinsot (*Encyclopédie des sciences occultes*, 1925) and in little curiosities such as B. Portier's *Le Carré diabolique de 9* (The Magic Square of 9) published in Algiers in 1902. On French occultism, which is the only non-English-language aspect that I bother with very much in this present book due to restrictions of size (among other reasons, of course), the big names besides Collin de Plancy and Guillot de Givry are "Paul Christian" (dealt with in the text here) and "Papus" (G.-A.-V. Encausse, 1865–1916). There are also L. de Gérin-Ricard (excellent for *sectes occultes* in Cagliostro's era), P. Geyraud on *L'Occultisme à Paris*, and, above all "Éliphas Lévy," author of (among other books) *Philosophie occulte* (two volumes, 1865) and many posthumous productions such as *Le Science des esprits* (1894), *Les Livres des splendeurs* (1894), *Le Clef des grands mystères* (1897), and *Le Livre des sages* (1911).

The tradition of popularizers and enthusiasts continues. None of the recent writers is likely to challenge the long runs of such as "Cheiro" (1898), Westcott (1890), Kozminsky (1912), or even "Sephariel" (W. G. Old, 1913). Some writers from a slightly later time (such as Leonard Bosman of *The Meaning and Philosophy of Numbers*, first published 1932, republished 1974) have been given new life in reprints. F. G. Lieb's *Sight Unseen: A Journal-*

252 The Complete Book of Numerology

The Misterious Characters of Letters deliverd by Honorious call'd the Theban Alphabet.

A B C D E F G H I K L M
N O P Q R S T V X Y Z

The Characters of Celestial Writing

Lamed Caph Jod Theth Cheth Zain Vau He Daleth Gimel Beth Aleph

Tau Shin Res Kuff Zade Pe Ain Samech Nun Mem

The Writing call'd Malachim

Caph Jod Theth Cheth Zain Vau He Daleth Gimel Beth Aleph

Pesh Kuff Zade Pe Ain Samech Samech Schin Tau Nun Mem Lamed

The Writing call'd Passing the River

Lamed Caph Jod Theth Cheth Zain Vau He Daleth Gimel Beth Aleph

Tau Schin Resh Kuff Zade Pe Ain Samech Nun Mem

ist *Visits the Occult* (1939) was fun in its day, and J. Fletcher's *The Symbolism of the Divine Comedy* (Columbia) is the sort of university press book that scholars keep writing over and over (like *Shakespeare's Women, Women in Shakespeare, Gender & Genre in Shakespeare*, etc.). Old books on numerology still consulted include E. C. Wilson's *You and the Universe* (1922), J. A. Coe's *Numerology* (1924), A. S. Raleigh's *The Hermetic Science of Motion and Number* (1924), A. Y. Taylor's *Numerology Made Plain* (1925), K. Adams's *Numerology Up-to-Date* (1925), C. C. Stewart's *Bulwer-Lytton as Occultist* (1927), W. Gibson's *The Science of Numerology* (1927). As World War I gave a boost to mediumship, so, after World War I, in the twenties, numerology had something of a vogue. Then it settled down to a quieter, steady pace.

Publications on Numerology

No one's book on the topic did nearly so well as "Cheiro"'s, probably because his book on palmistry was and remains standard and maybe even more because his predictions were astoundingly accurate. He predicted a decade before Mrs. Wallis Simpson appeared on the world stage that the Prince of Wales once he became King would give up his throne for the love of a woman. This was even more right on the money than Pearce's horoscope of George V, the father of Edward VIII and the younger brother who succeeded him as George VI. Celebrity clients always inspire confidence, and the prediction of newsworthy events is regarded as more significant than the foretelling of unimportant ones in the lives of ordinary people.

I must say just a little note about the literature of numerology but about the numerology in literature. So that will be the content of the next section, and after that, my work is done. You will have the numerically powerful 21 sections I intended from the start, all the matter that I can readably put into a book of reasonable size and price. I trust that numerology will do well in the market. If the (admittedly fiddled) bestseller lists of the *New York Times* are any guide, numerology has many of the things that most readers want. Those seem to be works on (a) self-improvement, (b) advice for the lovelorn and love-torn, (c) colorful characters of doubtful morality, and (d) general guides on how to make the most of your life, whether the advice comes from some human starlet or even Miss Piggy. I hope my book on numbers will be read by large numbers! However, you have to be careful of your oracles. "I see large numbers for your book!" Fine, but large numbers sold or (like most books these days) large numbers returned unsold by the booksellers? Well, it has the right number of sections and the right number of pages, not counting the index, which I did not make, but I don't think the extras could cause much numerological trouble.

254 The Complete Book of Numerology

Numerology has been around for thousands of years, and so it is no surprise that it has entered in classical literature, into medieval literature to a great extent (as in *Sir Gawain and the Green Knight* and famous works of Hrabanus Maurus, Boccaccio, Chaucer, Dante, and the tractates of Cataluña discussed by John Scott Lucas in *Corónia* 31:1, 2002, 55-67), into Shakespeare's *The Tempest* and other dramas of his superstitious age, into the poetry of Edmund Spenser (see Shohachi Fukuda, pp. 37-63 in *Spenser Studies* 19, 2004) and John Donne (Kate Gartner Frost's *Holy Delight*, 1990) and George Herbert and the Metaphysicals and even such minor poets as Maria Moulesworth. It has entered into the visions of Saint Theresa of Jesus and other mystics, even the great William Blake, into the works of Romantics such as Shelley and Keats, into Pushkin and Tolstoi and other Russian masters, into Borges in our time, and will continue. P. J. Klemp has an article: "Numerology and English Renaissance Literature: Twentieth-Century Studies," *Bulletin of Bibliography* 40: 4 (December 1983), 231–241, but ten pages are not adequate to the task. Numerology also figures largely in C. A. Patrides's very scholarly *Premises and Motifs in Renaissance Thought and Literature* (1982). A specialist study could be written about numerology in the writings of any era or any country. John MacQueen covers English literature interestingly in *Numerology* (1985), and there is much else available along the lines of *Symbolic Language of the Scriptures, Number in Scripture, Symbolism of Freemasonry*, etc. Go to the library, or look at books for sale online.

The next section will present something about numerology in literature. Certainly it will not be complete. It is but one section, if the last really important section, of this small book.

א	לה	לד	ג	לב	ו
ל	ח	כח	כז	יא	ז
כד	כג	יה	יו	יד	טי
יג	יז	כא	כב	כ	יח
יב	כו	ט	י	כט	כה
לא	ב	ד	לג	ה	לו

20
Numerology and Literature

ר

"All things have a number," wrote Philolaus *c.* 450 B.C., in the Pythagorean tradition. So it was inevitable that numbers would be often reflected in writings of all types. To give the history of numerology in all writing would require a summary of world literature from the earliest times, and, on top of that, there would be the matter of certain popular numbers connected to the occult in some perhaps haphazard way (42 among the Egyptians, for instance) of which notice would have to be taken. Here, however, a few examples will suffice to make the point that numerology has shaped literature since writing began.

There are clay tablets, epigraphy, and other evidence of numerology in curses and spells from the earliest times. Take 7, the favorite number of many of you, and therefore one I turn to often in these pages. You are not alone in your preference for 7. There is the proof of numerology in the 7 places that claimed the birth of Homer and his 7 purported burial places. (There is also in that disagreement about alleged fact, something that ought to give confident explicators of numbers some pause.) There are other numbers also at work in Homer's epic (on the nine-year siege of Troy), but 7 is likewise there: Consider the shield of Achilles on which is pictured the various occupations of the ancient world, with a wavy border

One of the great rediscoveries of the Renaissance was Ptolemy (90–168 A.D.), *Almagest* (The Greatest) astronomer, astrologer, geocentrist, geographer.

suggesting the sea all around the rather flat earth. The shield consists of 7 layers of protection, suggesting magical properties.

Folklore likes numbers as in the Finnish tale of Mount Kippumaki with its "9 caves, each of them 9 cubits deep, in which magicians store humanity's pain and suffering," in Schimmel's words. Take fairytales (with giants 9 cubits high) and heroic tales in which sometimes 9 obstacles challenge the hero. Hercules had 12, but Beowulf faces only 3 trials, and 3 tries abound in simple jokes to this day. Then there is proverbial wisdom with many 9s, as well as other mystic numbers. Greek mythology has 9 muses, and Apollo with his lyre controls the muses and creates the harmony of the 9 spheres. In religion, Christ dies on the rood 9 hours after sunrise, and Odin hangs on the tree 9 days. In literature, Herodotus wrote in 9 books, and so did Plotinus and other ancient writers. Sometimes the urge was for 12 books or 22. Each choice followed a number tradition.

Remember Shakespeare's witches in the Scottish Play (theatrical superstition says never mention the title *Macbeth*)? They chant:

> Thrice to thine, and thrice to mine,
> And thrice again, to make up nine.
> Peace! The charm's wound up.

Shakespeare's audience would have found that very satisfactory and understandable. I happen, as a professor of literature, to have begun my studies in the occult in order to understand the superstitions that shaped Shakespeare's plays, for plays are one of the very best ways of learning about the conventions, the shared beliefs and preferences, of a dramatist and his time. Shakespeare was steeped in religion, rather more clinging to his father's Roman Catholicism than the Protestantism of his own generation, and Shakespeare and all his contemporaries knew a great deal about folk belief. In Shakespeare's day, that was antiquarianism, because the term *folklore* was not yet coined. Now it is a major literary discipline, and popular culture is rapidly becoming one, you know.

The folk often introduced numbers into their popular superstitions. One of the earliest of recorded methods of fortune-telling was to observe birds. They did, of course, come from the heavens. Folklore says that one magpie is a bad sign (death), but more have different messages for us:

> One is sorrow, two is mirth,
> Three's a wedding, four's a birth.
> Five's a christening, six a dearth.
> Seven's heaven, eight is hell,
> And nine's The Devil his own sel'.

The numbers appear to be somehow connected to meanings here. One might expect 1 to be a better omen than 2, and Seventh Heaven seems to

The Witch of Endor calls up the dead for King Saul (whose very name suggests he follows his own desire, not the dictates of The Almighty). This is black magic and strictly forbidden to all in the Judeo-Christian tradition. Numerology is likewise transgressive but gains some excuse from its attachment to the science of mathematics.

have occasioned not only the 7 here. What is the meaning of 6 and 8? Why is 9, the divine number, connected to the antithesis of the divine, The Devil? That is hard to see unless one assumes that 7 and 8 lead to the connection here. Investigating anything, always ask why as well as what.

The backgrounds of folk rhymes can be extremely complicated. I shall cite just one of the children's rhymes to show this. You may know the U.S. counting-out rhyme that begins:

> Eeny, meeny, miney moe,
> Catch a nigger by his toe . . .

Or it used to begin like that when I was a child. We have all grown up a little since then. Today *tiger* or something like that is more politically correct. A version from the U.K. of the counting-out rhyme goes like this:

> Eena, meena, mona, mite,
> Basca, lora, hora, bite.
> Hugga, bucca, bau;
> Eggs, butter, cheese, bread,
> Stick, stock, stone dead, o-u-t!

Now let us let loose the scholar Charles Francis Potter (who wrote on "Eeeny, meeny, miny, moe" in *Funk & Wagnall's Standard Dictionary of Folklore, Mythology and Legend*, 2 vols., 1949). As Mary and Herbert Knapp in *One Potato, Two Potato: The Folklore of American Children* (1976, page 5) put it:

> The Reverend Charles Francis Potter points out that when the Romans decided to wipe out Druidism in England around 61 A.D., they sent troops over the Menai Strait to cut down the sacred trees on the island of Mona, now Anglesea. The words *lora* and *hora* in the rhyme mean "binding straps" and "hour" in Latin. *Bucca* means "goblin" in Cornish. The foods mentioned are traditionally associated with magic, and "eeny" stands for "one" in ancient counting jargon used by the shepherds in [the] West [of] England.

I want to make a point with this, so be patient with me. I suggest to you that our reaction to the explanation ought to be one of suspicion. I lost it when we got to eggs, butter, cheese, bread as foods "traditionally associated with magic." I know the magical traditions, and that is a desperate and dumb leap. Don't you feel a little uneasy about it, suspecting that it is more ingenious than convincing? Part of the know-it-all (or most of it) explanation is clever, but not nearly as ingenious as a little joke that convulsed me with laughter when I was about six. That joke involved the names of four kittens, Eeny, Meeny, Miny, and Paderewski—"Eeny was the eeniest, Meeny was the meany-ist, Miny was the miny-est, and

Paderewski was the peein'-ist." That childish fun reminds me to say that in numerology or indeed in any decoding, we ought to try to be as convincing as we are clever, and we ought to keep some sense of likelihood. We must retain a sense of proportion.

That said, we must agree that it is fun to play with words.

> My dog Lima loves to roam.
> One day he came wand'ring home.
> Full of burrs and quite unclean—
> Where the hell has Lima been?

(If you say "bin," you miss it.) Or what about this?

> "Would you hit a lady with a baby?"
> "No, I would hit her with a brick!"

DO NOT LET THEM WATCH ME EXIT BUT LET THEM BRING ME BACK FOR AN ENCORE. LET THEM SHUT UP THEIR SHOPS AND COME TO WATCH MY PERFOMANCE. YES, YES, FOR I ADJURE YOU IN THE NAME OF THE 7 LETTERS THAT ARE TATTOOED ON THE CHEST OF THE FATHER, WHICH ARE A 7 [TIMES], I 7 [TIMES], I 7 [TIMES], O 7 [TIMES], YES, YES, THAT YOU OBEY MY SPEECH, AT THIS MOMENT BEFORE IT PASSES, AND ANOITHER ONE TAKES ITS PLACE, AND YOU APPEAR TO ME IN A VISION THAT IS NOT TERRIFYING, THROUGH THE POWER OF THEV HOLY FATHER.

YAK, MERIAK, SEMIAK, THE THREE MIGHTY DECANS, WHO STAND OVER THE BED OF THE TREE OF LIFE, GIVE SWEETNESS TO MY THROAT.

I AM SEVERUS, SON OF ANNA.
NOW, NOW, PRESTO, NOW, NOW!

Such play makes poets and lovers of literature. Hamlet's "words, words, words" entrance us all. If writers play with words, so can we all. If they have something to say, we are free to hear it our own way, adopt or adapt in our own way. The interpretation of texts cannot be avoided. It cannot be denied that puns are fun (even if they are the lowest form of wit as the bun is the lowest form of wheat) and that it is a delight to pick out meanings or double meanings (or provide them). In any case, whatever the writer wrote, the reader will revise in the light of her or his own experience, wit, and wisdom. If any.

Some ages are more accepting of the message directly delivered. Ours happens to be an age in which readers dislike too much didacticism and prefer more independence, hate being lectured, reject instruction. We often prefer to make meaning rather than detect it. Some other ages have searched more for the writer's meaning, preferably a secret meaning, inherent in the encryption, not ingeniously put in there by a reader. That was their way; it arose from and expressed a psychology and a world view different from ours.

The Hebrew scholars rejoiced to find deep and dark meanings. This penchant they seem to have inherited from the Babylonians, those omen seekers who thought every comet came trailing a message, and from others who believed that letters could be numbers and numbers could yield letters. This led to a search for signs in all things. Later Saint Augustine warned that "all signs are things but not all things are signs," and yet he sought various levels of meaning and produced an incredibly numerological reading of all Scriptures. Everyone was looking for secret doctrines, maybe even esoteric powers. After all, writing itself was regarded as a sort of magic.

Every new technological development looks rather magical at first. Our grandparents would have marveled at microwaves cooking our food and our sending radio messages out into space in the hope that we are not the only intelligent beings in the cosmos. The first person to make a few marks that enabled him to remember some details or, better, could convey those ideas to others at a distance of time or place, was a marvel. The first person to tie a few knots in a cord and send it as a message to someone else in on the secret must have felt very special. The fellow must have believed himself inspired who first figured out that the knots could be tied in such a way that they could only be deciphered by someone who wrapped the cord around another stick of an agreed upon diameter. Invention. Technology.

The Chinese with their brush strokes must have closely connected numbers to ideograms. They wrote ideograms on bones and used them for divination. They set up a class of mandarins who tried very hard to keep power by controlling offices; they got their offices by reading and writing and like the Egyptian writers of hieroglyphs. Those experts were anxious to keep the secrets from the common people. Today's communication power-elite are the computer literate people. Their machines perform wonders. The computer experts used to be geeks and nerds and now are regarded as geniuses. I heard just today of some new chip that performs in one second 400 million operations. Isn't that pretty magical?

The Scandinavians were in awe of runes and the powers they were supposed to command. In writing we must expect not only communication, but even control and magic and secret or powerful communication.

Here (quoted in V. F. Hooper's *Medieval Number Symbolism*, of which you will hear more elsewhere) is Philo Iudæus. Although he was a Jew of the first century A.D. he sounds very medieval as he writes on *Genesis* (which Jews call the first book of the Five Books of Moses). If words can contain secrets, why not look for them, Philo thought, especially in the writings of masters who had picked up magical secrets in Egypt, such as Moses? Philo is going to tell us not only what has been written but precisely what, in his opinion, we "must understand." He is going to tell us how to deconstruct or how to decode. He is going to set patterns for religious exegesis for a long time to come.

When, therefore, Moses says, "God completed his work on the sixth day," we must understand that he is speaking not of a number of days, but that he takes six as a perfect number. Since it is the first number which is equal in its parts, in the half, and the third, and sixth parts, and since it is produced by the multiplication of two unequal factors, two and three. And the numbers two and three exceed the incorporeality which exists in the unity because the number two is an image of matter, being divided into two parts and dissected like matter. And the number three is an image of a solid body, because a solid can be divided according to a threefold division. Not but what it is also akin to the motions of organic animals. For an organic body is naturally capable of motion in six directions, forward, backwards, upwards, downwards, to the right, and to the left. And at all events he [Moses, supposed author of the Five Books under the inspiration of God] desires to show that the races of mortal, and also of immortal beings, exist according to their appropriate numbers; measuring mortal beings, as I have said, by the number six, and the blessed and immortal beings by the number seven. First, therefore, having desisted from the creation of mortal creatures on the seventh day, he [God] began the formation of other and more divine beings.

You have to watch out for those *therefores, fors,* and *becauses,* but at least you see that this learned rabbi (which means teacher, not priest), performing his close examination of the text characteristic of Talmudic scholars and writing at the time when Christianity, was not so far as it was later to be from Judaism from which it sprang. He is early in the connecting of Judaism to Christianity. He is engaging in the interpretation, often innovational if injudicious, of Holy Scripture that was to spread all over Christendom, survive the Dark Ages, and to be the mark of the Scholastics of the Age of Faith. The Jews were not only "the people of the book," but in addition to the Scriptures, they revered the commentaries of the Talmud and the Mishnah, and they possessed a long mystical, hermetic tradition. Christians also looked upon the sacred writings as subject for contemplation and comment, some of it departing wildly from the text into the most obscure corners of theology.

What theology did not tackle, mysticism might attempt. Magicians undertook to work miracles by anagrammatizing the Name of Power. Actually, they really did not know it, for *Adonai* (Lord) is just a title, not the Name, and *Jehovah* (I AM) was an evasion of a Name. Orthodox Jews say that if I give you the Name of God in print, the world will come to an end. I have decided not to do it. You do not need it. HE IS, and that is all you really know on earth and all you need to know.

When God refused to give His Name (lest Moses have power over Him, for the Name is part of the Self), God said to Moses simply "I AM." What did He *mean*? What *is* the Name? "Enquiring minds want to know." With it, we could *do a number* on God Himself!

Clerics were those who could read and write in medieval Europe, and so inescapable theological and didactic elements inform all literature of the Middle Ages. We see this always, not just in sermons. Petrus Bungus, who saw 13 as unlucky and 11 as transgressive because it went beyond the 10 of the commandments, produced for preachers a *Mysticæ numerorum significationis liber* or *Book of the Mystical Significations of Numbers*. We see numerology in other religious writings and not only the hermetic and mystical writings on the occult. Numbers were universally believed to be intimately connected to all truth.

Medieval encyclopedists such as Rhabanus Maurus (introducing Arabic ideas) and Isidore of Seville (numerology in early Spain still remains to be investigated by scholars) are almost essential to the reading of medieval literature in the light of numerology. Scholars in their pride drifted away from Occam's Razor. William of Occam, who died about the middle of the fourteenth century, was a no-nonsense antidote to the verbose and intellectually wobbly speculations of philosophers. His method (called Occam's Razor) sliced through the garbage: When confronted with a number of possible explanations, Occam said, choose the simplest one.

Edmund Spenser did not go about writing his epic poem, which he first thought he would base on the Arthurian legends and cover all the public and private virtues using what was called the Matter of Britain, without an ambitious plan, and his plan was too monstrous, too medieval in scope for him to complete all the books planned for his epic poem. In the part of *The Faerie Queene* that we have, at least one thing was determined, dared, and done, and that was to put in not only allegory but numerology. Had Spenser finished this big project there might have been a lot more numerology. In the poem (III, 2, 50) numbers in magic, for example, are referred to by the "agèd nurse," beldames being relied upon in those days to have special knowledge of magical practice.

In their prejudice, the men of the time announced that the reason witchcraft was practiced by so many old women was that women were less intelligent, more gullible, more easily seduced by The Devil than men were. Today numerology suffers from the fact that most of the published writers on the subject are women, and many of them are attractive and ambitious young women, facts that make their intellectual capacities all the more suspect according to male chauvinists. As women have, in the face of such bigotry, invaded the profession of law, for example, and contributed (along with their male tort millionaires) to increasing public scorn for the profession, so women writing about numerology (and to a certain extent about astrology) have lowered the reputation of this kind of writing in the minds of many bigots. We prefer, it seems, prophets to prophetesses. But the witch is the traditional figure of magic, the wizard coming a poor second.

So in Spenser, the witch, or, if you like, wise woman, shows her magic:

> Then taking thrise three hairs from off her head
> Them trebly breaded [braided] in a three fold lace,
> And round the pots mouth, bound the thread,
> And after having whisperèd a space
> Certaine sad words, with hollow voice and bace [base],
> She to the virgin said, thrise said she it:
> Come daughter come, come; spit upon my face,
> Spit thrise upon me, thrice upon me spit;
> Th'uneven number for this businesse is most fit.

Spit is part of the person and therefore can be used in magic as Christ used His sputum in performing miracles. It is supposed to transfer power.

You will find numerology not only in the esoteric magical writings and early science and philosophy but also in such Anglo-Saxon poems as "The Pearl" and the Middle English long poem of *Sir Gawain and the Green Knight*. In *Gawain*, the 5-pointed star or Seal of Solomon is on his shield where one might have expected a cross, as with Spenser's Red Cross Knight, but the star of Gawain is the right way up and not reversed as in Satanism, for Gawain is something like a good magician battling an evil one.

Numerology, no matter how much you yearn for a simple story of derring-do without the frills and furbelows, is everywhere to be found in the romances of chivalry, especially those of the paladins of Charlemagne such as *Le Chanson de Roland*. Many French epics of the sort were translated into English. Even better known to English readers are the romances of Arthur and his Round Table (variously said to involve 50, 150, or 250 knights, each number with numerological meaning, of course). These were exceedingly popular in the Middle Ages and revived, as in Lord Tennyson's *The Idylls of the King*, in Victorian times. In modern times we have had T. H. White's delightful novel of *The Sword in the Stone* and much more.

As modern writers of popular literature like to beef up their detective stories with precinct procedures, best-selling authors like to pad adventure stories with exact details of submarine technology or law-firm machinations or White House shenanigans, and even horror writers cram their books with extraneous materials, so the popular writers of chivalric romances, epics, and other works of old literature loved allegory and symbolism and numerology and all sorts of filigree. Theirs was no "less is more" approach. To use a current pun, they went for baroque.

Chaucer's Wife of Bath has 5 husbands (like the Samaritan Woman whom Jesus encounters). She knows all about astrology and numbers.

You cannot read Chaucer's *The Canterbury Tales*, which begins with an astrological reference to spring, intelligently without a knowledge of numerology as well as of Roman Catholicism.

The really big test of your understanding of those elements comes when you tackle the *Divine Comedy* of Dante. Hooper says that most of his *Medieval Number Symbolism: Its Sources, Meaning, and Influence on Thought and Expression* (1969) is based upon the work of others:

> A great deal of scholarly work has already been done on the primitive, astrological, and Pythagorean symbolism to which my early chapters are devoted. Without pretending to make any contribution to these fields, I have nevertheless deemed it necessary to summarize.

And I have drawn much from his summary, but when it comes to his chapter on "The Beauty of Order—Dante," I think you ought to read Hooper's work; it is fine. Dante and Milton are two poets everyone should read.

Dante could not but have shared some medieval beliefs regarding astrology, numerology, and other early attempts at real science, from alchemy to physiognomy. In the *Divine Comedy*, Dante's guide in Hell, Virgil, says regarding date of birth: *nascio sub Iulio, ancor che fosse tardi*. However, in numerology one cannot state one's birth date as in the reign of Julius (Caesar) "albeit late." One must have an exact date and basically the correct hour and minute and place of birth in order to cast a horoscope.

This is not the place for a serious examination of the literature of science, although numerology is involved with mathematics, physics, and natural philosophy, as well as with pseudoscience which gave birth to chemistry.

The story of alchemy, on which much was written because alchemists had powerful and sometimes royal patrons, may be said to have started in England with Robert of Chester (twelfth century). We must say something of alchemy because of its connections to numerology. It was in the forties of that century that Robert the Englishman (Robert de Ketene or de Retines), who was picking up Arabic lore in Spain, first translated the Koran into Latin (for Peter the Venerable, Abbot of Cluny in France—it was not printed for 400 years). Also in that century appeared the first English alchemist of whom we know, Robert of Chester. *Alchemy* comes from the Arabic for "the black land" (the black soil of the Nile Delta); it is Egyptian in origin but may have had even older origins, including Chaldean and Babylonian and Chinese. It incorporates elements of even earlier astrology and chemistry, magic and medicine.

Jabir ibn Hayyan (eighth century) was the most famous alchemist in Europe, Greek science having disappeared in the Dark Ages. Jabir the son of Hayyan was so famous that in the fourteenth century an alchemist was still using his name. The vast and classic work of M.-P.-E. Berthelot is *Collection des anciens alcimistes grecs*, 1888. Robert of Chester translated from the Arabic of Marianus *The Book of the Composition of Alchemie*, a step in the direction of real science. A major step forward in science was taken by Roger Bacon, author of *De Secretis artis naturæ*, 1249). Alchemy long continued, mixing science and superstition, with such works as George Ripley's *The Compound of Alchymie conteining Twelve Gates* (1474), Thomas Norton's *The Ordinall of Alkimie* (1477, published by Michael Maier in *Tripus aureus*, 1618), and by the extraordinary Elias Ashmole. Ashmole's *Theatrum chemicum Britannicum*, collected 209 treatises (1652). Ashmole was a member of an astrologers' club with Sir William Dugdale and Dr. Grew (after whom Linnæus named a genus of plants). A famous library is still named for Ashmole, the Ashmolean.

The poet Dryden cast the horoscopes of his children and was accurate. The playwright Congreve has an astrologer called Foresight in *Love for Love*. All England in their era was in love with horoscopes. In France it was the custom to present the new baby naked to an adept who looked at the physiognomy, read the palms, and cast the horoscope. Charles I asked for the most likely time of his escape from imprisonment. Charles II was a greater believer.

France's royal family was given prophecies by Nostradamus, and a later seer told Charles IX he would live as many days as he could spin around on his heel, standing on one leg, nonstop for exactly an hour. So the king did that daily. Nor must we fail to mention (as seems inevitable in all of my books on the occult) Paracelsus.

What is more useful, perhaps, is to note that Carl Jung (Swiss psychiatrist, 1875–1961) wrote importantly on *Psychology and Alchemy*. That is a work I highly recommend, and I even suggest you consider his opinions on astrology.

I leap now to numerology in psychoanalysis. I give you a rather amusing case of dream interpretation, the stock in trade of Freud and his followers, from Wilhelm Stekel's *The Interpretation of Dreams: New Developments* (1943, pages 372–373). Stekel, like Jung, was in the Freudian tradition, but he shared Jung's belief that Freud was wrong in tracing neuroses to infancy; Jung asserted that neuroses were the products not of infancy nor even inherited problems but produced by current maladjustment. This piece coming up may be enough to explain why in connection with the literature of science I do not permit myself to get much involved in numerology's frequent appearance.

Here is Dr. Stekel and the new form of conversation (with some old symbol hunting) that Freud's talking cure introduced. I shall translate the latinities that these sex-obsessed physicians break into for reasons of dignity or decency, as they see it:

St. Marcellus, from the doorway of the Cathedral of Nôtre Dame, Paris. The bishop's crozier is thrust into the mouth of the dragon of evil—or it originally was, but was shortened because what we really have here is the shaft of light (knowledge) of the alchemists kindling the fire of the *athenor* to produce the philosophers' stone.

Numerology and Literature

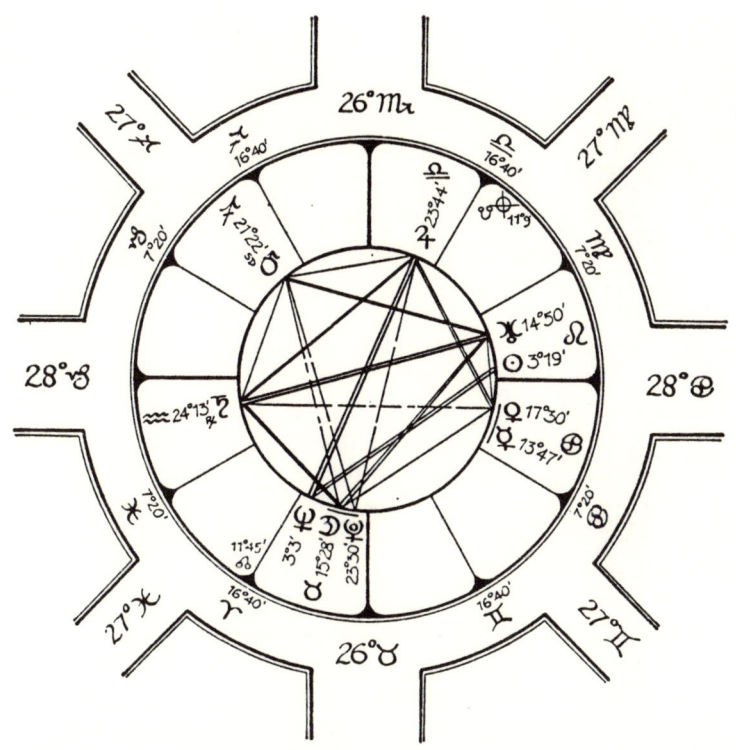

The horoscope of Carl Gustave Jung. From Michael R. Meyer's *Handbook for the Humanistic Astrologer* (1974).

For eighteen months the illness has been complicated by anxiety states. These are so severe that she can no longer go out unaccompanied. She was advised to visit a mountain health resort. There she became worse than ever, coming into contact with various ladies who gave her enthusiastic descriptions of their husbands' or lovers' ars amandi [art of loving], whilst she has never been able to enjoy an orgasm because her husband has ejaculatio praecox [premature ejaculation]. One of these ladies advised her to put herself in my hands. [Freudian slip?] The result of analytical treatment, conducted by myself and Frau Hilda Stekel in collaboration, was amazing. She was rather simple-minded, and it was hard to make her understand the nature of her parapathy. Nevertheless she achieved remarkable progress, and after two months she was entirely freed from both anxiety states and attacks of vomiting. Towards the end of the treatment she had the following dream:

> *In the year 1890 Empress Maria Theresa lost her son. Today it is a hundred years since he died.*

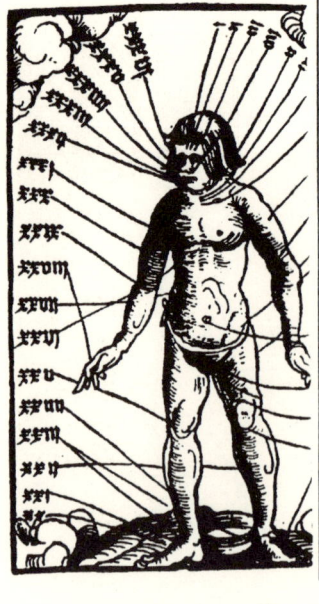

The patient promptly remarked: "Of course that is absurd. It's much more than a hundred years.

"What associates have you to this dream?," I asked.

"I have always been inclined to compare my mother-in-law to Maria Theresa, for she, too, had a great many children. My mother-in-law and my husband were greatly attached to one another. The former died six months ago. I should explain my dream as follows. I have known my husband for nine years. These nine years seem almost like an eternity—a century at least."

The number 1690 is over-determined. She had been married for seven years (1 + 6), 9 relates to the nine months of pregnancy, 0 to the failure of the orgasm, on the 20th of October (the 10th month) she was married, 10 is for her a fateful number (when she has had vomiting attacks they have always lasted ten days). She has known her husband for nine years, and the result is nil. It seems to her as long as a century.

What she has failed to recognize is her own fixation upon her father-in-law, a man-about-town who "stands his drink very well" and is a confirmed woman-hunter. Empress Maria Theresa symbolizes the leading figure in the mental drama, namely the aforesaid old gentleman who is still very much all there and helps her to refurbish her Electra attitude toward her own father. She wishes her husband would die. Then without remorse she could give herself up to her father-in-law. These relationships are illustrated by another of her dreams:

> *I am standing in the kitchen. It is dark. My father-in-law comes in to fetch some water, stumbles, and falls over me in to the floor, so that he is lying on me.*

I say elsewhere in writing about the interpretation of dreams that they are full of valuable information and I stress that in dreams we have not simply thoughts but experiences, that although there are certain universals, our dream vocabularies are idiolects: we give personal significances to all symbols, including numbers. That is why dreams have often to be subjected to careful, even professional, interpretation before they will yield the realizations that no dream book of symbols and numbers can effectively provide on a one-size-fits-all basis.

Numerology and Literature 269

Pharaoh has his dream interpreted by Joseph while a counselor and Potiphar's wife look on. The biblical characters (as is the custom in medieval art) wear medieval clothes. This emphasizes the contemporary significance of the depictions.

And now, a score of comments of a numerological importance from other sources.

These may score a few points with you and they may give some hint of the widespread interest in our subject evidenced by some interesting writers. Read the following remarks. Take time to think about them.

The talisman of Jupiter featuring the number 34, to be carried for peace and prosperity.

20 THOUGHTS PERTAINING TO NUMEROLOGY

In ancient China, a just and wise monarch ruled between 2205 and 2198 B.C.E. [Before the Common Era, usually B.C. Before Christ]; this was the emperor Yu, known for his great wisdom and care. Kungfutse [Kung Fu Tzu, that is Confucius] tells that the emperor had once been occupied with building a dam on the Yellow River to stop the floods. While he was sitting on the bank of the river, immersed in thought, a divine turtle named Hi appeared to him. On the turtle's back, there was a figure with number signs, which, transcribed into modern numerals, looked like this:

4 9 2
3 5 7
8 1 6

One immediately sees that the square is grouped around the number 5, which was highly esteemed in ancient China. All the horizontal and vertical lines produce the sum of 15, as do the diagonals. The even numbers are placed in the corners, the odd ones between them.

—Annemarie Schimmel, *The Mystery of Numbers* (1993)

❊

I am 1 who becomes 2, I am 2 who becomes 4, I am 4 who becomes 8, I am the one [god] after that.

—Gnostic Egyptian inscription of the 22nd Dynasty, quoted in Vincent Foster Hopper, *Medieval Number Symbolism* (1969)

❊

The gods name the fifty names of Nanib [the Babylonian god of the Sun] (= Marduk), and the name of 50 becomes sacred to him, so that even in the time of Gudea [Judea] a temple was actually dedicated to the number 50.

—Maurice H. Farbridge, *Studies in Biblical and Semitic Symbolism* (1923)

❊

It is therefore more certain and less hazardous to await the fulfillment of the prophecy [regarding the coming of The Beast of *Revelations*, the date of the Apocalypse] than to be making surmises, and casting about for any names that may present themselves, inasmuch as many names can be found possessing the number mentioned [666]; and the same question will after all remain unsolved.

—Saint Irenæus (c. 140–202), *Against Heresies* V: 30

❊

The letters of the name of the evil demon who is prince of this world [Satan] are the same as those of the Name of God—Tetra-grammaton [JHVH] – and he who knows how to effect their transposition can extract one from the other.

—Pico della Mirandola (1483–1494)

❊

Take 7 prickles from 7 palm trees, 7 chips from 7 beams, 7 nails from 7 bridges, 7 ashes from 7 ovens, 7 scoops of earth from 7 door sockets, 7 pieces of pitch from 7 ships, 7 handfuls of cumin, and 7 hairs from the head of an old dog, and tie them to the neck-hole of the shirt with a white twisted cord [to cure a tertian fever].

—Joshua Trachtenberg, *Jewish Magic and Superstition* (1974)

❊

[Benvenuto Cellini] actually met his Sicilian Angelica in Naples on the very last day of the month which the spirits had set as the term.

—E. M. Butler, *Ritual Magic* (1949)

❊

The Indo-Germanic heritage with the special place of the 9 can be observed in ancient Greece. The river Styx in the netherworld has 9 twists, and feasts are prepared to honor Apollo in Delphi every ninth year. . . . a feast in honor of Zeus was celebrated on the Lycean mountain every ninth year. There were reportedly even human sacrifices, but the person who performed the ritual slaying was, as it is told, banished from the country for 9 years. During the feast of Dionysus at Patra, 9 men and 9 women celebrated the ritual. Apollo, accompanied by the 9 Muses, carried the lyre with 9—or as we saw earlier, 7—strings, and according to one version of the myth, the labor of his mother, Leto, lasted for nine days and 9 nights, and Eileithya, who assisted the poor mother, received from her a necklace of 9 parts. One wonders if this "necklace" has any connection with the umbilical cord, which brings blood and nourishment to the embryo during the 9 months of gestation.

—Annemarie Schimmel, *The Mystery of Numbers* (1993)

❋

It is to be understood that there be in the year four quarters that is called Vere, Hiems, Aestas, and Autumnus [winter, spring, summer, autumn]. These be the four seasons in the year, as Primetime is the Spring of the year as February, March, April, these three months. Then cometh Summer, as May, June, and July; and those three months every herb, grain, and tree is in his kind and in his most strength and fairness even at the highest. Then cometh Autumn as August, September, and October, that all these fruits waxeth ripe and be gathered and housed. Then cometh November, December, and January, and these three months be in the Winter, the time of little profit.

We Shepherds say that the age of a man is seventy-two year [the Bible says four score and ten, 70], and this we liken to but one whole year. For evermore we take six years for every month, as January or February and so forth: for as the year changeth by the twelve months into twelve sundry manners, so doth a man change himself twelve times in his life, so be that he live to seventy-two, for three times six maketh eighteen, and six times six maketh thirty-six, and then is a man at the best and also at the highest, and twelve times six maketh seventy-two, and that is the age of a man.

Thus must ye reckon for every month six year or else it may be understood by the four quarters and seasons of the year. So is divided man into four parts [Galen to the medieval mind divided everything into four elements—Fire, Water, Earth, Air—as you know, and with these there were four humours or controlling liquids in the human body] as to youth, strength, wisdom, and age; he to be eighteen year young, eighteen year strong, eighteen year in wisdom, and the fourth eighteen year to go to the full age of seventy-two.

—Anonymous, *The Kalandar and Compost of Shepherds* (much older but first printed 1493, first English translation *c.* 1518)

❋

And all your fortune lies beneath your hat.

—John Oldham (1653–1683), *A Satire addressed to a Friend*

❋

All are inclined to believe what they covet, from a lottery-ticket up to a passport to paradise.
> —George, Lord Byron in his journal for 27 November 1813

❋

To believe in your own thought, to believe what is true for you in your own heart is true for all men—that is genius.
> —Ralph Waldo Emerson (1803–1882), *Self-Reliance*

❋

Faith, n. Belief without evidence in what is told by one who speaks without knowledge, of things without parallel.
> —Ambrose Bierce (1842–1914?), *The Devil's Dictionary*

❋

To become a popular religion, it is only necessary for a superstition to enslave a philosophy.
> —Dean William Ralph Inge, *Outspoken Essays II* (1922)

❋

One of the ways to recognize error is the fact that it is universal.
> —Jean Giraudoux, *Tiger at the Gates* (1925, translated by Christopher Fry, 1963)

❋

One of the peculiar sins of the twentieth century which we've developed to a very high level is the sin of credulity. It has been said that when human beings stop believing in God they believe in nothing. The truth is worse: they believe in anything.
> —Malcolm Muggeridge on BBC Radio, 23 March 1966

❋

About astrology and palmistry [and numerology?]: they are good because they make people vivid and full of possibilities. They are communism at its best. Everybody has a birthday and almost everybody has a palm.

—Kurt Vonnegut Jr., *Wampeters, Foma and Granfallons* (1974)

❋

The so-called science of biorhythm is nothing more than glorified numerology that, on the basis of a simple birth date and some supposed research, generates infantile notions about predetermined cycles that govern human existence. It is one of the purest—and simplest—forms of idiocy to assume the mantle of logic and science.

—James Randi, *Flim-Flam: Psychics, ESP, Unicorns and Other Delusions* (1982)

❋

Muppet: It's here! It's here! My correspondence course!
Kermit the Frog: Your correspondence course?
Muppet: It's called "How to Be a Superhero"! It comes complete with a helmet, a cape, a red shirt, and an instruction book called "Invincibility Made Easy."
Kermit the Frog: I don't believe it.
Muppet: Chapter Ten—"How to Fly. Flying is a simple matter of belief. Anyone can fly as long as he believes that he can."
Kermit the Frog: I can't watch this.

—Jim Henson's "The Muppet Show", CBS-TV, 18 February 1980

❋

Future, n. That period of time in which our affairs prosper, our friends are true and our happiness is assured.

—Ambrose Bierce (1842–1914?), *The Devil's Dictionary*

21
Conclusion

שש

So we come to the end of my necessarily subjective and limited take on numerology, and we must agree that numerology is not as much a science as an art, though perhaps more up to date in its lack of hierarchy than the other, ancient and medieval, occult sciences, or pseudosciences, as I have continually been cautious enough to add. Numerology appeals to moderns more than most occult matters because it looks rather technological and egalitarian. It seems to be, like what Ezekiel saw, wheels within wheels, "way up in the middle of the air," but visible from here, mechanical and spiritual:

> And the little wheel ran by faith,
> And the big wheel ran by the grace of God . . .

And numerology is available to all, 1 to 9 (and there is no 10 because "nobody's perfect"). Very modern, nonsexist, just right for our contemporary therapeutic culture, just right for a time in which even the traditional Christian denominations are becoming increasingly evangelical and charismatic, more superstitious some might say.

Here in this conclusion, you will not find summarized all the findings or opinions expressed in this book. It is not that kind of book. If you are the cold, practical sort who looks at the conclusion first (and maybe exclusively) in the volumes you pick up, this is not what you were expecting. Read the book. This is a good-bye rather than a précis. If you want to know what is in here, read the book in the old-fashioned way. What do you do with all the time you save by consuming instant food, including intellectual nourishment?

I hope you have found this book pleasant as well as informative. That has been the aim of all the books in this series. Moreover, I always try to be helpful. In this book I suggest that numerology may be useful. You may think numerology is nonsense, a joke, even a forbidden practice, but I contend that numerology is, like psychoanalysis, a wonderful way of conducting a conversation not with prenestine fates out there, in my view, but with one's innermost self. I see nothing wrong with communing with that if reason does not fly out the window. I think self-help did not end with Samuel Smiles (if you know who that is) and if you do not know who that is, I am not going to walk away from you in a haughty contempt. It may be that you and I are both very literate except on different subjects. It is quite possible that each knows things the other does not, so mutual respect seems called for.

It is in that self-reliant and self-improving aspect that is unquestionably real, rather than in any purported connection to the supernatural, that the advantage of numerology resides. In that is its appeal in the modern world to people who want all the pieces to be provided for them when some new construction is desired, not to have to supply a great deal from a storeroom of common culture that the diversity and speed of our modern world has depleted or demolished.

Some of my readers will ask why I bother to write about numerology at all if I am not a total believer in its claims. Others will accuse me, perhaps, of being too credulous and of paying the subject more attention than it deserves. Still others will want to know why I do not come down conclusively on one side or the other and say: Believe in it, or reject it out of hand. Is numerology important or is it not? I leave the final decision to you.

It is certainly of some importance that many people over a long period of time have believed in its claims, whether those claims are well-founded or not. Similarly, old beliefs that demons could possess us or newer ones such as the claims of UFOlogists that alien beings have visited our planet and even abducted some of us will continue to be debated. Neither the believers nor the unbelievers will ever be able to persuade unwilling opponents in the debate. What is not debatable, it seems to me, is that there is and should be abiding interest in all kinds of belief firmly held by some and at the same time completely rejected by others. What explains these disagreements about what is real and what is not? What are we to do with problems we cannot conclusively solve and so-called facts on which we cannot agree?

Remember, too, that whether you share belief in the mystic powers of numbers, or in devils and demons and extraterrestrial creatures, or you do

Conclusion

not, you live in a world in which it is a reality that other people hold fast to strange beliefs. That affects you, whether you like it or not, whether you think other people are deluded or not. Superstition is incontrovertibly real however it skews reality. It has real effects.

Numerology lets you dabble in superstition without burning noxious perfumes or chanting demonic evocations, and it is not seriously harmful to body or soul. It may not make it possible for you to communicate with Something, divinities or demons or forces Out There, but it promises to open up channels to the conflicting entities in your own unconscious mind and from that source rather than from oracles you may obtain knowledge and you may get direction.

This improvement may occur even if you play with the numbers as toys and regard numerology merely as a diverting game. In addition to entertaining or even revealing something about the mind of the individual, the history of numerology likewise reveals something about human nature and the history of religion and of society.

The fact that nature and those histories contain some things that are nonsense, are sometimes a joke, even unnerving, is well worth recognizing and demands understanding, however you come to the realization.

The K'AMÊ'A of Iron (Mars, 5 columns).

11	24	7	20	3
4	12	25	8	16
17	5	13	21	9
10	18	1	14	22
23	6	19	2	15

יא	כד	ז	כ	ג
ד	יב	כה	ח	יו
יז	ה	יג	כא	ט
י	יח	א	יד	כב
כג	ו	יט	ב	יה

Whether these five times five figures are added up vertically, horizontally or diagonally the total is 65, or in Hebrew letters A = 1, D = 4, N = 50 and Y = 10, i.e. 'ADÔNÂY a name of God. The total of the five columns of figures is 325, which is the number of the Spirit and Demon of the planet.

Sir E.A. Wallis Budge, *Amulets and Talismans* (1968).

DOGME ET RITUEL
DE LA
HAUTE MAGIE
PAR ÉLIPHAS LÉVI

TOME PREMIER
DOGME — 8 FIGURES

PARIS
GERMER BAILLIÈRE, LIBRAIRE-ÉDITEUR
17, RUE DE L'ÉCOLE-DE-MÉDECINE
LONDRES | MADRID
H. BAILLIÈRE, 219, Regent-street. | CH. BAILLY-BAILLIÈRE.
NEW-YORK, CH. BAILLIÈRE.
1856

This is a book about numerology for everyone, not the true believers nor the unbelievers alone. I dare say it will make numerology understandable to many who have never considered it before and even tell those who have long studied and practiced numerology a few things they did not know before. I think that is a lot to have accomplished in a popular book. Inevitably it will leave a lot of people not fully satisfied. Being unsatisfied is part of the human condition and not the worst type of impetus to keep living, looking, and thinking. Considering a contentious subject such as this, we can all to some degree come to understand other people better and better understand ourselves. Those are no bad things.

At this point I hope you will permit me on our brief acquaintance to offer some heartfelt advice. I would suggest you consider copying not on myself—though numerology tells me that with my December 5 date of birth I can expect quick mind, versatility, sociability, good adjustment and other good things, no "challenge" or impediment, though I must accept change and be ever energetic if I desire achievement and power, which proud and pushy as I am I do—no, not me, but Holly Golightly, Truman Capote's adventurous heroine in *Breakfast at Tiffany's*. Holly stated with her characteristic verve:

> Another thing. I've thrown away my horoscopes. I must have spent a dollar on every goddam star in the goddam planetarium. It's a bore, but the answer is good things only happen to you if you're good. Good? Honest is more what I mean. Not law-type honest—I'd rob a grave, I'd steal two-bits off a dead man's eyes [put there

as the fare for Charon, ferryman on The Styx] if I thought it would contribute to the day's enjoyment—but unto-thyself-type honest. Be anything but a coward, a pretender, an emotional crook, a whore: I'd rather have anything than a dishonest heart.

With or without fiddling with numbers (maybe in the light of astrology, too, with birth date, "house," configuration of the planets and particularly the ascendant then, day of the week, place in a 9-year personal cycle with peaks at 9s and lows at 4 1/2 so watch out and at the end of each cycle pause and reflect like The Hermit in the Tarot pack, expect special milestones at year 25 and year 57, and on and on), be *good* like that—and hope and work for and try to *earn* good luck. Don't rely on it just falling into your lap. And never count on anything good or bad lasting: Andrew "Jack" Whittaker Jr. of West Virginia won $314.9 million in the lottery in December 2002 and in August 2003 had over half a million in cashier's checks stolen from his SUV, in January 2004 was twice arrested for different offences and also had $100,000 stolen from his parked car—and the story went on. Do not plan on keeping it, do not plan on getting it. Joshua Riven in *As Luck Would Have It* tells of a man who played the lottery for the very first time after years of rationally resisting the temptation and won millions. Asked if he would play again, the winner said he would not. "I still know the odds," he said.

I end here with the words that "Éliphas Lévi" wrote on 1 September 1859 and used to conclude his *History of Magic* (whose "Key to the Great Mysteries will be established on the number four—which is that of the enigmatic forms of the sphinx and of elementary manifestations, it is also the number of square and force"):

> The writer of these books gives lessons willingly to serious and interested persons of these ["secrets of Jewish Kabalism and of Supreme Magic—whether that of Zoroaster or of Hermes"]; but once and for all he desires to forewarn his readers that he tells no fortunes, does not teach divination, makes no predictions, composes no philtres and lends himself to no sorcery and no evocation. He is a man of science, not a man of deception. He condemns energetically whatsoever is condemned by religion, and hence he must not be confounded with persons who can be approached without hesitation on a question of applying their knowledge to a dangerous or illicit use. For the rest he welcomes honest criticism, but he fails to understand certain hostilities. Serious study and conscientious labour are superior to all attacks; and the first blessings which they procure, for those who can appreciate them, are profound peace and universal benevolence.
>
> **Farewell. God Bless. Blessed Be.**

Index

African dominoes, 119
Agrippa, Cornelius, 199–200
Alchemist, The (illus.), 233
alchemy, 265
alchymy, 174
aleph (Hebrew letter), 206
alphabet, origin of, 206
Alphabet of the Magi (illus.), 184
Althotas, and Cagliostro, 175
American symbolism and number 13, 106–107
Amulet of Jupiter (illus.), 45
Amulets and Talismans (illus.), 277
anagrams, 208
Anaxagoras, 242
Ashmole, Elias, 265
astrological signs, 51–52
astrology, 50–55, 240
astrology signs, Southern, 194
Ateersata, 180
auras, and color, 171–172
ayin (Hebrew letter), 208

Bacon, Roger, 173, 265
Balsamo, Giuseppe. *see* Cagliostro
Balsamo, Joseph, 174
Basilica chymica oder alchymistisch königlich Kleynod (illus.), 244
Berthelot, M.-P.-E., 265

beth (Hebrew letter), 206
Bible
    meaning of 40 days, 95
Bible code, 210
bibliomancy, 173
birthstones, 52–54, 160–161
"black man" (Devil), 165
Black Mass, The, 165–166
Blavatsky, Helena Petrovna (illus.), 151
bones, throwing, 119
Book of Formation (*Sepher Yetzirah*), 211
breastplate of the High Priest of the Jews, 53–54, 119
Breitmann, Hans, 236
Buddha, 67

Cagliostro, 173–189
Cagliostro (illus.), 179
Cardan, Jerome (illus.), 241
Case, John, 175
Challenge numbers, 32–34
Charlemagne, 264
Chaucer, 264
"Cheiro," 60–61, 235–243
    best places to live according to, 238
    color recommendations, 168–169
    and palmistry, 235–236
chi, 68

281

Chinese astrology
  cycles of, 68
  demons in, 70
  signs or "houses" of, 66
Chinese ideograms, 260
Chinese ideographs, 206
Christ, birth of, 60, 239
churches, and fortune-telling, 16
Clement XII, 179
coat of arms of Count Cagliostro (illus.), 188
codes
  Bible, 210
  and colors, 172
  common, 210–211
  encryption, 80–83
  and Shakespeare, 239
colors
  and days of the week, 170
  favorite, meaning of, 167–169
  and Hebrew letters, 160–161
  and musical notes, 171
  symbolism of, 163–166
common codes, 210–211
Complete Book of Dreams and What They Mean, The (Ashley), 109
Complete Book of Superstition, Prophecy, and Luck, The (Ashley), 192, 216
conception of child, planned, 155
Confucius, 270
Cornerstone number, 47, 156–157
Count Alessandro di Cagliostro. *see* Cagliostro
cypher (*sephiroth*), 209

daleth (Hebrew letter), 206
Dante, 264–265
DaVinci Code, The, 247
days of the week and color, 170
decans, 54–55
Devil, The, 165
Devine Design, 238
diacritical marks, handling of, 19
dice, 119–146
Digital number, 45
divinities (*elohim*), 209
Dragon, significance of in Chinese astrology, 67
dreams, and symbolism, 93–95
Dumas, Alexandre, 174, 176

Egyptian hieroglyphics, 206, 260

Egyptian magic, 179
Eight
  basic meaning of, 27–28
  basic personality type, 43
  color for personality number, 166
  Heart's Desire number, 78
  personality number and karma, 154
Eleven
  basic meaning of, 28
  color for personality number, 166
  Heart's Desire number, 79
elohim (divinities), 209
English Grand Lodge, 180
even numbers
  characteristics of (Life Path number), 100–102
  significance of, 25
  superstitions about, 91–94
evil days, verses about, 216
Expression numbers, 24

faith healers, 92
Fatima, 95
Faust in his study, by Rembrandt (illus.), 6
favorite color, meaning of, 167–169
Favorite numbers, 85–90
fear of 13. *see* triskaidekaphobia
Feliciani, Lorenza, 175–179
feng shui, 72
Fifth pentacle of Mars (illus.), 169
figure for winning lotteries (illus.), 117
Five
  basic meaning of, 26–27
  basic personality type, 42–43
  color for personality number, 166
  Heart's Desire number, 77–78
  personality number and karma, 153
forenames, 38
Four
  basic meaning of, 26
  basic personality type, 42
  color for personality number, 166
  Heart's Desire number, 77
  personality number and karma, 153
France, history of, 60
Franklin, Benjamin, 180
freemasons (masons), 179–181
Freud, Sigmund, 266
Friday the 13th, 106, 226

Galen (Claudius Galenus), 23–24

Index 283

gambling, 109–118
Gébelin, 181–183
gematria, 208
gems (gemstones), 52–54, 160–163
German Jew, A (illus.), 204
gimel (Hebrew letter), 206
Grand Copt (Copht). *see* Cagliostro
graphology, 198
Greek gods, 242
Grimoire of Honorius, 97

hands as a sign of ill health, 242
hand size, 242
Harmon, Louis. *see* "Cheiro"
Harmonious numbers, 31–32
Hayyan, Jabir ibn, 265
he (Hebrew letter), 206
health, and numerology, 60–61
Heart number. *see* Heart's Desire number
Heart's Desire number
  finding, 44, 75–76
  meaning of, 76–79
Heaven, size of, 56
Hebrew alphabet, 206–208
"Hebrew" system of numerology, described, 20–21, 201
Hepburn, Katharine, 201
herbs, 61–62
Hermetic scripts (illus.), 212
heth (Hebrew letter), 206
hieroglyphics, 206
Hitler, Adolph, 174
Holy Inquisition, 178–179
Holy Inquisition torture chamber (illus.), 178
Homer, 255
Horoscope of Death (illus.), 188
human psyche, elements within, 30

I Ching, 72, 120, 202–203
ideographs, 206
ides of March, 215
illuminatus, 180
Image number, 44–45

Jacobins, 180
Japanese astrology, 66, 72
Jung, Carl, 266
Jung, Carl, horoscope of (illus.), 267

kaph (Hebrew letter), 208

karma, 47, 149–157
King, John, 238
Knights of Malta, 175
Knights Templar, 181
koph (Hebrew letter), 208

lamed (Hebrew letter), 208
Leland, Charles Godfrey, 236
levitation, 70
lifeline, 242–243
Life Path
  birthday, significance of, 49
  colors, 168
  cycles of, 32–34
  place of birth, significance of, 54
  time of birth, significance of, 54–56
  year of birth, significance of, 55
Life Path numbers
  even numbers, characteristics of, 100–102
  meaning of, 58–59
  odd numbers, characteristics of, 100–102
Life Path numbers, meaning of, 58–59
Lindbergh baby, 97
lottery, playing of, 109–118
Lourdes, 95
lucky and unlucky numbers according to religion, tradition, or superstition, 219–232
Lucky numbers, 85–90

magic, 185–186
Magic Seals or Talismans (illus.), 233
Masonic initiations, 180
Masonic lodge, 180
masons. *see* freemasons
Master numbers, 24
mem (Hebrew letter), 208
Mesopotamia, 30
Minor expression number, 169–170
miracle cures, 95
modifiers, 24
Mount Kippumaki, 256
musical notes and color, 171

names, 156–157
  changing of, 46–47
  ethnic, 40
  significance of, 37–47, 156, 159
  variations of, 38
necromancer, 186
necromancy, 191

nicknames, 38
Nine
  basic meaning of, 28
  basic personality type, 44
  color for personality number, 166
  Heart's Desire number, 78–79
  personality number and karma, 154–155
non-English letters, handling of, 19
Norton, Thomas, 265
notariqon, 208
numerology
  defined, 2
  history of, 16–18
nun (Hebrew letter), 208

odd numbers
  characteristics of (Life Path number), 98, 100–102
  significance of, 25
  superstitions about, 91–94
omens, 197
One
  basic meaning of, 25
  basic personality type, 42
  color for personality number, 166
  Heart's Desire number, 76–77
  personality number and karma, 152
onomastics (the study of names), 39, 192
Oracle at Delphi, 122
oracles, 121, 173

palmistry, 235–236, 240, 242–243
Paracelsus, 266
past lives, 149–157
pe (Hebrew letter), 208
personality numbers, 155–156
personality types, basic, 24–29
Pharaoh's dream interpreted by Joseph (illus.), 269
Philolaus, 255
phrenology, 191–192, 198
physiognomy, 198
place of birth, significance of, 54
Plato, 221–223
Potter, Charles Francis, 258
predictions, 210
predictions of death, 238
psychiatry, 30–31
Ptolemy (illus.), 255
Pythagoras, 30, 184, 239

qooph (Hebrew letter), 208

recurring numbers, 85–90
Regiomontanus (illus.), 217
reincarnation, 149
Reisman, David, 31
Religion and the significance of 7, 195–196
resh (Hebrew letter), 208
Ripley, George, 265
ritual magic and colors, 163–166
Robert of Chester, 265
Rooster, significance of in Chinese astrology, 67
"root" numbers, 237
Rosicrucians, 183
Rosy Cross, 181, 183
Russell, Bertrand, 30, 239

Saint Anthony, 215
Saint Augustine, 260
Saint Distaff's Day, 215
Saint Fillan, 215
Saint Marcellus (illus.), 266
samekh (Hebrew letter), 208
Santería, 166
Sardinia, 215
Satanists, 165
Saturnalia, 239
Scottish Rite, 180
Sepher Yetzirah (Book of Formation), 211
sephiroth (cypher), 209
September 11, 2001, 88
Seven
  basic meaning of, 27
  basic personality type, 43
  color for personality number, 166
  Heart's Desire number, 78
  personality number and karma, 154
Seventh Heaven, 195
Shakespeare, 256
shield of Achilles, 255–256
shin (Hebrew letter), 208
"short name numbers", 169–170
Shroud of Turin, 96, 172
Six
  basic meaning of, 27
  basic personality type, 43
  color for personality number, 166
  Heart's Desire number, 78
  personality number and karma, 153–154
Skelton, John, 80–81

Index

skeltonics, 80–81
Soul and Spirit (illus.), 82
Southern Astrology Signs, 194
Spenser, Edmund, 262
Stekel, Wilhelm, 266
substitution codes, 81
superstitions
  ides of March, 215
  lucky and unlucky numbers, 104
  odd and even numbers, 91–94
surnames, 39
symbolism in dreams, 93–95

talisman of Jupiter (illus.), 269
talismans, schedule for making (illus.), 219
Talismans for the days of the week (illus.), 224
Tarot cards, 18, 184–185
tav (Hebrew letter), 208
taw (Hebrew letter), 208
tea leaves, reading of, 198
Temple of Isis, 180, 187
Temple of Solomon, 181
temurah, 208
teth (Hebrew letter), 206
"The Dread of the '13' Unfounded," 237
Thirteen, 72, 196–197
Thirteen colonies, 106–107
Three
  basic meaning of, 26
  basic personality type, 42
  color for personality number, 166
  Heart's Desire number, 77
  personality number and karma, 153
three angel trumpeters announce the Apocalypse (illus.), 220
time of birth, significance of, 54–56
Torah, 210
Tree of the Holy Kabbalah, The (illus.), 207

triskaidekaphobia, 103–109
Turkish amulet (illus.), 214
Twelve Days of Christmas, 215
Twenty-two
  basic meaning of, 28–29
  color for personality number, 166
  Heart's Desire number, 79
Two
  basic meaning of, 25–26
  basic personality type, 42
  color for personality number, 166
  Heart's Desire number, 77
  personality number and karma, 152–153
tzade (Hebrew letter), 208

Unlucky numbers, 104–107

Vertical Tabulation, 62–63
Virgil, 173, 265
Virgin Mary
  visions of, 95–96
Voodoo, 166
voodoo doll, 166
vowels, in Hebrew, 209

Washington, George, 180
waw (Hebrew letter), 206
What's in a Name? (Ashley), 40, 192
Wheel of Fortune, The (illus.), 148
White, T. H., 264
Wicca, 165
Witch of Endor, The (illus.), 257

year of birth, significance of, 55
yin and *yang*, 65
yod (Hebrew letter), 208
York Rite, 180

Zodiac, signs (houses) of, 51–52